T0345001

Topics in Empirical
International Economics

**A National Bureau
of Economic Research
Conference Report**

Topics in Empirical
International Economics
A Festschrift in Honor
of Robert E. Lipsey

Edited by **Magnus Blomström and
Linda S. Goldberg**

The University of Chicago Press

Chicago and London

MAGNUS BLOMSTRÖM is professor of economics at the Stockholm School of Economics, president of the European Institute of Japanese Studies in Stockholm, a research fellow of the Centre for Economic Policy Research (CEPR), London, and a research associate of the National Bureau of Economic Research. LINDA S. GOLDBERG is assistant vice president of international research at the Federal Reserve Bank of New York and a faculty research fellow of the National Bureau of Economic Research.

The University of Chicago Press, Chicago 60637
The University of Chicago Press, Ltd., London
© 2001 by the National Bureau of Economic Research
All rights reserved. Published 2001
Printed in the United States of America
10 09 08 07 06 05 04 03 02 01   1 2 3 4 5
ISBN: 0-226-06083-7 (cloth)

Library of Congress Cataloging-in-Publication Data

Topics in empirical international economics : a festschrift in honor of Robert E. Lipsey / edited by Magnus Blomström and Linda S. Goldberg.
    p.   cm. — (A National Bureau of Economic Research conference report)
    Contains edited versions of papers from a conference held at the Federal Reserve Bank of New York, Dec. 3–4, 1998.
    Includes bibliographical references and index.
    ISBN 0-226-06083-7 (cloth : alk. paper)
    1. International economic relations—Congresses. 2. International trade—Congresses. I. Lipsey, Robert E. II. Blomström, Magnus. III. Goldberg, Linda S. IV. National Bureau of Economic Research. V. Series.

    HF1359 .T666 2001
    337—dc21

                                  00-048010

Contents

Acknowledgments

This volume contains edited versions of papers presented at the conference Topics in Empirical International Economics: A Festschrift in Honor of Robert E. Lipsey, held at the Federal Reserve Bank of New York, on 3–4 December 1998.

The NBER provided excellent logistical support, as well as support for the North America–based conference participants. The Federal Reserve Bank of New York graciously hosted the conference. The Stockholm School of Economics supported the Sweden-based participants and hosted an elegant reception for conference participants. Special thanks are due to Martin Feldstein for his warm and witty tribute to Bob Lipsey at the main conference dinner at the Federal Reserve Bank of New York.

We greatly appreciate the editorial support for this volume. Two anonymous reviewers, for the NBER and the University of Chicago Press, made very helpful comments and suggestions on the volume. We also greatly appreciate the editorial assistance of Helena Fitz-Patrick of the NBER's Publications Department in preparing the volume for publication.

Introduction

Magnus Blomström and Linda S. Goldberg

Understanding the complex world of economics requires simplification in the form of theories and models. Using the insights from theories and models also requires data on the real world: A solid empirical base is needed for all but the most esoteric research. Robert E. Lipsey is one of the economists who have most significantly contributed to this empirical base. During more than fifty years at the National Bureau of Economic Research (NBER), Bob Lipsey has published many influential contributions in the broad field of empirical international economics. Colleagues have described Bob Lipsey as "a master of understated yet authoritative empirical research, and a meticulous creator and defender of measurements of the highest quality and interest" and noted that "his is the work that definitely supports or refutes perceptions, slogans, and 'stylized facts.'" This Festschrift is in honor of Bob Lipsey's contributions to economic research and his great efforts to promote the work and careers of other international economists, including all of the contributors to this volume.

Robert Lipsey got an early start at the NBER. After courses at the Juilliard School of Music, a B.A. from Columbia University, and a year of graduate work at Columbia, the eighteen-year-old Lipsey joined the Bureau in 1945, working as an assistant to Geoffrey H. Moore and Solomon Fabricant. He later received a Ph.D. from Columbia, after writing a char-

Magnus Blomström is professor of economics at the Stockholm School of Economics, president of the European Institute of Japanese Studies in Stockholm, a research fellow of the Centre for Economic Policy Research (CEPR), London, and a research associate of the National Bureau of Economic Research. Linda S. Goldberg is assistant vice president of international research at the Federal Reserve Bank of New York and a faculty research fellow of the National Bureau of Economic Research.

acteristically rich and insightful thesis entitled "Price and Quantity Trends in the Foreign Trade of the United States." During his more than fifty-five years at the Bureau, Lipsey has at various times been a research associate, the director of international and financial studies, the vice president for research, and, most recently, director of the Bureau's New York Office, a post which he has held since 1978. He also taught at Columbia for several years, and became professor of economics at Queens College, City University of New York, in 1967. He is professor emeritus of Queens College and the Graduate Center of the City University of New York (CUNY).

Bob Lipsey's extensive research agenda covers four wide research areas, which are all represented among the contributions to this volume: international trade (particularly the role of prices); international comparisons of prices and output; multinational firms, international direct investment, and other capital movements; and relative national economic growth and capital formation.

The work on prices and quantities in international trade, both historical and current, was the earliest. It began with his dissertation on prices and quantities in U.S. trade, later published as Lipsey (1963) and continued with later essays on trade and U.S. economic development (1971, forthcoming). The data series for 1879 to 1913 have become the standard source for that period and have contributed to the debate about long-term trends in the terms of trade.

Studies of more recent times and other countries began with the book Lipsey coauthored with Irving Kravis (Kravis and Lipsey 1971). Further contributions, with Kravis (1972, 1982) and Bushe and Kravis (1986) analyzed prices and trade in the machinery sector, showing the advantages of the newly developed data in measuring price and income elasticities. The price collection and weighting methods were explained in Lipsey, Molinari, and Kravis (1991).

A second area of research has been that of international comparisons of prices and output, mainly with Irving Kravis, and later with Birgitta Swedenborg, based on the data produced by the United Nations International Comparison Program (ICP). The ICP is a worldwide program aimed at developing measures for calculating purchasing power parities and comparing real output, consumption, and investment across many countries, replacing the often grossly misleading comparisons based on exchange rates. The program is summarized in Kravis and Lipsey (1991), and recent developments are described in Heston and Lipsey (1999). The measures of international price levels are indispensable for studies of purchasing power parity and real exchange rates. Examples of this research are Kravis and Lipsey (1983, 1987a, 1988), and Lipsey and Swedenborg (1996, 1999).

Lipsey's international investment research, the third broad area, is almost as long-standing and has earned him considerable international fame. One well-known subtheme from this work concerns the distinction between countries and firms in analyses of competitiveness and comparative advantage (see, e.g., Lipsey and Kravis 1985; Blomström and Lipsey 1989; and Kravis and Lipsey 1992). Capital, technology, and other factors of production are mobile across international borders within multinational corporations (MNCs). This means that MNCs may maintain or strengthen their competitiveness by relocating their production facilities, even when the competitiveness or market shares of the home country decline. For instance, contrary to popular belief, U.S. multinational firms have remained competitive in world markets since World War II, while the dominant position (by some measures) of the United States has weakened over the same period. Moreover, national policies aimed at improving the competitiveness of the country may fail if they create or subsidize assets which then can be exploited both at home and abroad.

Another important subtheme is the measurement of the internationalization of production (see, e.g., Lipsey, Blomström, and Ramstetter 1998). One surprising conclusion from this work is that the ratio of international production (i.e., operations of MNCs outside their home country) to total world production is relatively small, and that the vast majority of production is still carried out by national producers within their own borders. A related research area in which Bob Lipsey has played a prominent role is the analysis of the home-country effects of foreign direct investment (FDI). His early studies examined the relation between home-country exports and FDI, and found complementarity rather than substitution between the two (Lipsey and Weiss 1981, 1984). Later contributions have also looked at effects on investment, employment, and wages (Stevens and Lipsey 1992; Aitken, Harrison, and Lipsey 1996; Blomström, Fors, and Lipsey 1997).

Lipsey's research on relative national growth and capital formation is his fourth major area of work. Kravis and Lipsey (1984) and Blomström, Lipsey, and Zejan (1994, 1996) all analyze different aspects of growth and convergence between "rich" and "poor" countries. One conclusion is that the income distribution among countries is remarkably fluid; another is that the net "catch-up" was particularly strong for the poorest developing countries, contradicting the idea that there has been a "convergence club" confined to relatively well-off countries. Moreover, it appears that growth induces subsequent capital formation more than capital formation induces subsequent growth. Kravis and Lipsey (1987b) and Kirova and Lipsey (1998) document other important aspects of growth and capital formation. Contrary to popular impressions at that time, productive investment and capital formation by the United States did not lag strongly behind those of its peer countries, once appropriate corrections were made to measure education, defense, consumer durables, and research and development (R&D) capital. Rather than slipping toward mediocrity, Lipsey argued that the United States seemed to be holding its position in the relative-growth race reasonably securely, presaging the developments observed late in the 1990s.

Many of these research programs involved extensive efforts at data development. In addition, he has been involved in several pure data improvement projects, starting with a volume on construction data (Lipsey and Preston 1966). A more recent one was a project aimed at organizing and distributing a consistent and comprehensive data set on international trade flows (Feenstra, Lipsey, and Bowen 1997). Like the ICP project, it is likely that this data set will facilitate much new empirical research in the area.

Our brief comments just touch the surface of Bob Lipsey's career as a productive and influential researcher, as well as a meticulous creator of measurements of the highest quality and relevance. While his academic work has been widely read and quoted, the long list of publications still underestimates his contributions to the international economics community and the NBER.

As director of international and financial studies, as vice president of NBER, and at NBER meetings of the International Trade and Investment group, the International Finance and Macroeconomics group, and the Productivity group, Bob has been a consistent source of well-grounded insights and factual perspectives on issues related to empirical international economics. Bob has also been a steady and willing mentor to a broader group of colleagues in the research and policy communities, and to the many students whom he has taught and inspired. Through his work at Queens College and the City University of New York, Bob has demonstrated a genuine respect for scholars of many different backgrounds. This respect has often been admired and appreciated, and his inspirations have been long lasting.

All of the contributors to this volume have been inspired by and have benefited in various ways from Bob Lipsey's work, comments, and advice. In the following section we briefly overview the chapters by these contributors.

Organization of the Text

The book is organized around three wide research areas: international comparisons of output and prices, multinational firms, and international trade and exchange rates. The collection of essays consists of eight papers, original and serious contributions by scholars in these areas. Each of the papers is followed by a detailed comment written by an established participant in the specific field.

International Comparisons of Output and Prices

The first part of the volume consists of two papers on international comparisons of prices and output, the area where Robert Lipsey made his earliest contributions. Following in the Lipsey tradition, both papers are original, creative, and careful empirical approaches to understanding international linkages.

In the opening essay, Michael Knetter and Matthew Slaughter present some new measures of product-market integration based on price and quantity data. Globalization—the integration of national economies—has become one of the most widely used buzzwords of the late twentieth century. Yet there are remarkably few statistical measures of product-market integration across time, countries, and goods. Knetter and Slaughter's approach is to provide a time series perspective on macroeconomic price convergence, thereby rounding out the findings of a literature that generally has had a more cross-sectional emphasis. The idea is very nice: The authors measure equilibria outcomes—the prices and quantities generated in various markets—and then examine whether these outcomes are consistent with sizable changes in the magnitudes of barriers separating national markets for goods. The authors also provide theoretical context for interpreting these outcomes, using the standard Heckscher-Ohlin model and a second "HO plus production fragmentation" approach. Ultimately, the data on price dispersion provide little evidence that product markets in developed countries have become more integrated in recent decades. Data on relative prices provide more mixed results internationally. Quantity evidence suggests that product markets have integrated since the 1970s, but at quite different rates over time.

In the second chapter of the volume, Robert Baldwin uses an original methodology to infer relative factor price changes from quantitative data. He first proceeds by discussing the difficulties with existing approaches that study the implications of trade for relative wages. Basically, there is an indeterminacy of the commodity composition of trade in models with two or more factors and at least as many goods as factors. As a consequence, it is useful to interpret the Heckscher-Ohlin theorem in terms of the exchange of a country's relatively abundant productive factors for its relatively scarce factors. Testing this theorem empirically invariably involves calculating the factor content of the goods and services traded internationally. Some economists have relied on the behavior of factor proportions within and among industries to draw conclusions about the causes of observed factor price changes. Baldwin investigates the appropriateness of linking these measures to factor price changes within the general equilibrium framework used by trade economists. His clear and sensible conclusions are important for a broad spectrum of studies: Baldwin emphasizes that only under special assumptions are such linkages between factor proportions and factor prices justified.

Multinational Corporations

A second important and ongoing component of Robert Lipsey's research deals with untangling the reasons for and implications of the multinational corporation. In chapter 3, James Markusen and Keith Maskus provide a fundamental contribution to our understanding of multinational firms. Analytically, the authors begin by extending the recent theory referred to as the *knowledge-capital model*. This modeling approach, which generates motives for both horizontal and vertical multinational production, is used to derive analytically strong and subtle predictions about a range of activities undertaken by producers. For example, a key issue is the foreign affiliates' pattern of production for local markets versus their production for exports. Markusen and Maskus elegantly demonstrate that the producer's decision is a function of country and partner characteristics such as market size and relative endowments.

Further demonstrating the gains from exploiting their own absolute and comparative advantages, Markusen and Maskus explore the model's implications using data on foreign affiliate production and sales to the host-country market and for export markets. The authors find that the ratio of production for export sale to production for local sale depends negatively on market size, investment, and trade costs in the host country, and positively on the relative abundance of skilled labor in the parent country (or the skilled labor scarcity of the host country). Export sales by affiliates are particularly important when the parent is both skilled-labor abundant and small. Overall, this paper clearly follows in the tradition of Bob Lipsey by providing a rich set of empirical findings and a particularly lucid set of interpretations.

The fourth chapter, by Birgitta Swedenborg, takes on one of the long-debated questions raised by the growth of multinational companies: namely, whether growth of production abroad substitutes for or is complementary to production growth at home. Swedenborg revisits this and related issues in a new way for Sweden, a large net foreign investor and the only country other than the United States for which there exist comprehensive firm-level data. The novelty of Swedenborg's analysis is that it uses panel data for Swedish MNCs, covering a thirty-year period in order to answer those questions that are essentially dynamic in nature. The careful results broadly confirm earlier findings based on cross-sectional analyses, but reveal too that the latter tend to overestimate the relationship between variables over time. Two-stage least squares (2SLS) analysis reaffirms that the partial effect of foreign production on exports is negative in the case of products that are "substitutes" and positive for "complements," and that the net effect is zero. The overall relationship between foreign and domestic growth in production is positive, due to economies of firm size in R&D and headquarter services, which benefit both home and foreign operations.

Over the years, Bob Lipsey has analyzed not only MNC behavior in terms of production and trade, but also the home-country effects of foreign investment. That is also the topic of chapter 5, in which Gunnar Fors and Ari Kokko examine the effects of outward foreign direct investment on economic structure within the home countries of the multinational corporations, as opposed to the implications for destination countries, as is often emphasized in the literature. Drawing on a detailed plant-level database covering seventeen of the largest Swedish MNCs, Fors and Kokko find that the changes taking place within the MNCs are significantly larger than those recognized in most earlier studies. The establishment and closures, and associated employment, of domestic and foreign plants owned by the seventeen MNCs demonstrate that rapid changes in the structure of production in the home country are possible over relatively short periods of time. Fors and Kokko find no simple pattern in the relocations of production, although econometric analysis suggests that home-country operations were becoming relatively less labor intensive as a result of the structural changes.

International Trade and Exchange Rates

The third section of the volume presents three papers that pay homage to Robert Lipsey's extensive work toward both creating data sets and considering broad policy questions that arise due to international openness. The availability of new theoretical paradigms, including the so-called New Open Economy Macroeconomics approach to studying international linkages, allows for a reexamination of long-standing issues of pricing, choice of exchange rate systems, and the structure of production activity. The availability of new data and the incidence of expanded trade have triggered new research and important policy questions.

In chapter 6, Michael Devereux and Charles Engel elegantly address a number of themes that have often been the subject of Bob Lipsey's research. The broad debate entered by the authors concerns the issue of the choice of exchange rate regime—fixed or floating—and the interaction between this decision and the type of price-setting rules and production structures found within and across economies. Clearly, the paper is inspired by a number of important phenomena and issues central to Bob's work: the determinants and patterns in both relative prices and nominal exchange rates across countries, and, as we have previously emphasized, the behavior of multinationals. The methodology is within the developing New Open Economy Macro school, wherein in a dynamic, intertemporal general equilibrium framework is carefully crafted and analyzed.

Devereux and Engel consider different types of price stickiness: Nominal prices can be sticky in the currency of the consumer, as referred to by "pricing-to-market," or prices can be set in the currency of the producer. Using this carefully executed dynamic framework, Devereux and Engel argue that when prices are set in producers' currencies, floating exchange rates are preferred if the country is large enough in international markets or not too risk averse. On the other hand, floating exchange rates are always preferred if prices are set in consumers' currencies, because floating exchange rates allow domestic consumption to be insulated from foreign monetary shocks. The gains from floating exchange rates are greater when there is internationalized production. While the issue of exchange rate regime choice undoubtedly will continue to be debated in international economics, Devereux and Engel make a convincing theoretical case that the debate should carefully consider dominant pricing behaviors and the incidence of multinational production.

The next paper in the volume also follows in the tradition of Robert Lipsey. In chapter 7, David Richardson and Chi Zhang map and interpret U.S. comparative advantage across time, trading partners, and sectors at an increasing level of commodity detail. They use Bela Balassa's index of revealed comparative advantage (RCA), measured from U.S. export data. The authors call some of their indexes RRCA indexes—in which they measure regional revealed comparative advantage by groups of U.S. trading partners. U.S. patterns of comparative advantage seem to be different in different parts of the world, and these differences seem to have changed between 1980 and 1995, the period covered by the authors' data. The data reveal that aggregation issues are important, and that U.S. comparative advantage is quite diverse across sectors. Furthermore, more finely disaggregated sectoral data reveal some subproducts that have strong comparative advantage, and others that do not. Quantitatively, the United States has comparative advantage in all regions in differentiated producer goods and generally has comparative disadvantage in standardized producer goods and consumer goods of all sorts.

The final chapter of the volume, chapter 8, by Drusilla Brown, Alan Deardorff, and Robert Stern, addresses a topic that has rarely been studied by international economists but is of real policy interest. They examine issues of child labor exploitation in developing countries, and the variety of trade and other policy options and programs that are available in the United States and other industrialized countries to deter such exploitation. These deterrents include U.S. trade policies, economic and technical assistance provided through the International Labour Organization (ILO), supranational measures working through the ILO or the World Trade Organization, codes of conduct, and consumer labeling. The authors present a theoretical model of family labor supply that is embedded in a standard Heckscher-Ohlin general equilibrium model of production and trade. Using this model, the authors argue that the total labor supply of the family varies when the wages of parent and child move together, in comparison with results when the wage of only one family member changes. The implication is that well-meaning policy proponents can make some conditions worse. For example, policy prescriptions that are initially targeted at the child and expected to improve the child's welfare may lead to perverse outcomes and leave the child worse off. These considerations are important for our broader understanding of the consequences of globalization and of a country's sources of comparative advantage.

In summation, this volume pulls together many talented and influential contributors to empirical international economics. Their writings represent serious and substantial contributions to the areas of empirical international economics that span the breadth of fields to which Bob Lipsey has himself contributed. The comments on the papers, by Bruce Blonigen, James Harrigan, Ann Harrison, Edward Leamer, Anna Schwartz, Robert Staiger, Guy Stevens, and Kei-Mu Yi, also provide insightful perspectives on individual papers and the broader topics addressed in the volume. Through these writings and in many immeasurable ways, we pay homage to Bob Lipsey, a great man and an influential economist.

References

Aitken, B., A. Harrison, and R. E. Lipsey. 1996. Wages and foreign ownership: A comparative study of Mexico, Venezuela, and the United States. *Journal of International Economics* 40 (3/4): 345–71. NBER Reprint no. 2132.

Blomström, M., G. Fors, and R. E. Lipsey. 1997. Foreign direct investment and employment: Home country experience in the United States and Sweden. *Economic Journal* 107 (November): 1787–97.

Blomström, M., and R. E. Lipsey. 1989. The export performance of U.S. and Swedish multinationals. *Review of Income and Wealth* ser. 35, no. 3 (September): 245–64. NBER Reprint no. 1397.

Blomström, M., R. E. Lipsey, and M. Zejan. 1994. What explains the growth of developing countries? In *Convergence of productivity: Cross-national studies and historical evidence,* ed. W. J. Baumol, R. R. Nelson, and E. N. Wolff, 243–59. Oxford: Oxford University Press. NBER Reprint no. 1924.

———. 1996. Is fixed investment the key to economic growth? *Quarterly Journal of Economics* 111 (1): 269–76. NBER Reprint no. 2065.

Bushe, D. M., I. B. Kravis, and R. E. Lipsey. 1986. Prices, activity, and machinery exports: An analysis based on new price data. *Review of Economics and Statistics* 68 (2): 248–55. NBER Reprint no. 764.

Feenstra, R. C., R. E. Lipsey, and H. P. Bowen. 1997. World trade flows, 1970–1992, with production and tariff data. NBER Working Paper no. 5910. Cambridge, Mass.: National Bureau of Economic Research, January.

Heston, A., and R. E. Lipsey, eds. 1999. *International and interarea comparisons of income, output, and prices.* Studies in Income and Wealth, vol. 61. Chicago: University of Chicago Press.

Kirova, M. S., and R. E. Lipsey. 1998. Measuring real investment: Trends in the United States and international comparisons. *Review of the Federal Reserve Bank of St. Louis* 80 (1): 3–18.

Kravis, I. B., and R. E. Lipsey. 1971. *Price competitiveness in world trade.* New York: National Bureau of Economic Research.

———. 1972. The elasticity of substitution as a variable in world trade. In *International comparisons of prices and output,* ed. D. J. Daly, 369–98. Studies in Income and Wealth, vol. 37. New York: National Bureau of Economic Research.

———. 1982. Prices and market shares in the international machinery trade. *Review of Economics and Statistics* 64 (1): 110–16. NBER Reprint no. 252.

———. 1983. Toward an explanation of national price levels. Princeton Studies in International Finance no. 52. Princeton University, International Finance Section, November.

———. 1984. The diffusion of economic growth in the world economy, 1950–1980. In *International comparisons of productivity and causes of the slowdown,* ed. J. W. Kendrick, 109–51. Cambridge, Mass.: Ballinger Publishing Co.

———. 1987a. The assessment of national price levels. In *Real-financial linkages among open economies,* ed. S. W. Arndt and J. D. Richardson, 97–134. Cambridge, Mass.: MIT Press. NBER Reprint no. 1043.

———. 1987b. *Saving and economic growth: Is the United States really falling behind?* Washington, D.C.: American Council of Life Insurance.

———. 1988. National price levels and the prices of tradables and nontradables. *American Economic Review* 78 (2): 474–78. NBER Reprint no. 1087.

———. 1991. The International Comparison Program: Current status and problems. In *International economic transactions: Issues in measurement and empirical research,* ed. P. Hooper and J. D. Richardson, 437–68. Studies in Income and Wealth, vol. 55. Chicago: University of Chicago Press.

———. 1992. Sources of competitiveness of the U.S. and of its multinational firms. *Review of Economics and Statistics* 74 (2): 193–201. NBER Reprint no. 1757.

Lipsey, R. E. 1963. *Price and quantity trends in the foreign trade of the United States.* Princeton, N.J.: Princeton University Press.

———. 1971. Foreign trade. In *American economic growth: An economist's history of the United States,* ed. L. Davis, R. Easterlin, and W. Parker, 548–81. New York: Harper and Row.

———. Forthcoming. U.S. foreign trade and the balance of payments, 1800–1913. In *The Cambridge economic history of the United States,* vol. 2, ed. S. Engerman and R. Gallman. New York: Cambridge University Press.

Lipsey, R. E., M. Blomström, and E. D. Ramstetter. 1998. Internationalized production in world output. In *Geography and ownership as bases for economic accounting,* ed. R. E. Baldwin, R. E. Lipsey, and J. D. Richardson, 83–138. Studies in Income and Wealth, vol. 59. Chicago: University of Chicago Press.

Lipsey, R. E., and I. B. Kravis. 1985. The competitive position of U.S. manufacturing firms. *Banca Nazionale del Lavoro Quarterly Review* 153 (June): 127–54. NBER Reprint no. 659.

Lipsey, R. E., L. Molinari, and I. B. Kravis. 1991. Measures of prices and price competitiveness in international trade in manufactured goods. In *International economic transactions: Issues in measurement and empirical research,* ed. P. Hooper and J. D. Richardson, 144–95. Studies in Income and Wealth, vol. 55. Chicago: University of Chicago Press.

Lipsey, R. E., and D. Preston. 1966. *Source book of statistics relating to construction.* New York: National Bureau of Economic Research.

Lipsey, R. E., and B. Swedenborg. 1996. The high cost of eating: Causes of international differences in consumer food prices. *Review of Income and Wealth* ser. 42, no. 2 (June): 181–94.

———. 1999. Wage dispersion and country price levels. In *International and interarea comparisons of income, output, and prices,* ed. A. Heston and R. E. Lipsey, 453–77. Studies in Income and Wealth, vol. 61. Chicago: University of Chicago Press.

Lipsey, R. E., and M. Y. Weiss. 1981. Foreign production and exports in manufacturing industries. *Review of Economics and Statistics* 63 (4): 488–94. NBER Reprint no. 240.

———. 1984. Foreign production and exports of individual firms. *Review of Economics and Statistics* 66 (2): 304–8. NBER Reprint no. 558.

Stevens, G. V. G., and R. E. Lipsey. 1992. Interactions between domestic and foreign investment. *Journal of International Money and Finance* 11 (1): 40–62. NBER Reprint no. 1715.

I

International Comparisons of Output and Prices

Measuring Product-Market Integration

Michael M. Knetter and Matthew J. Slaughter

1.1 Introduction

Globalization—the integration of national economies—has become one of the most widely used buzzwords of the late twentieth century. It is frequently given credit or blame for all manner of economic outcomes. While many signs of globalization are quite obvious, it is hard to say whether market integration is more important for economic performance today than it was thirty years ago. But one thing is certain: Few people have done more to advance our understanding of the manifold dimensions of economic integration than Robert Lipsey. Lipsey and numerous co-authors have chronicled market integration in all its dimensions—the behavior of relative prices, national price levels, volume flows of traded goods, and volume flows of foreign direct investment—in as much detail as anyone (e.g., Lipsey 1963). As a result, much of what we know about the extent of international economic integration is due to him. In this paper we try to make a further contribution to that understanding, particularly in the area of the integration of markets for traded goods.

What drives globalization? In financial markets, integration has been driven by declines in both natural and political trade barriers. For example, the proliferation of computer technology has drastically cheapened trading and communication; at the same time, policy makers have elimi-

Michael M. Knetter is professor of international economics at the Tuck School of Business, Dartmouth College, and a research associate of the National Bureau of Economic Research. Matthew J. Slaughter is assistant professor of economics at Dartmouth College and a faculty research fellow of the National Bureau of Economic Research.

For helpful comments the authors especially thank Jim Harrigan; they also thank the other participants at the Festschrift conference. For excellent research assistance the authors thank Rob Simik. For financial support Slaughter thanks the Russell Sage Foundation.

nated a wide range of restrictions on international capital flows. The results are clear in terms of both quantities and prices. In 1973 the daily turnover in worldwide foreign exchange trading averaged about $10 billion; today this quantity has increased more than a hundredfold to well over $1 trillion. And across many countries, covered interest parity holds much more closely today than it did twenty years ago. In light of this evidence on both quantities and prices, there is a consensus that financial markets are much more integrated today than they were twenty years ago.

Many of the same forces driving financial market integration have also been operating in goods markets, so it is tempting to conclude that product markets have integrated as well. Natural trade barriers have fallen with improvements in transportation such as supertankers and wide-body jets. On the political side, successive General Agreement on Tariffs and Trade (GATT) rounds have greatly reduced tariffs on manufactures and have expanded the scope of liberalization to many nonmanufacturing sectors as well. In addition to multilateral liberalization, many countries have also lowered barriers through regional arrangements such as the European Union (EU) and the North American Free Trade Agreement (NAFTA).

Other factors have been working against product-market integration, however. First, the many regional trading blocs that have formed in recent years can divert trade as well as create it. Second, as tariff barriers have declined, many countries have increasingly resorted to nontariff barriers (NTBs) to impede trade. Arrangements such as the Multi-Fiber Arrangement (MFA) and "voluntary" export restraints in the U.S. automobile market have proliferated. The aggressive use of antidumping laws to protect domestic industries is common in the United States and Europe. Recent complaints levied by U.S. steel makers remind us of the importance of these tools in restricting the flow of goods and distorting prices. Rough measures of the existence of NTBs, such as coverage ratios, are available, but these measures do little to gauge the extent to which NTBs actually inhibit trade. Unlike tariff rates, they do not tell us how great a wedge is created between prices of similar goods in different markets. Overall, with the decline of natural trade barriers and tariffs on the one hand and the rise of regional blocs and NTBs on the other, it is difficult to say a priori just how much more integrated product markets have become in recent years.[1]

In this paper we present some new price- and quantity-based measures of product-market integration. Documenting trends in market integration is interesting in itself; but it will also help us understand the link between

---

1. Widely available volume measures, such as trade/GDP ratios, may really reflect something about the nature of economic growth rather than the integration of product markets. Harrigan (1993) provides direct evidence on how much trade barriers reduce import volumes. Using a 1983 sample of OECD countries, he finds that tariffs and transportation costs reduce import volumes much more than NTBs do.

countries' trade policies and their economic performance. Do countries grow faster as their product markets become more connected to those of other countries? Has product-market integration contributed to rising income inequality in countries? By studying product-market integration in multiple dimensions—across countries, industries, and time—we hope to assemble some facts on integration that will permit more powerful tests of the impact of integration on national economic performance.

This paper is organized as follows. Section 1.2 discusses the process of economic integration and its implications for economic outcomes. Section 1.3 presents our data and framework for analyzing product price evidence on integration. Section 1.4 presents our data and framework for analyzing quantity evidence on integration. Section 1.5 concludes.

1.2   Perspectives on Economic Integration

Before discussing the conceptual issues that underlie the measurement of product-market integration, it is worth remembering why we care about this integration in the first place. Economic integration has many consequences for the operation of a market economy. First, it can affect an economy's response to monetary and fiscal policies. In each case, tighter connections between domestic and foreign markets can reduce the potency of conventional demand stimuli. For example, increased lending by domestic banks or increased spending by domestic consumers may be directed at foreign firms. Second, greater integration can allow external factors to exert greater influence on domestic outcomes. For example, increased product-market competition from less developed countries might be contributing to the ongoing rise in the U.S. skill premium. The exact degree to which economic integration affects domestic outcomes remains open to speculation, however. In part, this is because we have only rough metrics by which to measure the extent of integration, especially in product markets. Our paper aims to provide some new measures.

Broadly speaking, there are two ways to proceed in measuring product-market integration. One approach would be to assemble direct evidence on the magnitude of barriers between national markets. Included here would be shipping costs, tariffs, and any other barriers that make costly the international movement of goods. In general, we expect the degree of market integration to vary inversely with the magnitude of these barriers.

Available data on tariff rates and transport costs certainly confirm the view that markets have become more integrated in recent years. Figure 1.1 presents some evidence of declining U.S. barriers. Average tariff rates cover all U.S. manufacturing imports; each year's rate measures the total tariff revenue collected, divided by the value of all dutiable imports. Average transportation costs also cover all U.S. manufacturing; each year's rate measures the cost, insurance, and freight for all U.S. imports, divided by

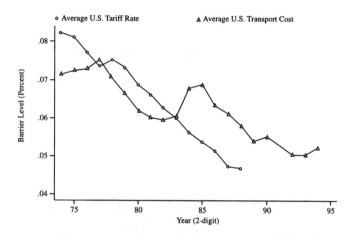

Fig. 1.1 Declining U.S. trade barriers

Source: Feenstra (1996).

Note: Data cover all U.S. manufacturing. Tariff rate is defined as total manufacturing duties collected divided by total manufacturing free on board (f.o.b.) imports. Transportation cost is defined as the difference between total manufacturing imports valued cost, insurance, freight (c.i.f.) and f.o.b. divided by total manufacturing f.o.b. imports.

the value (excluding the shipping costs) of all imports. These data come from Feenstra (1996). As figure 1.1 shows, average U.S. tariffs and transportation costs have generally been declining the past twenty years. This suggests that U.S. product markets have become more integrated with world markets.

These direct measures of integration are suggestive, but they face at least three important limitations. First, these ex post measures omit the cost of prohibitive barriers—that is, tariffs or transportation costs that are so high that U.S. imports are zero. Second, these tariff measures completely omit all NTBs. This matters because NTBs, both intended and unintended, are now the primary barriers between countries in many product categories. Third, even if NTB data were readily available they likely could not be easily quantified as a cost of moving goods. Details of NTBs vary so much by product that it would be hard to systematically assemble such information. On all counts, these measures may overstate the degree of product-market integration.

These limitations suggest the need for an alternative approach to measuring economic integration. This is to examine equilibrium outcomes—the prices and quantities generated in various markets—to see if they are consistent with a marked change in the magnitude of barriers separating national markets for goods. For example, price equalization for a good would suggest that trade barriers for that good had been eliminated. This is the approach we use in this paper.

One advantage of this approach is that, relative to measuring barriers, measuring outcomes offers more hope for comparability of data across countries, product categories, and time, thanks in part to the efforts of Robert Lipsey through initiatives such as the International Comparisons Program (ICP) and the NBER World Trade Flows Database. For efforts to measure globalization across lots of dimensions, this advantage is particularly important. One disadvantage of this approach is it does not link outcomes back to barriers. Without these links one cannot rule out the possibility that changes in outcomes are caused by forces other than declining barriers, such as economic growth. Increased trade flows among a set of countries might be caused by declining trade barriers. As Helpman (1987) has shown, however, it might also be caused by convergence of country incomes—which in turn may be caused by forces such as technological convergence or factor accumulation. We acknowledge this disadvantage of outcome-based measures, yet point out that for many important issues, outcome-based integration matters regardless of the cause(s). For example, if changes in a country's relative product prices are raising domestic wage inequality, that outcome is the same for workers whether it is caused by reduced transportation costs or by growth abroad.

To date, most descriptions of product-market integration have focused on trade volumes rather than on trade prices.[2] However, in standard models, trade benefits a country both by compelling its producers to reallocate resources across industries and by presenting its consumers with an improved range of options. The mechanism that generates these gains is a change in the vector of traded-goods prices facing the country. As these prices come to match those of the world, a country benefits by specializing in its comparative-advantage goods and exporting them in exchange for the rest of the world's comparative-advantage goods. The potential benefits of facing world prices are not limited to these gains from reallocating resources. At least three additional gains from facing world prices arise in some models: reduced market power for firms and thus smaller price-cost margins in the imperfect-competition models from new trade theory, higher firm productivity via reduced X-inefficiencies, and greater capital accumulation. Thus, trade theory makes clear that an important—if not the most important—aspect of goods-market integration is facing world prices of traded goods.

While it may be true that prices carry the important economic signals associated with increased market integration, it is also true that in most cases, these signals will lead firms and consumers to make new allocation decisions. The patterns of production and consumption (and thus, of imports and exports) are almost certain to change in concert with the change

---

2. See, e.g., Krugman (1995) or Irwin (1996). Another popular strain of the literature on integration relies on gravity models of trade volumes.

in prices. Therefore, it is of great interest to look at quantity data as well in assessing the changing extent of economic integration across countries.

Given our decision to measure integration with price and quantity outcomes, it is important to clarify how reductions in natural and political trade barriers change these equilibrium outcomes. To do this we outline these changes from two alternative perspectives. The first is the standard Heckscher-Ohlin (HO) model, in which the key determinant of trade is international differences in relative factor endowments. In the textbook two-good setup, we imagine that one country specializes in cars and the other in shirts, and that they trade to satisfy their preferences. When barriers fall, countries specialize more in production (production becomes more dissimilar across the countries) and trade more with each other. Our second perspective also presumes endowment differences, but here the product space actually evolves as a result of the opportunity to trade. The production of the car may become fragmented into the production of car components. The country that specializes in shirts may now make the fabric for the car seats. The country that specializes in cars may now make the machines that make shirts. We call this second model *HO plus production fragmentation*.[3] Feenstra (1998, 13) describes this model as characterized by "the increased use of imported [intermediate] inputs, and narrowing of production activities within each country."

In both models, declining trade barriers permit production reorganization according to comparative advantage. In the standard model, there is no real distinction between "industries" and "activities." In the modified model, the distinction is quite important. Specialization occurs on the basis of comparative advantage in activities. This distinction matters because data are organized by industry, rather than activity. As a result, the normal patterns of specialization by industry, which seem natural from the perspective of the standard HO model, may not arise in the data if vertical specialization is occurring within industries according to activity. In the rest of this section we briefly discuss these differences. We start with prices.

First, consider prices charged to various destination markets by exporters in a particular source country. With integration, price dispersion across destination markets should decline over time in the standard HO world. This follows from the law of one price (LOP). As barriers preventing cross-country arbitrage decline, a particular source country must charge increasingly uniform prices to destination markets. In the HO-fragmentation world, things are less clear because integration can change the activity composition of exports. For example, initially a country might export fully

---

3. What we are calling "fragmentation" has been labeled differently by various authors: "kaleidoscope comparative advantage" (Bhagwati and Dehejia 1994), "slicing the value chain" (Krugman 1995), and "delocalization" (Leamer 1998).

assembled cars. Declining barriers might lead the country to export partially assembled cars to certain markets and fully assembled cars to other markets. If there are destination-specific differences in goods arising as a result of specialization by activity, then price dispersion across destinations need not decline. In fact, it could easily increase.

Second, consider relative price structure for producer goods within each country. With integration, the relative price structure should become more similar across countries over time in the standard HO world. Again, this follows from the LOP. But in the HO-fragmentation world, relative producer prices need not become more similar across countries. Industry-level producer prices might actually become less similar across countries as the mix of activities within each industry becomes less similar across countries, thanks to greater specialization by activity.

Third, consider relative consumer prices for final goods (across all industries) within each country. If consumers worldwide share similar tastes for consumption in terms of industries, then integration should make these relative prices more similar across countries. Note that this is true even from the HO-fragmentation perspective. Within-industry activities matter in price dispersion for intermediate goods, but not for final goods.

We now consider how integration from these two perspectives affects quantities of both trade and production. In a multilateral world, with either standard HO or HO-fragmentation we expect to see rising trade "incidence" in terms of the frequency of bilateral trade flows for each industry. However, in the standard HO world all this trade would be interindustry trade, whereas in the HO-fragmentation world much of it would be intraindustry trade of activities within industries.

Production patterns should also look different across the two perspectives. In the standard HO world, if countries focus production on comparative-advantage industries, then the vector of output shares should grow more dissimilar across countries over time for given factor endowments. In the HO-fragmentation world, however, the product mix might grow more similar across countries over time. Consider the example of automobile production for these two cases. With integration in the standard HO model, countries with a comparative advantage in automobiles would increase their automobile shares of domestic production, while countries with a comparative disadvantage would reduce their automobile shares. But in the HO-fragmentation world, most (perhaps all) countries move into some aspect of car production: Different countries focus on different activities, but many might have at least some output in the car industry. Another different feature of the HO-fragmentation world is that the share of domestic value added in industry gross output might fall across industries and countries as countries increasingly rely on imported intermediate inputs. The standard HO world does not carry this prediction.

In general, the predicted effects of integration on industry-level data are less clear for the HO-fragmentation model than for the standard HO model. While this is not a new idea, it is an important empirical consideration because most readily available international data are at high enough levels of aggregation to mask particular activities. Feenstra (1998) provides rich anecdotal and systematic evidence that production fragmentation has increased in recent years.

1.3   Evidence from Prices

The absolute version of the LOP provides one natural benchmark for assessing the integration of markets. Presumably, globalization would reduce the magnitude of deviations from the LOP. Another benchmark might involve relative prices: Globalization should force countries to face increasingly similar relative-price vectors for traded goods. This definition might be attractive in instances in which misalignments of exchange rates might generate substantial short-run deviations from the absolute or relative LOP.

The usefulness of these benchmarks is limited by data constraints, however. There are no comprehensive data on local-currency prices of identical products across countries. Thus, any attempt to measure integration using product prices will typically require a compromise in one of the three dimensions emphasized previously: comprehensiveness, unit of measure (e.g., comparing measures such as indexes whose levels are arbitrary), or product differentiation. Although much research has tested the relative LOP (e.g., Kravis and Lipsey 1977), most of this work says nothing about the changing degree of integration. Somewhat ironically, the movement from segmented to integrated markets would appear in the data as a departure from the relative LOP (or, alternatively, as pricing-to-market). In general, it is difficult to study price convergence with indexes—which contain no information about price levels.

1.3.1   The Behavior of Deviations from the Law of One Price

It may seem obvious that deviations from the LOP should be decreasing as markets integrate, but it is less clear whether absolute or relative (i.e., percentage) deviations from the LOP are what matters. Therefore, it is worth considering what price dispersion actually reveals about integration.

Theoretically, price discrimination across markets arises as a result of (1) differences in demand characteristics across groups of consumers (in our case, the groups refer to countries) and (2) the ability of firms to exploit differences in demand because of costs of resale across markets. Our definition of increased market integration is that the costs of resale are falling relative to other costs in the economy, either because nations have reduced barriers to the free flow of goods across borders or because transport and information costs have decreased between markets.[4] These definitions of price discrimination and market integration have important consequences for measurement and interpretation.

First, it is important to recognize that the degree of price dispersion we observe in the data is not purely a function of market integration. Variation in demand elasticities due to underlying variation in fundamentals such as income, exchange rates, or availability of substitutes can give rise to variation in price dispersion as well. Unfortunately, the precise link between these fundamental factors and the dispersion in demand elasticities is likely to be quite complicated and difficult to discern in the amount of data we have available. We will make no explicit attempt to control for them, but merely note their potential impact on our findings.

Second, it is important to account for the fact that resale costs may be rising in nominal terms, but falling relative to other costs. Ideally, we would like to know whether the permissible range of price dispersion is rising or falling relative to the product price itself. To capture this concept we will use the coefficient of variation (CV), which equals the standard deviation of the prices across countries within a given period divided by the mean of prices across countries for that period. A falling CV will be interpreted as falling resale costs and increased integration.

We study the dispersion of prices across markets and over time for four different types of price data: German export unit values, U.S. export unit values, the Big Mac, and *The Economist*. Each of these samples has nominal prices, converted if necessary into units of a common currency. The data samples vary in the length of time they span (German data, 1975–87; U.S. data, 1973–87; Big Mac data, 1986–97; *The Economist* data, 1967–91) and the destinations they include, although in general these data measure prices in OECD countries only. It is more difficult to get comparable price data in nominal currency units for many of the less developed economies. For evidence on integration between the developed and less developed countries, which has arguably been a more important phenomenon in recent decades, we will turn to quantity data in the next section.

Table 1.1 reports the estimated linear trend in the CVs calculated for each of sixteen U.S. export unit value series from 1973 to 1987. For each industry, the CV is calculated for each year across the set of destinations in the sample. Then the time series of CVs for that industry are regressed on a constant and a linear time trend. The cross section of destination markets includes between five and eight countries, typically including Canada, Japan, Germany, and the United Kingdom, plus one or more other European markets. Because the set of destinations is not fixed across products, the variation in results across industries may partly reflect variation

---

4. It is important to measure resale costs relative to other costs in order to abstract from the effects of inflation.

Table 1.1   Trends in U.S. Export-Price Dispersion, 1973–1987

Industry	Trend	Std. Error	t-Statistic
Aluminum foil	0.0383	0.0039	9.78
Aluminum oxide	−0.0274	0.0111	−2.47
Integrated circuit	0.0068	0.0053	1.28
Kraft linerboard paper	−0.0036	0.0020	−1.77
Autos, over 8 cylinders	0.0108	0.0043	2.51
Primary cell batteries	0.0071	0.0203	0.35
Photocopier paper	0.0040	0.0067	0.60
Putty	0.0054	0.0048	1.14
Cigarettes	0.0102	0.0015	6.74
Industrial lacquers	0.0097	0.0059	1.63
Nitrile rubber	−0.0053	0.0056	−0.96
Raw cotton	0.0060	0.0059	1.02
Autos, under 8 cylinders	0.0023	0.0012	1.92
Titanium dioxide	0.0162	0.0128	1.26
Bourbon whiskey	−0.0086	0.0035	−2.47
Yellow corn	0.1880	0.0320	5.87

Source: U.S. Department of Commerce.
Note: Each trend is the coefficient estimate of annual export-price dispersion regressed on a time trend. Annual export-price dispersion is measured as the coefficient of variation in bilateral U.S. export unit values across all destination markets. Each regression contains fourteen observations.

in the markets in the sample. If price dispersion were declining steadily, we would expect the regression to yield a negative coefficient. In fact, only four of the sixteen estimates are negative and only two of them are significant at conventional levels. About four of the positive coefficients are statistically significant.

Table 1.2 reports the analogous regressions for twenty-nine German export industries from 1975 to 1987. The cross section of destinations is similar to that in the U.S. sample, except that the United States replaces Germany as a destination in each industry. In this sample, a small majority of cases (sixteen out of twenty-nine) show a declining trend, although only five *t*-statistics are below −2.20, which is required for statistical significance at the 5 percent level for a two-tailed test with eleven degrees of freedom. In contrast, nine out of thirteen positive coefficients are statistically significant. One factor that may help explain the number of significant positive coefficients in this set of regressions is the overvaluation of the dollar in the second half of the data sample. In general, deutsche mark prices of shipments to the United States rose sharply relative to the deutsche mark prices of shipments to other markets during the dollar's rise from 1980 to 1985. However, we obtained similar qualitative results when we repeated the regressions excluding the United States from the sample of German export destinations. Therefore, it is clear that the overvaluation of the dollar was not by itself responsible for the significant trend increase in price dispersion across German export markets.

Table 1.2   **Trends in German Export-Price Dispersion, 1975–1987**

Industry	Trend	Std. Error	t-Statistic
Aluminum oxide	−0.0080	0.0086	−0.92
Autos, 1.5 to 2-liter	0.0095	0.0024	3.94
Autos, 2 to 3-liter	−0.0058	0.0012	−4.65
Autos, over 3-liter	−0.0091	0.0044	−2.07
Glykocides	0.0052	0.0045	1.16
Induction furnaces	−0.0169	0.0065	−2.60
Record players	−0.0136	0.0077	−1.78
Razor blades	0.0055	0.0044	1.24
Pneumatic tires	−0.0005	0.0021	−0.22
Platinum plating	0.0117	0.0021	5.51
Aluminum hydroxide	0.0087	0.0034	2.52
Autos, under 1.5-liter	0.0193	0.0069	2.80
Titanium pigment	−0.0143	0.0033	−4.28
Titanium dioxide	0.0052	0.0087	0.60
Aldehyde derivatives	−0.0211	0.0207	−1.02
Hydrocarbons	−0.0066	0.0055	−1.19
Hydrogen	0.0080	0.0022	3.67
Vitamin A	0.0197	0.0078	2.54
Vitamin C	−0.0022	0.0023	−0.94
Beer	−0.0081	0.0023	−3.48
Synthetic dyes	−0.0026	0.0027	−0.97
Special dyes	0.0090	0.0026	3.41
Glazed ceramic tiles	−0.0021	0.0030	−0.72
Calcium	−0.0234	0.0099	−2.36
Olive oil	−0.0064	0.0045	−1.42
Sandals	0.0332	0.0047	7.08
Semi-finished platinum	0.0059	0.0036	1.63
Cocoa powder	−0.0013	0.0045	−0.29
Women's blouses	0.0322	0.0048	6.69

Source: Statistisches Bundesamt.
Note: Each trend is the coefficient estimate of annual export-price dispersion regressed on a time trend. Annual export-price dispersion is measured as the coefficient of variation in bilateral German export unit values across all destination markets.

One problem with the results for the U.S. and German exports is that in each case the data are based on unit values of shipments. The unit-value data are susceptible to quality change. If product varieties have become more specialized in a destination-specific manner over time, this may account for increasing dispersion in unit values (see Lipsey 1963 for a detailed analysis of these issues). Arbitrage forces are not as strong when product substitutability is low. While there are no comprehensive data on identical products, it is quite easy to get price data for the Big Mac and *The Economist* (cover or newsstand price) on a local-currency basis for a number of markets.

While Big Macs and *The Economist* do not strike people as classic "tradables" for which trade arbitrages away international price differentials, there are still good reasons to expect that prices for these goods should converge as a result of market integration. First, many of the inputs used in producing a Big Mac (flour, beef) or a magazine (paper) are in fact tradable goods. As these prices converge across countries, prices of the final goods should as well. Second, if product-market integration induces factor-price convergence across countries, then we have further reason to think the prices of these goods might converge across markets.

What do these data show us about price dispersion? Results for the Big Mac prices are reported in table 1.3 for three different samples. The first sample uses prices from twelve different markets, but excludes the 1987 observation (which is missing for half of these markets). The regression shows a slight, but insignificant, tendency for dispersion to fall over time for the ten annual data points. If we restrict the sample to the six markets for which prices are available in all eleven periods, there is an increase in the estimated convergence trend, but the coefficient is still not statistically significant. Finally, if we exclude the United States from the sample of six, the remaining five markets—Belgium, the United Kingdom, France, the Netherlands, and Germany—do show a significant trend toward lower dispersion. This might be expected since European integration is taking hold over this period and exchange rates are perhaps more tightly linked.

Results for *The Economist* are shown in table 1.4. These data cover the longest time span of any of our data: 1967 to 1991. The whole sample of eleven markets shows little evidence of trend. This result does not change markedly when the United States is excluded. When the United States, the United Kingdom, and Ireland are removed from the sample, the remaining set of European and Scandinavian markets does show some tendency toward reduced dispersion. If we restrict the sample of countries to the same six used for the Big Mac, we see significantly lower dispersion over time.

What do we take away from the reported evidence on price dispersion? Basically, that there is little evidence in the data that product markets in developed economies have become more closely linked in the 1970s and 1980s. That may be a result of the fact that this set of countries was already fairly integrated by the 1970s. We do note that with the Big Mac and *The*

Table 1.3	Trends in Price Convergence for the Big Mac, 1986–1997		
Country Group	Trend	Std. Error	*t*-Statistic
Big Mac 12	−0.0014	0.0023	−0.62
Big Mac 6	−0.0029	0.0026	−1.14
Big Mac 5	−0.0069	0.0020	−3.44

Source: The Economist, various issues.

Note: Each trend is the coefficient estimate of annual price dispersion regressed on a time trend. Annual price dispersion is measured as the coefficient of variation in Big Mac prices across all countries in the country group. Country groups are defined in the text.

Table 1.4   **Trends in Price Convergence for *The Economist*, 1961–1991**

Country Group	Trend	Std. Error	*t*-Statistic
Economist 11	0.0003	0.0010	0.25
Economist 10	0.0005	0.0010	0.47
Economist 8	−0.0014	0.0008	−1.77
Big Mac 6	−0.0049	0.0012	−4.01
Big Mac 5	−0.0028	0.0014	−1.94

Source: The Economist, various issues.

Note: Each trend is the coefficient estimate of annual price dispersion regressed on a time trend. Annual price dispersion is measured as the coefficient of variation in prices of *The Economist* across all countries in the country group. Country groups are defined in the text.

Economist there is some evidence that countries in Europe may be more closely linked today than they were ten or twenty years ago. This is not surprising.

1.3.2   The Behavior of Relative Prices

Our second approach to looking for integration of national economies in price data is to examine whether countries seem to be converging toward a common set of internal relative prices. This approach is appropriate for two reasons. First, resource-allocation decisions within a country are a function of relative prices. Second, the best source of information on internal relative prices for fairly detailed product categories is found in the International Comparisons Program data. This collection effort was spearheaded by a group of scholars that included Robert Lipsey.

While the ICP data exist in principle for many countries at five-year intervals from 1970 to the present, we were only able to obtain the data for 1975, 1980, and 1985. We focus on the two endpoints and ask whether the relative prices within countries are converging toward a common benchmark. This requires a choice of benchmark. Ideally one would like a "world price" that would prevail in an open market, but by definition, this does not exist. Instead, we pick individual countries as a benchmark: first the United States, then Germany.

To measure variation relative to the base country, we first normalize the data by multiplying each country's price for a given product by the reciprocal of the base-country price of that product. This is done for all products, ensuring that the price vector for the base country is a vector of ones. For each other country in the sample, we compute the coefficient of variation of the prices across individual products. If the country has a relative price structure identical to that of the base country, the CV will equal zero, since the price vector will be a constant. Specifically, each element of the price vector for a particular country would be equal to the exchange rate (local currency per unit of base-country currency) between the particular country and the base country that prevailed for this set of products. Since that exchange rate need not equal the actual market exchange rate, prices in the two countries need not be equal to have a common relative price structure.[5] On the other hand, as prices within a country depart from the cross-category mean price, the CV rises.

Table 1.5 reports the CV of internal relative prices for seventeen countries in 1975 and 1985 benchmarked against the U.S. relative price structure. The CV is calculated for two separate groupings of goods—producer goods and consumer goods—and for the total.[6] The measure for producer goods is based on a sample of only three products and should be judged accordingly. The cross-country variation in the CVs seems to correlate with stages of economic development. Most developed countries in the sample have lower CVs than the less developed countries.[7] This might reflect the different degrees of nontraded services included in product prices, especially for certain consumer goods.

Turning to the time dimension of the U.S.-benchmarked sample, there is a large decline in the calculated CVs between 1975 and 1985 for Korea and India, and to a lesser extent for Japan, Belgium, and France. This suggests some convergence toward common relative prices between the United States and these countries. On the other hand, the CVs for the Philippines and Thailand increase by large amounts between the two periods, suggesting a movement toward more diverse relative prices vis-à-vis the United States. Overall, this relative-price evidence shows that linkages are much closer between the United States and the other developed countries than they are between the United States and developing countries. Furthermore, the big movements in relative prices suggest either convergence or roughly no change with respect to some developed countries, while there are signs of convergence and divergence with respect to the set of developing countries.

Turning to the German-benchmarked sample (see table 1.6), one feature that stands out is how small the CVs are vis-à-vis other continental European countries. It seems that relative prices within Europe were already quite close to the relative prices in Germany. The only notable changes

---

5. It is easy to imagine how a sudden currency swing might cause systematic violations in the law of one price without necessarily altering the relative price structure between two markets.

6. Note that the CV for the total is not equal to the average of the two subgroups. This is primarily because the two subgroups may have different means. Looking within the subgroup does not capture this additional source of change in the overall coefficient of variation.

7. The raw data also reveal another interesting feature: The less developed countries tend to have higher relative prices for producer vs. consumer goods relative to the United States. Other developed countries' distortions relative to U.S. prices seem to be unrelated to the broad groupings of producer and consumer goods. We note that some of the developing countries (e.g., Poland) had extensive government intervention in product markets during our sample period. That said, however, we have chosen to include countries with available data without making judgments about this issue.

Table 1.5   **Dispersion in National Relative Prices Relative to U.S. Relative Prices**

	1975			1985		
Country	All Goods	Consumer Goods	Producer Goods	All Goods	Consumer Goods	Producer Goods
Austria	0.23	0.20	0.10	0.21	0.22	0.18
Belgium	0.28	0.30	0.14	0.18	0.18	0.19
Denmark	0.27	0.29	0.20	0.30	0.30	0.28
France	0.26	0.28	0.09	0.19	0.19	0.20
Germany	0.23	0.23	0.23	0.24	0.25	0.16
India	0.69	0.79	0.07	0.42	0.41	0.13
Ireland	0.33	0.36	0.15	0.31	0.33	0.27
Italy	0.30	0.31	0.13	0.26	0.28	0.20
Japan	0.37	0.37	0.28	0.29	0.29	0.15
Kenya	0.47	0.42	0.20	0.46	0.48	n.a.
Korea	0.76	0.83	0.20	0.38	0.39	0.34
Netherlands	0.23	0.22	0.17	0.29	0.31	0.18
Philippines	0.61	0.61	0.20	0.88	0.36	1.02
Poland	0.37	0.41	0.12	0.35	0.34	0.41
Spain	0.26	0.25	0.04	0.26	0.26	0.22
Thailand	0.48	0.42	0.12	0.60	0.47	0.16
United Kingdom	0.35	0.38	0.06	0.30	0.31	0.26

Source: International Comparisons Program, from World Bank (1993).
Note: Each cell reports the coefficient of variation in the country's price basket. For each product, price levels have been normalized worldwide such that the U.S. price equals one. n.a. = not available.

Table 1.6   **Dispersion in National Relative Prices Relative to German Relative Prices**

	1975			1985		
Country	All Goods	Consumer Goods	Producer Goods	All Goods	Consumer Goods	Producer Goods
Austria	0.22	0.19	0.28	0.12	0.12	0.14
Belgium	0.16	0.17	0.10	0.15	0.16	0.05
Denmark	0.18	0.16	0.31	0.19	0.18	0.27
France	0.17	0.18	0.16	0.15	0.17	0.05
India	0.61	0.69	0.14	0.58	0.63	0.26
Ireland	0.28	0.28	0.30	0.26	0.28	0.21
Italy	0.22	0.22	0.20	0.16	0.17	0.11
Japan	0.48	0.46	0.45	0.34	0.35	0.03
Kenya	0.46	0.37	0.37	0.38	0.38	n.a.
Korea	0.96	1.03	0.30	0.48	0.51	0.40
Netherlands	0.12	0.11	0.08	0.12	0.12	0.08
Philippines	0.60	0.61	0.37	0.97	0.48	1.09
Poland	0.35	0.37	0.29	0.46	0.47	0.39
Spain	0.44	0.48	0.21	0.25	0.24	0.20
Thailand	0.49	0.52	0.16	0.73	0.69	0.27
United Kingdom	0.25	0.27	0.15	0.21	0.22	0.20
United States	0.31	0.32	0.21	0.22	0.24	0.14

Source: International Comparisons Program, from World Bank (1993).
Note: Each cell reports the coefficient of variation in the country's price basket. For each product, price levels have been normalized worldwide such that the German price equals one. n.a. = not available.

among this set of countries were declines by Austria and Italy. Price dispersion is somewhat greater vis-à-vis the United Kingdom and Ireland, with only slight declines in the CVs over the decade. Looking outside European markets, we see that CVs declined markedly for Japan, Kenya, Korea, and the United States. They rose for the Philippines, Poland, and Thailand. This evidence seems broadly consistent with what was observed in the U.S. sample. Relative prices are much more similar within the developed economies, and the main tendency among developed markets is toward further convergence of prices. However, with developing countries, we see cases of both convergence and divergence over this decade.

Taken together, the totality of price evidence we have examined here points to increased linkages between the developed economies over recent decades, especially within the European markets, which were already quite closely integrated with each other. It is more difficult to tell what the price evidence says about integration between developed and developing countries, partly due to lack of data. For the data we have at present, the results are mixed.

1.4   Evidence from Quantities

1.4.1   Market "Thickness": Evidence from Trade Flows

Our first quantity-based integration measure looks at how "thick" product markets are in terms of breadth of trade flows. Define the categorical variable Z_{ijkt} to be equal to one if country j has some positive value of exports to country k in industry i during year t, and zero otherwise. If there are N countries in the world at time t, then for each industry i there can be up to $[(N) \times (N - 1)]$ total bilateral trade flows. One possible measure of market "thickness" might be the share of total possible bilateral trade flows for which trade actually happens. This thickness measure can be calculated for each industry-year as follows:

$$(1) \qquad \theta_{it} + \left\{ \frac{\cdot_j \cdot_{k \cdot j} Z_{ijkt}}{[(N) \times (N - 1)]_t} \right\}.$$

By construction, the thickness measure θ_{it} ranges from zero to one and reports the share of total possible bilateral trade "hits" in which trade actually happened. If every (no) country-pair worldwide has two-way trade in industry i at time t, then θ_{it} equals one (zero). We interpret higher values of θ_{it} to indicate a thicker world market. In accounting for the incidence of trade (i.e., because Z_{ijkt} is categorical), note that this measure does not incorporate any information about trade volumes. Given this property, we intend for this measure to capture the competitiveness of product markets under the assumption that competitiveness depends "on the margin" on the incidence of trade regardless of the volume of that trade. We hypothesize that globalization might increase market thickness over time, insofar as lower trade barriers permit more bilateral trade hits. Of course, lower barriers might have countervailing effects as well: If national production mixes become more specialized, for some industries there might be fewer exporters and thus fewer bilateral trade hits. Whatever the case, we think the θ_{it} measure is informative.

To construct θ_{it} we use the world trade data in Feenstra, Lipsey, and Bowen (1997). These data cover thirty-four manufacturing industries (as defined by the Bureau of Economic Analysis) from 1970 through 1992. We try two different sets of countries: the twenty-four original OECD countries, and "the world" defined as 122 countries with trade data available for all twenty-three years of the sample. In addition, each observation of θ_{it} from the world group of countries is decomposed into four components: exports from an OECD country to another OECD country (oo); exports from an OECD country to a non-OECD country (on); exports from a non-OECD country to an OECD country (no); and exports from a non-OECD country to a non-OECD country (nn). That is, for each industry-year observation of the world sample:

$$(2) \qquad \theta_{it} = \theta_{ioot} + \theta_{iont} + \theta_{inot} + \theta_{innt}.$$

Each of the four components is constructed by varying the countries j and k in Z_{ijkt}. For example, for θ_{iont} the set of j exporting countries is the OECD and the set of k importing countries is the non-OECD. By keeping $N = 122$ for all four components we end up with equation (2). With this decomposition, we can see how changes in θ_{it} are accounted for by major country groupings.[8]

Table 1.7 reports some summary statistics for the OECD sample, the world sample, and the four components of the world sample. Note that on average, markets are much thicker within the OECD sample than within the broader sample. This squares with the general fact that most world trade is among OECD countries. Within the world sample, note that total exports from non-OECD countries account for about two-thirds of all bilateral trade "hits." These summary statistics mask a lot of heterogeneity across industries. Table 1.8 reports the mean thickness indexes for all thirty-four industries for both the OECD and full-world samples. Over the full time series, in both samples tobacco products is the thinnest market (0.53 in the OECD, 0.07 in the world) while miscellaneous food products is the thickest market (0.97 in the OECD, 0.31 in the world).

8. One concern we have in constructing our trade-thickness measures is whether the raw data contain threshold levels of trade required for a nonzero entry and, relatedly, how these threshold levels change over time. Any discrete changes in thresholds might cause discrete changes in trade thickness. The available data documentation did not flag any problems here, but we highlight the issue nevertheless.

Table 1.7   **Summary Statistics for Trade-Thickness Measures**

Variable	Mean	Std. Deviation	Minimum	Maximum
θ_{it} OECD	0.851	0.088	0.496	0.994
θ_{it} World	0.200	0.054	0.061	0.362
θ_{ioot}	0.029	0.003	0.017	0.034
θ_{iont}	0.035	0.016	0.005	0.089
θ_{inot}	0.082	0.018	0.028	0.122
θ_{innt}	0.054	0.022	0.009	0.135

Source: Feenstra, Lipsey, and Bowen (1997).
Note: These variables are trade-thickness measures as defined by equations (1) and (2) in the text. The sample contains 782 observations (34 industries × 23 years).

To see how market thickness has evolved over time, we pooled the industry thickness measures and regressed them on a full set of industry dummy variables (ID, which control for time-invariant differences in market integration across industries) and a time trend:

$$(3) \qquad \theta_{it} = \alpha(ID)_i + \beta t + e_{it},$$

where e_{it} is an additive error term. For both our thickness measures (OECD and world) the time trend in equation (3) had a significantly positive coefficient estimate, suggesting that markets have been thickening over time. Regressions with a time trend, however, do not allow us to see whether the pace of integration has varied over time. To do this we replace the time trend in equation (3) with a full set of time dummies (TD) and estimate equation (3'):

$$(3') \qquad \theta_{it} = \alpha(ID)_i + \beta(TD)_t + u_{it}.$$

Table 1.9 reports the parameter estimates on the time dummies from equation (3') using the world sample and all six thickness measures: those from the OECD sample, those from the world sample, and the four world components as described in equation (2). The key message of table 1.9 is that the market-thickening process looked very different in the 1970s and 1980s. During the 1970s the coefficients on the time dummies increased almost uniformly for all six thickness measures. This indicates that market thickening proceeded continually throughout the 1970s.

The 1980s looked very different, however. After 1979 the coefficients on the time dummies *decreased* for some time, and only after some additional time did they return to their 1979 level. This suggests that market thickening proceeded much less uniformly during the 1980s. The extent of this thickening slowdown varies among thickness measures. Among the OECD countries the slowdown lasted the shortest period: For the OECD-sample θ_{it} the time dummies return to their 1979 levels in 1984, and for θ_{ioot} the

Table 1.8   Average Trade-Thickness Measures by Industry

Industry Name	θ_{it} OECD	θ_{it} World
Grain-mill and bakery products	0.780	0.147
Beverages	0.832	0.162
Tobacco products	0.535	0.072
Miscellaneous food products	0.974	0.308
Apparel and textile products	0.967	0.307
Leather products	0.877	0.200
Pulp, paper, and board mills	0.801	0.168
Other paper products	0.834	0.177
Printing and publishing	0.874	0.188
Drugs	0.863	0.218
Soaps, cleaners, and toilet goods	0.789	0.153
Agricultural chemicals	0.672	0.145
Industrial chemicals and synthetics	0.914	0.258
Other chemical products	0.885	0.218
Rubber products	0.852	0.197
Miscellaneous plastic products	0.889	0.191
Ferrous metal products	0.836	0.182
Nonferrous metal products	0.908	0.219
Fabricated metal products	0.926	0.257
Farm and garden machinery	0.785	0.124
Construction, mining, and related machinery	0.836	0.189
Computer and office equipment	0.835	0.167
Other nonelectric machinery	0.932	0.278
Household appliances	0.841	0.177
Audio, video, and communication equipment	0.892	0.222
Electronic components and accessories	0.762	0.115
Other electrical machinery	0.897	0.236
Motor vehicles and equipment	0.858	0.228
Other transportation equipment	0.839	0.188
Lumber, wood, furniture, and fixtures	0.857	0.214
Glass products	0.845	0.178
Stone, clay, and other mineral products	0.889	0.210
Instruments and related products	0.898	0.248
Other manufactures	0.948	0.254

Source: Feenstra, Lipsey, and Bowen (1997).

Note: These variables are average trade-thickness measures as defined by equation (1) in the text. The sample contains 782 observations (34 industries × 23 years).

1979 level held steady until 1985. Trade flows involving non-OECD countries took longer to rebound—particularly exports from non-OECD countries. For the world-sample θ_{it} the time dummies do not return to the 1979 level until 1988. The other three components of the world-sample θ_{it} returned as follows: θ_{iont} 1986, θ_{inot} 1989, and θ_{innt} 1988. Figure 1.2 summarizes the difference across decades for all manufacturing together by averaging θ_{it} across all thirty-four industries in each year. The rise in the 1970s and subsequent stalling in the 1980s is clear. Figure 1.3 shows the same

Table 1.9   **Time-Series Trends in Trade-Thickness Measures**

	θ_{it} OECD	θ_{it} World	θ_{ioot}	θ_{iont}	θ_{inot}	θ_{innt}
1970	0.899	0.223	0.031	0.049	0.081	0.062
1971	0.909	0.227	0.031	0.050	0.082	0.064
1972	0.918	0.232	0.031	0.051	0.083	0.066
1973	0.933	0.239	0.032	0.054	0.085	0.068
1974	0.936	0.244	0.032	0.054	0.086	0.071
1975	0.933	0.246	0.032	0.055	0.087	0.073
1976	0.935	0.248	0.032	0.055	0.087	0.074
1977	0.935	0.253	0.032	0.056	0.089	0.076
1978	0.939	0.264	0.032	0.058	0.095	0.079
1979	0.942	0.265	0.032	0.059	0.095	0.079
1980	0.929	0.248	0.032	0.054	0.089	0.072
1981	0.933	0.248	0.032	0.055	0.089	0.072
1982	0.933	0.247	0.032	0.055	0.090	0.070
1983	0.936	0.244	0.032	0.055	0.089	0.068
1984	0.944	0.244	0.032	0.055	0.090	0.066
1985	0.951	0.249	0.033	0.056	0.092	0.068
1986	0.962	0.256	0.033	0.059	0.092	0.072
1987	0.971	0.263	0.033	0.061	0.094	0.075
1988	0.983	0.269	0.034	0.064	0.093	0.079
1989	0.989	0.275	0.034	0.064	0.095	0.081
1990	0.998	0.283	0.034	0.065	0.096	0.087
1991	1.001	0.284	0.034	0.065	0.095	0.089
1992	1.004	0.293	0.034	0.068	0.098	0.093

Source: Feenstra, Lipsey, and Bowen (1997).

Note: Each column is a different trade-thickness measure as defined in equations (1) and (2) in the text. For each thickness measure, each row reports the coefficient estimate on that year's time dummy variable from regression equation (3′). All regressions contain 782 observations.

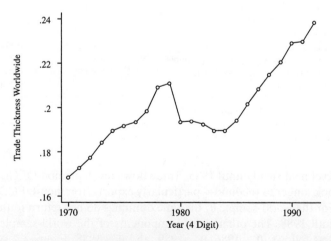

Fig. 1.2   World trade thickness: all manufacturing
Source: Feenstra, Lipsey, and Bowen (1997).
Note: Each year plots the thickness of world trade (as defined in eq. [1]) averaged across all thirty-four manufacturing industries.

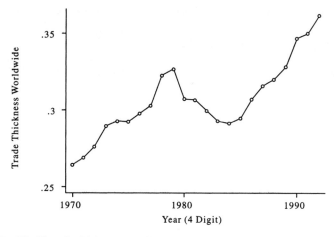

Fig. 1.3   World trade thickness: textiles and apparel
Source: Feenstra, Lipsey, and Bowen (1997).
Note: Each year plots the thickness of world trade (as defined in eq. [1]) for the textiles and apparel industry.

pattern for a single industry, textiles and apparel. The pattern in this figure is repeated in many other industries; altogether they give rise to figure 1.2.

In interpreting regression results from equation (3′) as evidence of integration, we reiterate our caveat that our analysis does not link outcomes back to trade barriers. Without these links we cannot rule out the possibility that changes in outcomes are caused by forces other than declining barriers, such as economic growth. To address this issue we reestimated equation (3′) by adding in additional regressors to control for forces affecting θ_{it} other than declining barriers as proxied by time dummies. Our choice of regressors, as with our empirical strategy more generally, does not follow from a specific trade model. Instead, we chose measures aimed at capturing cross-country differences in endowments, tastes, technology, and the resulting international dispersion of production.

In table 1.10 we report estimation results for equation (3′) augmented by three alternative controls: cross-country dispersion in capital-to-labor endowment ratios, cross-country dispersion in GDP per worker, and cross-country dispersion in industry production. We intend for these three controls to capture the role of endowments, of tastes and technology, and of the equilibrium international dispersion of production, respectively. The first two controls vary only over time; both come from the Penn World Tables assembled by Summers and Heston (1997). The third control is from UNIDO (1995); it varies by both time and industry. For each control, the dispersion of the variable of interest is constructed as the standard deviation of the log of that variable calculated by pooling across the rele-

Table 1.10   Time-Series Trends in Trade-Thickness Measures: Specifications with Controls

	θ_{it} OECD			θ_{it} World		
	Endowments	Per Capita GDP	Output	Endowments	Per Capita GDP	Output
1970	n.a.	n.a.	0.876	−0.055	n.a.	0.232
1971	0.030	0.052	0.888	−0.049	0.005	0.236
1972	0.058	0.086	0.898	−0.042	0.007	0.240
1973	0.096	0.107	0.914	−0.033	0.012	0.246
1974	0.118	0.129	0.918	−0.026	0.017	0.251
1975	0.126	0.167	0.916	−0.022	0.019	0.253
1976	0.139	0.182	0.917	−0.019	0.018	0.255
1977	0.148	0.207	0.918	−0.012	0.024	0.260
1978	0.168	0.205	0.922	0.001	0.036	0.270
1979	0.180	0.200	0.926	0.006	0.037	0.272
1980	0.174	0.182	0.914	−0.008	0.012	0.254
1981	0.184	0.186	0.917	−0.006	0.017	0.255
1982	0.189	0.200	0.917	−0.007	0.018	0.253
1983	0.196	0.204	0.919	−0.011	0.016	0.251
1984	0.205	0.200	0.927	−0.013	0.015	0.251
1985	0.209	0.209	0.935	−0.011	0.024	0.256
1986	0.220	0.235	0.947	−0.002	0.029	0.263
1987	0.229	0.260	0.956	−0.001	0.036	0.269
1988	0.241	0.268	0.968	0.001	0.039	0.275
1989	0.252	0.282	0.974	0.007	0.044	0.281
1990	0.263	0.341	0.982	0.012	0.055	0.290
1991	0.294	n.a.	0.986	0.002	n.a.	0.291
1992	0.339	n.a.	0.988	n.a.	n.a.	0.300

Source: Feenstra, Lipsey, and Bowen (1997), Summers and Heston (1997), UNIDO (1995).
Note: Each column is a different trade-thickness measure as defined in equation (1) in the text. For each thickness measure, each row reports the coefficient estimate on that year's time dummy variable from regression equation (3'), expanded to include the control regressor. Exact definitions of control variables are given in the text. All regressions contain 782 observations. n.a. = not available.

vant set of countries (i.e., the set of countries used in the thickness measure—either the OECD or the 122 countries in "the world").[9]

Table 1.10 reports results for six regressions: three for the OECD and three for the world, each estimates of equation (3') plus one of the control regressors.[10] The key message of this table is that the time-series patterns in our thickness measures appear robust to controlling for other plausible determinants of thickness. In all but one case, the general pattern remains

9. For our third control, the UNIDO data contain 28 three-digit International Standard Industrial Classification (ISIC) manufacturing industries. Our thickness measures are constructed for the thirty-four BEA manufacturing industries. We matched the UNIDO industries to the BEA industries as best we could without a true concordance; accordingly, we acknowledge that this procedure introduced some measurement error.
10. For the world sample, in the interest of brevity we report using just total world trade-hits thickness measure—i.e., only the left-hand side of equation (2).

Table 1.11   **Changes in World Trade Thickness**

Thickness Measure	θ_{ioot}	θ_{iont}	θ_{inot}	θ_{innt}
Level in 1970	0.028	0.028	0.074	0.044
Level in 1992	0.031	0.048	0.090	0.075
Change in level, 1970–92	0.003	0.020	0.016	0.031
Share of $\Delta\theta_{it}$ world	0.054	0.284	0.223	0.439

Source: Feenstra, Lipsey, and Bowen (1997).

Note: These levels and changes for each measure are averaged across all 34 industries in the sample. The thickness measures are defined in equation (2).

of rising thickness over the 1970s followed by a decline and then recovery in thickness over part or most of the 1980s. Only for the OECD sample using endowment dispersion do we find a much shorter decline period. As for the controls, both endowment and per capita GDP dispersion were very significantly positive in all specifications. The industry-output control was significantly positive at the 10 percent level for the OECD sample, but significantly negative at that level for the world sample.

Finally, table 1.11 reports how the worldwide trade thickening from 1970 to 1992 was allocated across the four components in equation (2). For each of the four components table 1.11 reports the level in 1970 and 1992, the level change between 1970 and 1992, and finally the share of the total level change in θ_{it} accounted for by that component, all averaged in each year across the thirty-four industries. Slightly less than half of the total increase in θ_{it} was accounted for by trade among non-OECD countries. About 28 percent was accounted for by exports from the OECD to non-OECD countries, while another 22 percent was accounted for by trade in the other direction. Only about 5 percent of the total increase was accounted for by trade among OECD countries.

1.4.2   The Geographic Dispersion of Production

Our second quantity-based integration measure is the degree of production concentration worldwide, measured with industry-year Herfindahl indexes of production. Let X_{jit} be the output of country j in industry i at time t. Then we define the following:

$$(4) \qquad \mathrm{Herf}X_{it} + \cdot_j \left(\frac{X_{jit}}{X_{\mathrm{world}it}} \right)^2.$$

By construction, $\mathrm{Herf}X_{it}$ ranges from zero to one. It equals one if a single country produces all the world's output in some industry-year, and it approaches zero as world production is spread evenly across all countries. In a standard HO model $\mathrm{Herf}X_{it}$ should increase with integration as world production becomes more specialized according to comparative

Table 1.12   Summary Statistics for World Production Dispersion

Variable	Mean	Std. Deviation	Minimum	Maximum
Value-added $\text{Herf}X_{it}$	0.164	0.063	0.064	0.465
Gross-output $\text{Herf}X_{it}$	0.133	0.045	0.056	0.346

Source: UNIDO (1995).
Note: These variables are Herfindahl indexes of production dispersion as defined by equation (4) in the text. The sample contains 644 observations (28 industries × 23 years).

advantage. In an HO-fragmentation world $\text{Herf}X_{it}$ might decline as production activities within industries spread across more countries. To construct $\text{Herf}X_{it}$ we use data from UNIDO (1995) covering the 28 three-digit ISIC manufacturing industries from 1970 through 1992, with "the world" defined as all countries with output data available for all twenty-three years of the sample. We have information on both value added and gross output; for completeness we use both, and thus measure X_{jit} in terms of either value added or gross output.[11]

Table 1.12 reports summary statistics for the two Herfindahl indexes. Note that, on average, $\text{Herf}X_{it}$ is slightly larger for value-added output than for gross output. To see how these indexes evolved over time we pooled all observations and regressed each $\text{Herf}X_{it}$ on a full set of industry dummy variables (which control for time-invariant differences in market integration across industries) and a time trend:

$$(5) \qquad \text{Herf}X_{it} = \alpha(\text{ID})_i + \beta t + e_{it},$$

where e_{it} is an additive error term. For both our output measures the time trend in equation (5) had a significantly negative coefficient estimate, suggesting that world production has become less concentrated over time. As before, however, regressions with a time trend do not allow us to see whether the pace of integration has varied over time. To do this we estimate equation (6).

$$(6) \qquad \text{Herf}X_{it} = \alpha(\text{ID})_i + \beta(\text{TD})_t + u_{it},$$

where, as before, TD is a full set of time dummies.

Table 1.13 reports the parameter estimates on the time dummies from equation (6) for both measures of $\text{Herf}X_{it}$. For each measure, table 1.13 also reports results for equation (6) modified by adding the world-endowment-dispersion control. As with trade thickness, here, too, the

11. Strictly speaking, the standard HO model refers to industry net outputs. We have data on value added and gross output, and we assume that the Herfindahl indexes rise for these output measures whenever it rises in terms of net output.

Table 1.13   **Time-Series Trends in World Production Dispersion**

	Gross-Output HerfX$_{it}$		Value-Added HerfX$_{it}$	
	None	Endowments	None	Endowments
1970	0.233	0.081	0.255	0.078
1971	0.214	0.063	0.250	0.074
1972	0.206	0.057	0.242	0.067
1973	0.195	0.046	0.222	0.048
1974	0.185	0.038	0.211	0.038
1975	0.179	0.032	0.198	0.027
1976	0.181	0.035	0.205	0.034
1977	0.174	0.030	0.206	0.036
1978	0.171	0.027	0.203	0.035
1979	0.164	0.022	0.197	0.031
1980	0.157	0.018	0.181	0.017
1981	0.166	0.027	0.196	0.033
1982	0.167	0.028	0.200	0.037
1983	0.171	0.031	0.203	0.039
1984	0.172	0.031	0.209	0.044
1985	0.172	0.030	0.210	0.044
1986	0.159	0.018	0.192	0.026
1987	0.158	0.014	0.193	0.024
1988	0.156	0.009	0.187	0.016
1989	0.152	0.009	0.185	0.013
1990	0.154	0.006	0.180	0.006
1991	0.148	0.006	0.181	0.000
1992	0.160	n.a.	0.187	n.a.

Source: UNIDO (1995) and Summers and Heston (1997).

Note: Each column is a Herfindahl index of production dispersion as defined in equation (4) in the text. For each dispersion measure, each row reports the coefficient estimate on that year's time dummy variable from regression equation (6). Exact definition of control variable is given in the text. All regressions contain 644 observations. n.a. = not available.

1970s and 1980s look different. Both measures of HerfX$_{it}$ had uniformly declining time dummies during the 1970s. But this trend reversed after 1980, with the time dummies increasing for several years before coming down again. This pattern holds even controlling for the world distribution of endowments (similar results were obtained using the other controls described earlier; for brevity we omit these). Figure 1.4 displays the difference across decades for all manufacturing together by averaging the gross-output HerfX$_{it}$ across all twenty-eight industries in each year. The fall in the 1970s and subsequent stalling in the 1980s is clear.

What these time-series patterns in HerfX$_{it}$ say about integration depends on which framework is applied. From the standard HO perspective the patterns suggest no integration in the 1970s, then greater integration in the 1980s. From the HO-fragmentation perspective the opposite is suggested: marked integration during the 1970s and then very little integration in the

Fig. 1.4   World production dispersion: all manufacturing
Source: UNIDO (1995).
Note: Each year plots the dispersion of world production (as defined in eq. [4]) averaged across all twenty-eight manufacturing industries.

1980s. We note that this latter interpretation is consistent with the trade-thickness evidence.

1.4.3   Production Fragmentation: Evidence from Value-Added and Gross Output

Our final quantity-based integration measure is the ratio of value added to gross output (VAGO) within industries. With the UNIDO data we can construct this ratio for each industry-year, $VAGO_{it}$, again for all 28 three-digit ISIC manufacturing industries from 1970 through 1992. In the full sample, $VAGO_{it}$ had a mean value of 0.376 (with a standard deviation of 0.102). In the HO-fragmentation world, with integration $VAGO_{it}$ should decline as countries focus on narrower mixes of activities within industries and import other activities as intermediate inputs. To test this we estimate

$$(7) \qquad VAGO_{it} = \alpha(ID)_i + \beta(TD)_t + u_{it},$$

where, as before, TD is a full set of time dummies. An important data caveat here is that $VAGO_{it}$ can change because of changing reliance on *domestic* intermediate inputs, not just foreign inputs. We have no data on imported intermediate inputs; our results should be interpreted accordingly.

Table 1.14 reports the parameter estimates on the time dummies from equation (7); it also reports results for equation (7) modified by adding the world-endowment-dispersion control. Again the 1970s and 1980s look different. With or without the control for endowments, the time dummies

Table 1.14   **Time-Series Trends in World (Value Added/Gross Output) Dispersion**

	None	Endowments
1970	0.423	0.066
1971	0.336	−0.019
1972	0.340	−0.012
1973	0.342	−0.007
1974	0.331	−0.016
1975	0.327	−0.018
1976	0.328	−0.015
1977	0.317	−0.023
1978	0.315	−0.023
1979	0.313	−0.021
1980	0.318	−0.011
1981	0.318	−0.010
1982	0.310	−0.017
1983	0.319	−0.010
1984	0.319	−0.012
1985	0.311	−0.023
1986	0.314	−0.019
1987	0.317	−0.023
1988	0.325	−0.020
1989	0.318	−0.027
1990	0.355	0.006
1991	0.329	0.034
1992	0.377	n.a.

Source: UNIDO (1995) and Summers and Heston (1997).

Note: Each row reports the coefficient estimate on that year's time dummy variable from regression equation (7), where the dependent variable is the ratio of value added to gross output. Exact definition of control variable is given in the text. All regressions contain 644 observations. n.a. = not available.

in equation (7) generally declined during the 1970s, then plateaued during the 1980s and increased sharply the last few years. Figure 1.5 displays these trends by averaging VAGO_{it} across all twenty-eight industries in each year. The fall in the 1970s and subsequent stalling is clear.

1.4.4   Summary of Quantity Evidence

Viewed from the HO-fragmentation perspective, our quantity evidence suggests that product markets have integrated since 1970 but at quite different rates over time. There was sizable, steady integration during the 1970s. The 1980s had very little integration overall: Integration actually reversed initially, only to recover this reversal by the end of the decade. We note that these decade differences broadly match the trend in U.S. natural trade barriers shown in figure 1.1. These differences also have a parallel in the recent product-price studies linking rising U.S. wage inequality with Stolper-Samuelson price effects. The consensus of these studies is that during the 1970s the U.S. relative price of unskilled-labor-

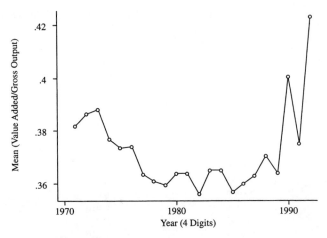

Fig. 1.5   World (value added/gross output): all manufacturing
Source: UNIDO (1995).
Note: Each year plots the ratio of value added to gross output averaged across all twenty-eight manufacturing industries.

intensive products declined, but that this decline did not continue during the 1980s. These price changes suggest that the U.S. economy liberalized during the 1970s but not in the 1980s—a split in timing that matches our quantity evidence.

In interpreting these integration measures, we reiterate our position that these measures do not link outcomes back to trade barriers. Without these links we cannot rule out the possibility that forces other than declining barriers, such as economic growth, drove the changes in outcomes. In our analysis we have included some first-pass controls for these other forces, such as cross-country dispersion of endowments and per capita income. Our outcomes-based integration measures look quite similar either way, so these measures hopefully relate to the underlying integration process.

1.5   Conclusion

In this paper we have presented some new price- and quantity-based measures of product-market integration. Our price measures do not permit very strong conclusions about the changing nature of market integration. Both the absolute and relative price information available does confirm that European countries seem to be moving toward a single market. There is little to suggest convergence toward common prices among Europe and the United States or the United Kingdom, however. We have limited price data on linkages between developed and developing countries. The developing-country evidence is mixed: Some countries seem to converge in relative prices but others do not. Our quantity evidence suggests that product markets have integrated since 1970, but at quite different rates over time. There was sizable, steady integration during the 1970s. But the 1980s had much less integration overall: It reversed initially and then recovered.

These new measures we regard as a first step in trying to quantify more accurately the process of product-market integration. We have tried to use data that are readily available to other researchers, to permit further steps in this direction. With refinement, we think measures such as these will help researchers understand the links between integration and domestic-economy outcomes.

References

Bhagwati, Jagdish, and Vivek Dehejia. 1994. Free trade and wages of the unskilled: Is Marx striking again? In *Trade and wages,* ed. J. Bhagwati and M. Kosters, 36–75. Washington, D.C.: American Enterprise Institute.

Feenstra, Robert C. 1996. U.S. imports, 1972–1994: Data and concordances. NBER Working Paper no. 5515. Cambridge, Mass.: National Bureau of Economic Research, March.

———. 1998. Integration of trade and the disintegration of production. *Journal of Economic Perspectives* 12 (fall): 31–50.

Feenstra, Robert C., Robert E. Lipsey, and Harry P. Bowen. 1997. World trade flows, 1970–1992, with production and tariff data. NBER Working Paper no. 5910. Cambridge, Mass.: National Bureau of Economic Research, January.

Harrigan, James. 1993. OECD imports and trade barriers in 1983. *Journal of International Economics* 35 (1/2): 91–111.

Helpman, Elhanan. 1987. Imperfect competition and international trade: Evidence from fourteen industrial countries. *Journal of the Japanese and International Economies* 1 (1): 62–81.

Irwin, Douglas A. 1996. The United States in a new global economy? A century's perspective. *American Economic Review* 86 (May): 41–46.

Kravis, Irving, and Robert E. Lipsey. 1977. Export prices and the transmission of inflation. *American Economic Review* 67 (February): 155–63.

Krugman, Paul R. 1995. Growing world trade: Causes and consequences. *Brookings Papers on Economic Activity,* no. 1:327–77.

Leamer, Edward E. 1998. In search of Stolper-Samuelson linkages between international trade and lower wages. In *Imports, exports and the American worker,* ed. Susan Collins, 141–214. Washington, D.C.: Brookings Institution.

Lipsey, Robert E. 1963. *Price and quantity trends in the foreign trade of the United States.* Princeton, N.J.: Princeton University Press.

Statistisches Bundesamt. Various issues. *Fachserie 7, Reihe 2, Aussenhandel nach Warren und Landern.* Weisbaden, Germany.

Summers, Robert, and Alan Heston. 1997. Penn World Tables, Mark 5.6. Available at http://www.nber.org/data.html.

United Nations Industrial Data Organization (UNIDO). 1995. *UNIDO database.* Available at http://www.unido.org/.

U.S. Department of Commerce. Various years. *U.S. exports: Schedule E. Commodity by country.* Washington, D.C.: GPO.

World Bank. 1993. *Purchasing power of currencies: Comparing national incomes using ICP data.* Washington, D.C.: World Bank.

Comment   James Harrigan

"Everyone knows" that product markets have become more internationally integrated in recent decades: Trade has grown faster than output, trade barriers and transport costs have fallen, and the word "globalization" has become almost as ubiquitous as the word "Lewinsky." Knetter and Slaughter's contribution in this paper is to try to confirm this conventional wisdom, and in the process they show how difficult it is to do so.

Rather than looking directly at the trends in trade and communications costs that are widely thought to be causing globalization, the authors look instead at outcomes. The main advantage of this strategy is pragmatic: Trade flows and international prices are easier to measure than trade and communications costs.[1] A crucial disadvantage, which the authors acknowledge, is that outcomes may change for reasons unrelated to changes in trade costs. This makes it important to control for the other determinants of changes in trade flows and international prices, but Knetter and Slaughter make only limited efforts in this regard.

Prices

Knetter and Slaughter have three types of price data: export unit values, the prices of a bad food and a good magazine, and relative internal prices from the International Comparisons Program (ICP).

Turning first to the export unit-value data, they ask, "Has dispersion of prices for the 'same' good decreased over time?" The answer appears to be no. The key problem here is the usual problem with unit values: If the composition of the category changes, then changes in its unit value only partially reflect changes in prices of specific goods. Nevertheless, the failure of unit-value dispersion to fall is weak evidence that barriers to arbitrage are still big enough to matter. This is not to say that resale costs haven't fallen, since a decline in costs from "prohibitive" to "half as big, but still prohibitive" will not show up in the data used here.

The data on Big Macs and *The Economist* don't suffer from comparability problems, but price differences surely reflect continuing high resale costs. No imaginable decline in transport costs will lead to Big Mac arbi-

James Harrigan is a senior economist at the Federal Reserve Bank of New York and a faculty research fellow of the National Bureau of Economic Research.

1. For some painstaking work on direct measurement of these costs, see Hummels (1999a, 1999b).

trage, and the timeliness of a weekly magazine makes it unlikely that arbitrage of *The Economist* will ever be profitable. The authors state that easier tradability of inputs should lead to price convergence in nontraded goods even if resale costs are prohibitive, but this is true only if the traded component of marginal costs is high and demand elasticities are similar across markets.[2] I conclude that the data on Big Macs and *The Economist* shed little light on product-market integration.

The ICP data are not ideal, primarily because they are final customer prices and therefore reflect differences in internal taxes and distribution margins across countries. The authors' methodology is also not ideal: Their conclusions depend on the base country, and they weight all goods equally. Nevertheless, some of the results are striking: Relative prices within continental Europe are very similar, and it appears that relative prices are becoming more similar among richer countries generally.

Quantities

In addition to price data, Knetter and Slaughter look at three types of quantity data: the number of bilateral trade flows, the dispersion of industry output levels, and the value-added share of gross output by industry.

If there are fixed costs to trade, then the number of bilateral trade flows in the world will increase if these costs fall, holding the distribution of output and demand fixed. The authors show that "market thickness" has increased over time, and this inference holds regardless of whether controls for output or demand are included in the analysis. This seems like solid evidence of increased market integration.

The second quantity analysis looks at the dispersion of production across countries using Herfindahl indexes. The motivation of this analysis is unclear, since the authors acknowledge that integration has no particular implications for the dispersion of production. As a tool for analyzing dispersion, a drawback of the Herfindahl index is that its value will change if relative country sizes change, even if the composition of outputs within each country stays constant. Expressing outputs as a share of GDP, and looking at differences in the output mix across countries, would address this shortcoming of the Herfindahl index.

The final data analysis tries to address the "production fragmentation" or "outsourcing" phenomenon by looking at trends in the ratio of value added to gross output: This may fall as fragmentation increases. As the authors recognize, however, fragmentation may increase with no increase in international integration, which means that the analysis sheds little light on the subject of the paper.

---

2. This is true unless nontraded prices are determined by traded prices in general equilibrium, as will be the case if there is perfect competition in all markets and at least as many traded goods/factors as there are nontraded goods/factors.

Conclusion

Of the six data analyses in the paper, two offer the most direct evidence of increased product-market integration: the ICP price data and the "market thickness" quantity data. The paper makes a contribution to a small but growing literature on measuring product-market integration, and the authors deserve credit for their contribution as well as for forthrightly acknowledging the limitations of their analysis.

References

Hummels, D. 1999a. Toward a geography of trade costs. University of Chicago Graduate School of Business. Mimeograph.

———. 1999b. Transportation costs and the growth of world trade. University of Chicago Graduate School of Business. Mimeograph.

Inferring Relative Factor Price Changes from Quantitative Data

Robert E. Baldwin

2.1 Introduction

As Travis (1964), Melvin (1968), and Vanek (1968) pointed out some thirty years ago, due to the indeterminacy of the commodity composition of trade in models with two or more factors and more goods than factors, it is useful to interpret the Heckscher-Ohlin theorem in terms of the exchange of a country's relatively abundant productive factors for its relatively scarce factors. Testing this theorem empirically now invariably involves calculating the factor content of the goods and services traded internationally.[1] Some economists have also recently utilized measures of the factor content of trade to draw inferences about the causes of observed changes in factor prices. In addition, other authors have relied upon another important quantitative relationship in trade theory, namely, the behavior of factor proportions within and among industries, to draw conclusions about the causes of factor price changes.

In the spirit of Bob Lipsey's lifelong practice of integrating careful empirical work with sound economic theory, sections 2.2 and 2.3 of this paper first investigate, within the general equilibrium framework utilized by trade economists, the theoretical appropriateness of linking these quantitative measures to factor price changes. The conclusion reached is that only under special assumptions are such linkages justified. Deardorff and Staiger (1988), Deardorff (1997), and Panagariya (1998) have specified sets

Robert E. Baldwin is the Hilldale Professor of Economics, emeritus, at the University of Wisconsin–Madison and a research associate of the National Bureau of Economic Research.

1. Interestingly, the first major empirical test of the Heckscher-Ohlin theorem by Leontief (1953) also involved calculations of the factor content of trade. However, Leontief did not present a formal theoretical model justifying this approach.

of assumptions under which the factor content of trade can be used to indicate the effects of trade on relative factor prices. Section 2.4 then presents empirical estimates of how trade may have affected the U.S. wage gap between more educated and less educated workers in recent years that are based on these assumptions. Section 2.5 summarizes the paper's main conclusions.

2.2   The Implications of Changes in the Factor Content of Trade in Trade Theory

Papers by Katz and Murphy (1992), Murphy and Welch (1991), and Sachs and Shatz (1994) illustrate the use of the factor content of trade to investigate the impact of trade on relative wages. Factor content calculations are utilized to estimate the effect of trade on the magnitude and sign of changes in relative demands for labor of different educational levels. Since the United States tends to export goods intensively using highly educated labor and to import goods intensively using less educated labor, they find that trade tends to increase the domestic demand for more educated labor and decrease the demand for less educated labor. Katz and Murphy (1992) find the impact of trade on the demand for all types of labor to be moderate in the late 1960s and 1970s, but quite significant in the 1980s. For example, they estimate that between 1979 and 1985, a period when the U.S. trade deficit was large and increasing, changes in trade across industries increased the relative demand for male college graduates by 0.55 percent, while reducing the relative demand for males who dropped out of school with eight to eleven years of education by 0.63 percent. They conclude that these trade-induced changes in relative demand moved in the correct direction to help explain the rising education differentials in the 1980s.

Consider the theoretical underpinning of these and similar statements in terms of the standard Heckscher-Ohlin model. To begin with the simplest version of this model, assume there are two freely trading countries, A and B, who both produce two goods, X and Y, utilizing two factors of production: less educated labor and more educated labor. Identical constant-returns-to-scale production functions are assumed for both countries, as are perfect competition, perfect internal mobility of factors, and identical homothetic preferences. Figure 2.1 depicts the trading equilibrium for the two countries in terms of the diagram first made familiar by Lancaster (1957) and Travis (1964) and later by Dixit and Norman (1980) and Helpman and Krugman (1985). Let O_{B1} indicate the total quantities of more educated and less educated labor (measured from O_A) that both countries possess initially; $O_A Q$ (equals $O_{B1} Q'$) the equilibrium total quantity of good X produced by both countries in equilibrium; and $O_A Q'$ (equals $O_{B1} Q$) the equilibrium total quantity of good Y produced by both coun-

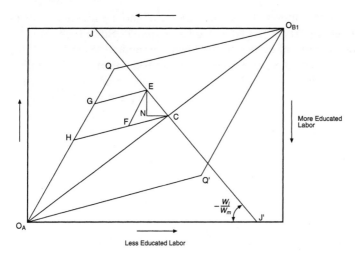

Fig. 2.1   Relationship between net factor content of trade and relative factor prices

tries. The slopes of these lines are the common equilibrium ratios of more educated to less educated labor used in producing the two goods.

Assume that E describes the distribution of more educated and less educated labor between the two countries, with country A's endowments of these factors measured from O_A and country B's endowments from O_{B1}.[2] Since E is above the diagonal, $O_A O_{B1}$, country A is relatively well endowed with more educated labor compared to country B, and country B is relatively well endowed with less educated labor compared with country A. Country A, therefore, exports the relatively more-educated-labor-intensive good, X, and imports the relatively less-educated-labor-intensive good, Y, while country B does the opposite. Since tastes are identical and homothetic, each country ends up consuming the two goods in the same proportions. Because each good is produced with the same factor proportions in both countries, this implies, in turn, that each country ends up, in effect, consuming more educated and less educated labor in the same proportions. Points on the diagonal $O_A O_{B1}$, such as C, satisfy this condition.

Let the equilibrium levels of production of X and Y for country A be $O_A G$ and GE, respectively, and the equilibrium levels of consumption of these goods, $O_A H$ and HC, respectively. Consequently, GH (equals EF) indicates the quantity of good X that country A exports as well as the amounts of more educated and less educated labor embodied in these exports. Similarly, FC indicates the quantity of good Y that country B imports and the proportions of more educated to less educated labor embod-

---

2. It is assumed that E lies within the parallelogram $O_A Q O_{B1} Q'$, so that factor price equalization between the two countries is achieved.

ied in these imports. Thus, net exports of more educated labor are *EN*, while net imports of less educated labor are *NC*. Since the value of exports (= the quantity of more educated labor embodied in exports × the wages of more educated labor + the quantity of less educated labor embodied in exports × the wages of less educated labor) equals the value of imports (the quantity of more educated labor embodied in imports × the wages of more educated labor + the quantity of less educated labor embodied in imports × the wages of less educated labor) in the absence of capital transfers, it follows that the ratio of the net exports of more educated labor to the net imports of less educated labor (the slope of the line *JECJ'*) equals the ratio of the wages of less educated labor to the wages of more educated labor.[3]

Next, consider the effects of a change in factor endowments in the two countries. To take the simplest case, assume that A's endowments remain unchanged but that the endowment of less educated labor in country B increases. This is depicted in figure 2.2, which is the same as figure 2.1 except that the point indicating the two countries' total endowments of the two factors shifts from O_{B1} to O_{B2}. The point describing the distribution of the total endowments between the two countries, namely, *E*, remains unchanged, but the diagonal indicating points where the two factors are consumed in equal proportions shifts downward from $O_A O_{B1}$ to $O_A O_{B2}$. As is familiar in this simple model, the increase in country B's supply of its relatively abundant factor, less educated labor, causes its production-possibilities curve for the two goods to shift outward in such a manner that, at any given price ratio of the two goods where both are produced, the output of the less-educated-labor-intensive good, Y, increases and the output of the more-educated-labor-intensive good decreases (the Rybczynski theorem). This, in turn, causes its offer curve of the less-educated-labor-intensive good Y for the more-educated-labor-intensive good B to shift outward. If the offer curve of country A of good X for good Y is less than infinitely elastic, the relative international price of good Y will then fall, the wages of less educated labor will fall, and the wages of more educated labor will rise (the Stolper-Samuelson theorem). Associated with the decline in the wages of less educated labor compared to the wages of more educated labor will be a decrease in the ratios of more educated to less educated labor used in producing the two goods (to keep the figure from

---

3. In equation terms, $w_m X_{Lm} + w_l X_{Ll} = w_m M_{Lm} + w_l M_{Ll}$, or $-(w_l/w_m) = (X_{Lm} - M_{Lm})/(X_{Ll} - M_{Ll})$, where w_m and w_l are the wages of more educated and less educated labor, respectively, while $X_{Lm} - M_{Lm}$ and $X_{Ll} - M_{Ll}$ are the net exports of more educated and less educated labor, respectively.

While increasing the number of goods beyond two in the two-factor Heckscher-Ohlin leads to an indeterminacy of the commodity composition of trade, it does not change this relationship between the factor content of trade and relative wages.

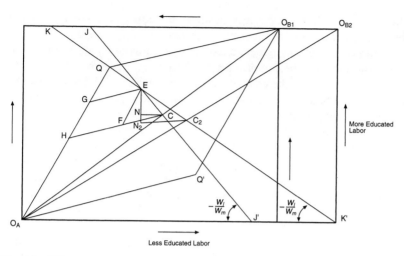

Fig. 2.2   Effects of change in factor endowments

becoming too cluttered, the resulting change in the parallelogram depicting the factor price equalization region is not shown).

Assume that C_2 is the new point of equal factor proportions consumption for the two countries, with the slope of the line between E and C_2,
namely, KEC_2K', indicating the new lower ratio of the wages of less educated to more educated labor. As in the first situation, the ratio of country
A's net exports of more educated labor, EN_2, to its net imports of less educated labor, N_2C_2, equals the equilibrium ratio of the wages of less educated to more educated labor. Thus, the change in relative wages can be
inferred from the change in net factor proportions embodied in traded
goods.

If, however, trade is not balanced, this relationship will no longer hold.
Assume that C is A's initial equilibrium consumption point when trade is
balanced. Next assume that country A's citizens borrow funds from country B and increase their expenditures on both their import and export
goods, thereby leading to an increase in imports and decrease in exports.[4]
A standard result of the literature on such transfers is that there will be no
change in the terms of trade if tastes domestically and abroad are identical
and homothetic so that the increased domestic spending on these goods is
matched by decreased spending on them abroad. The new equilibrium
point will still be on the diagonal O_AO_{B1} but closer to O_{B1}. Net exports of

---

4. The existence of the debt and the need to repay the loan will tend, of course, to reduce
spending in the future, but the initial effect on expenditures will be positive. Murphy and
Welch (1991) and Katz and Murphy (1992) take into account the increase in the trade deficit,
but Sachs and Shatz (1994) do not. See Deardorff and Hakura (1994, 93–94) for a more
detailed discussion of this issue.

more educated labor and net imports of less educated labor will change, but the relative prices of these two factors remain unchanged.

As noted earlier, the papers cited in the beginning of this section draw conclusions about the importance of changes in trade on relative factor prices by comparing the changes in the proportions of different educated groups embodied in net exports to the domestic supplies of these factors. However, there is no unique relationship in the simple $2 \times 2 \times 2$ Heckscher-Ohlin model between changes in the ratios of factors embodied in trade to the total supplies of these factors, and changes in relative factor prices. For example, with a more inelastic international demand for good Y by country A, the same decrease in the relative price of unskilled labor depicted in the shift in A's consumption of factors from C to C_2 could have been achieved with a smaller relative increase in B's endowment of less educated labor. In this case the ratio of the wages of less educated to more educated labor would still be indicated by the slope of the line KEC_2K', but the new factor-consumption point in equilibrium would be on this line but closer to E. The ratios of country A's less educated and more educated labor embodied in net exports to the endowments of these factors will be less at this new consumption point than at C_2, although factor prices will be unchanged.[5]

Suppose that the increase in the endowment of less educated labor had occurred in country A rather than country B because of, say, immigration into country A.[6] This will shift A's production possibilities curve such that, at any price ratio at which both goods are produced, the output of the less-educated-labor-intensive good Y will increase and the output of the more-educated-labor-intensive good X will decrease. This shift results in a decrease in country A's offer curve of good X for good Y so that, with an unchanged offer curve for country B, the price of the less-educated-labor-intensive good Y will decline relative to the price of good X and, in accordance with the Stolper-Samuelson theorem, the wages of less educated labor will fall relative to the wages of more educated labor. The decrease in the wages of less educated labor relative to more educated labor (and thus the decrease in the ratio of more educated labor to less educated labor embodied in net exports) could be the same as in the case in which the increase in the supply of less educated labor occurred in country B. Thus, it is not possible to distinguish between these two cases by focusing only on the factor content of trade. However, when observers

5. The factor content of more educated labor in exports could even decrease compared with C and thus give the incorrect signal concerning the direction of change of this factor price. Bhagwati and Dehejia (1994) also provide an example in which the ratios of factors embodied in net exports to the domestic supplies of these factors change, but relative factor prices do not.

6. The endowment point, E, in figure 2.1 will shift to the right by the amount of the increase in the endowment of less educated labor, for example, by $O_{B1}O_{B2}$.

express concerns about the effects of globalization on relative U.S. wages, they usually have in mind the first case, in which the increased wage gap is brought about by an exogenous increase in foreign supplies of goods intensively using less educated labor. In the second case, the wider wage gap is due to a change in domestic labor supply conditions that have general equilibrium implications for trade flows.

Technological progress in country A can also affect relative wages and the factor content ratio in a manner that cannot be distinguished from changes in these variables due to changed conditions in country B. For example, more rapid neutral technological progress in industry X than in industry Y in country A (with technological conditions unchanged in country B), or more rapid less-educated-labor-saving technical progress in the X sector, both reduce the relative wages of less educated labor without any change in international commodity prices. Since both good X and good Y are produced with lower ratios of more educated to less educated labor as the relative price of less educated labor declines, the ratio of more educated to less educated labor embodied in net exports falls along with the relative price of less educated labor.

In summary, since exogenous shocks originating either within a country's domestic economy or abroad can produce similar effects on a country's factor content of trade in a general equilibrium setting, it is in general not possible to use this measure as a means of distinguishing between foreign versus domestic causes of shifts in relative wages.[7] For similar reasons, measures of relative changes in the demand for different types of labor are also inadequate for attempting to determine the causes of changes in relative wages.

When the analytical framework is expanded to consider the more realistic situation of three or more factors and three or more goods, the ratio of the factor content of, say, more educated labor to less educated labor in net exports no longer can be used as a measure of the relative wages of these two factors. Consider, for example, a two-country, three-or-more-goods Heckscher-Ohlin model with three factors. In a depiction of the integrated free trade equilibrium, such as shown in figure 2.1 for two factors, the endowment point E would be a point in three-dimensional space. The trading equilibrium C, at which both countries consume the three factors in the same proportions, would also be represented by a point in this space. The differences in the quantities of each of the three factors between E and C would give the net trade in each factor in moving from autarky to free trade. This trade in the factors would be indicated by moving along a straight line from E to C. The relative prices of the three factors would be depicted as a plane that passed through both points E and C;

---

7. Deardorff and Hakura (1994), Deardorff (1997), and Leamer (1994, 1996b) all stress this point.

however, many different planes can be generated that rotate on a straight line between E and C. Consequently, unlike the two-factor case, there is no unique relationship between the factor content of trade and relative factor prices. Depending on the nature of technology and consumer preferences, a particular content of the three factors in net exports can be the result of many different price relationships among the three factors and trading relationships among the three factors. Consequently, one cannot draw inferences about the price relationship between any two of the factors (e.g., more educated and less educated labor) from the amounts of these factors embodied in trade. The observed net imports of less educated labor may, for example, be the result of exporting more educated labor for less educated labor and also exporting capital for less educated labor. Comparing exports of more educated labor with total imports of less educated labor to infer the price of less educated labor for more educated labor would be incorrect under these circumstances. The same point holds with regard to comparisons of the proportions of these factors embodied in trade.

2.3   The Implications of Changes in Factor Proportions within and among Industries in Trade Theory

As noted in section 2.1, some economists stress the importance of within-industry shifts in factor proportions in contrast to between-industry changes in these proportions in reaching conclusions about the relative importance of different factors that may have brought about the increase in wage inequality. The paper by Berman, Bound, and Griliches (1994) illustrates this approach. Berman et al. investigate the relative importance of skill-biased technological change, increased trade, and increases in defense spending in explaining the shift in demand away from unskilled and toward skilled labor in U.S. manufacturing over the 1980s. Utilizing skill indexes based on the relationship between hourly earnings and the occupational classifications of blue-collar and white-collar workers, they first show that a significant part of the skill upgrading between 1973 and 1987 was due to a shift in the economy from production (blue-collar) workers to nonproduction (white-collar) workers. (They present evidence that shows production workers to be less skilled than nonproduction workers.)[8] They then decompose the increase in the proportion of nonproduction workers in U.S. manufacturing into that part due to their increased use within industries and that part due to the shift in production toward industries using high proportions of such workers. For explaining the shift in employment toward nonproduction workers, the authors argue that increases in international trade (as measured by the ratio of imports plus exports of

---

8. Further evidence is presented in Berman, Machin, and Bound (1997).

manufactures to manufacturing shipments) and increases in military expenditures affect the skill composition of labor demand, primarily by shifting interindustry labor demand from industries intensive in the use of production workers to those intensive in the use of nonproduction workers. In contrast, they contend that biased technological change shifts the skill composition of labor demand within industries.

Berman et al. find that the within-industry component of the shifts in the demand for labor dominates the between-industry component. Furthermore, when they allocate employment in each of 450 industries to four sectors (domestic consumption, exports, imports, and defense procurement) and assume that imports replace employment in import-competing sectors, they find that the between-industry contribution of imports and exports to the rise in the share of nonproduction workers is small. Therefore, they conclude that the role of trade in shifting employment away from industries that intensively use production labor has been quite small.

The implications of these findings are best understood by analyzing the possible within-industry and between-industry factor proportion effects of various causes of the shifts in relative wages within a general equilibrium framework. Consider, for example, the effects of an increase in the share of international trade in GDP. While they do not discuss reasons that the ratio of a country's exports and imports to its output can increase, causes that seem to be consistent with what they have in mind are a reciprocal reduction in tariffs among countries or a general decrease in transportation costs. In these situations, trade could expand as a share of a country's GDP without any change in international prices of traded goods.

To examine the effects of such changes, again consider a standard two-factor (skilled labor and unskilled labor), two-good (a skilled-labor-intensive good and an unskilled-labor-intensive one), two-country Heckscher-Ohlin model with homothetic preferences, in which the home country exports the skilled-labor-intensive good and the foreign country exports the other good. The endowments of the two types of labor are assumed to remain fixed in the two countries. Even if the reciprocal reductions of tariffs or the decrease in transportation costs do not change the international prices of the two goods, these changes will increase the relative domestic price of each country's export good. If we further assume that labor coefficients are fixed in each country, each country's output levels for the two goods will not change, nor will there be any change in the use of skilled versus unskilled labor within each country. Under these circumstances there will be no within-industry or between-industry effects on the use of skilled versus unskilled labor. However, as the relative domestic prices of the goods change, the real wages of skilled labor will increase relative to the wages of unskilled labor in the home country and fall in the foreign country, in accordance with the Stolper-Samuelson theorem.

If factor coefficients are not fixed, the output of the skilled-labor-intensive good will expand in the home country, and its output of the unskilled-labor-intensive good will decline. These shifts tend to increase the demand for skilled labor relative to that for unskilled labor.[9] At the same time, in response to the changes in relative factor prices, there will be a substitution in production of unskilled labor for skilled labor in the home country, thereby decreasing the ratio of skilled labor to unskilled labor in the two industries.[10] The opposite will take place in the foreign country. Thus, as trade expands, both within-industry and between-industry shifts in the relative use of skilled and unskilled labor occur.[11] Both shifts take place concurrently.

Unskilled-labor-saving technical progress also brings about relative shifts in labor demand among and within industries. Consider, for example, the case in which technical progress that is saving of unskilled labor takes place to the same extent in both industries, in the sense that at unchanged factor prices the relative reduction in unit costs is the same in both sectors.[12] Besides the within-industry shift toward the greater use of skilled compared with unskilled labor in both sectors, the output of the unskilled-labor-intensive industry (the import-competing sector) will increase relative to the output of the skilled-labor-intensive industry (the export sector) at given product prices.[13] As long as the country is too small to affect its terms of trade, these within-industry and between-industry effects will not change relative factor prices. However, if the country is large in the sense of being able to affect its trading terms, the relative increase in the supply of the unskilled-labor-intensive good will tend to decrease the price of this good, thereby reducing the relative wages of unskilled workers. Nevertheless, if the labor coefficients are fixed under a given technology, there will be no further changes in relative outputs; but if substitution between the two factors is possible, these changes in the relative prices of the goods and factors will lead to further between-

9. The opposite will take place in the foreign country. For simplicity, it is again being assumed that the international price ratio does not change.

10. This is possible even though the country's total endowment of each factor remains fixed, since these ratios are weighted averages.

11. See Baldwin (1995, 27–30) for a diagrammatic explanation of this case and the example of unskilled-labor-saving technical progress discussed in the following paragraph.

12. In the standard Lerner diagram depicting unit value isoquants for the skilled-labor-intensive and unskilled-labor-intensive goods, technical progress defined in this manner shifts both unit value isoquants based on constant product prices toward the origin so that the lower constant outlay line that must be tangent to both isoquants in equilibrium has the same slope as the constant outlay line tangent to the initial unit value isoquants. In other words, with this uniform technical progress across sectors, relative factor prices remain unchanged if product prices remain unchanged. Since the technical change is unskilled labor saving, the ratio of skilled to unskilled labor used in producing both goods is, however, greater at the new tangency points than initially.

13. In this two-factor, two-good model, the output of the unskilled-labor-intensive good must increase relatively more than that of the skilled-labor-intensive good at given product prices in order to employ fully the available endowment of unskilled labor.

industry and within-industry shifts. The lower relative price of the unskilled-labor-intensive good will lead to a decrease in the output of this good relative to that of the skilled-labor-intensive good.

The relative decline in the wages of unskilled labor will also lead to a substitution of unskilled labor for skilled labor in each industry. Because of these offsetting forces, both the output of the skilled-labor-intensive good relative to the output of the unskilled-labor-intensive good and the ratio of skilled to unskilled labor used in producing the two goods could end up lower than their initial levels.

While this general equilibrium analysis supports the authors' conclusion that the increased use of skilled labor relative to that of unskilled labor within industries is consistent with unskilled-labor-saving technical progress' playing a dominant role in explaining the shift in relative wages in the 1980s, their factor use findings are not inconsistent with international trade's playing an important role in accounting for the increased wage inequality. As previously explained, the relative wages of unskilled workers could have fallen due to product price changes caused by increased trade without any (or with very little) between-industry or within-industry changes in the use of skilled versus unskilled labor. The increase in the wage gap brought about by increased trade under these circumstances could have been even greater than the increase associated with the within-industry factor use shifts documented by Berman et al. that are consistent with the technology hypothesis.

2.4 The Deardorff-Staiger Model for Inferring Relative Factor Price Changes from Changes in the Factor Content of Trade: An Empirical Analysis

Deardorff and Staiger (1988), Deardorff (1997), and Panagariya (1998) show that, under special conditions, changes in relative factor prices can be inferred from changes in the factor content of trade. Deardorff and Staiger (1988) demonstrate that there is an equivalent autarky equilibrium associated with each trading equilibrium for a country under trading conditions with incomplete specialization in the following sense.[14] If the factors embodied in the country's exports are subtracted from its initial factor endowments, and the factors embodied in the country's imports are added to its initial factor supplies (the factors embodied in trade being calculated with the country's own technology), then with the same prices of goods as prevailed in the trading equilibrium, a competitive production equilibrium exists in which the consumption of goods and factors is the same as in the trading equilibrium.

As these authors point out, the insight for this relationship is simply

14. It is not necessary to assume identical technologies across countries.

that changing the endowment of factors in this manner provides the country with an endowment equal to the factor content of equilibrium consumption. Thus, the constructed autarky equilibrium merely endows the economy with the factors needed to produce what it had consumed with trade, thereby obviating the need for trade at the prevailing prices of goods and factors. Deardorff and Staiger (1988) then proceed by making the strong assumption that both preference and production functions are Cobb-Douglas. Cobb-Douglas production functions imply that each factor earns a constant share of the revenue of each industry, while Cobb-Douglas preferences imply that consumers spend a constant share of their total expenditures, E, on each good. In autarky, where consumers' expenditures on any good equal the revenue of the industry producing the good, the two relationships together imply that each factor's total income (from employment in all industries) is a constant fraction of consumer expenditures. Thus, letting w_i be the return of the ith factor, L_i^a the endowment of this factor under autarky conditions, and c_i the constant fraction for the factor, the following relationship holds:

$$(1) \qquad w_i L_i^a = c_i E.$$

Next, consider two equilibria (numbered 1 and 2) that involve trade for this country. With trade, equation (1) does not apply directly. However, equilibrium factor prices with trade can be expressed in terms of what they would be without trade in an equivalent autarky equilibrium, the factor endowments of which are $B = L$ (the actual endowments) minus S (the factors needed to produce what is exported less the factors needed to produce replacements for what is imported). Thus, letting L^0 be the actual factor endowments of the country (assumed to be the same in both trading equilibria), the price of factor i in each trading equilibrium, w_i^2 and w_i^1, can be expressed in terms of total expenditures in each trading equilibrium, E^2 and E^1 (consumer preferences are assumed not to change), the unchanged endowment of the factor L_i^0, and the net contents of trade in the factor in the two trading equilibria, S_i^1 and S_i^2, as follows:

$$(2) \qquad w_i^t = \frac{c_i E^t}{L_i^0 - S_i^t}, \qquad t = 1, 2.$$

If we compare the price of factor i in the two trading equilibria, we have

$$(3) \qquad \frac{w_i^2}{w_i^1} = \frac{E^2(L_i^0 - S_i^1)}{E^1(L_i^0 - S_i^2)}.$$

If expenditures are the same in the two equilibria, the relationship can be simplified to

$$(4) \qquad \frac{w_i^2 - w_i^1}{w_i^1} = \frac{S_i^2 - S_i^1}{B_i^2}.$$

Consequently, with unchanged Cobb-Douglas preferences and technologies for a country and unchanged expenditures and factor endowments between two trading equilibria, the relative change in the price of any factor can be expressed in terms of the change in the content of trade in the factor and the factor endowment of the equivalent autarky equilibrium of the number 2 trading equilibrium (which equals the factor content of consumption in this equilibrium).

One use of this relationship is to ask the following question: What would the gap in wages between highly educated and less educated workers have looked like in (say) 1987, if, given U.S. factor endowments, preferences, technology, and expenditures in that year, U.S. trade policy had been adjusted to hold the factor content of U.S. net exports (measured in U.S. techniques of production for 1987) at (say) their 1977 levels?[15]

The equation for calculating the change in the wage gap under this hypothetical scenario is

$$
(5) \qquad \frac{w_h^{1987'} - w_l^{1987'}}{w_l^{1987'}} = \frac{\left(1 + \dfrac{S_h^{1977} - S_h^{1987}}{B_h^{1987'}}\right) w_h^{1987}}{\left(1 + \dfrac{S_l^{1977} - S_l^{1987}}{B_l^{1987'}}\right) w_l^{1987}} - 1,
$$

where the left side is the hypothetical wage gap between highly educated (h) and less educated (l) labor in 1987 as a ratio of the wages of less educated workers in the hypothetical 1987 economy that still exports in net factor terms what it had in 1977, S_i^t is the observed content of net exports of the ith factor (highly educated or less educated labor) in year t (1977 or 1987) measured in U.S. technologies of year t, and $B_i^{1987'}$ is the U.S. endowment of factor i in 1987 minus S_i^{1977}.[16] The difference between the

---

15. I am grateful to Robert Staiger for suggesting the use of equation (5) to test the effect of changes in the factor content of trade on relative wages.

16. In his characteristically witty and assertive style, Ed Leamer argues in his comment on this paper that, although one is neither making a technical error nor being illogical in empirically measuring the Deardorff-Staiger relationship between changes in the factor content of trade and relative changes in factor prices that holds under certain conditions, the researcher is "not making sense." According to Leamer, "the Stolper-Samuelson mapping of product prices into factor prices is the conceptually straightforward and direct setting in which to study how changes in trading opportunities are affecting U.S. wages. . . . Study prices, not quantities." However, since changes in domestic technological conditions affect wages independently from any resulting changes in product prices, it is necessary to assume no changes in domestic technology for it to be sufficient to focus only on the behavior of domestic prices in studying the forces affecting U.S. wages. One method of attempting to deal with the effects of changes in domestic technical conditions, which Leamer has utilized in other research (1996a), is to introduce measures of domestic changes in total factor productivity (TFP) into the analysis. However, as he also points out in that research, while changes in TFP directly affect wages, the price pass-through effects of these changes can range from none at all to a price pass-through equal to the productivity improvement. Arbitrary assumptions must be made about these pass-through effects in order to disentangle the price effects (and thus factor price effects) of changes brought about by changes in domestic technology from those brought about by other forces. Moreover, since these other forces

hypothetical wage gap calculated by this formula and the actual wage gap can be interpreted as that part of the gap attributable to the actual change in trade between 1987 and 1977.[17] Since the actual change in trade between these two years could be due to changes in U.S. factor endowments and preferences or technology as well as changes in foreign competition, it should be emphasized (see Deardorff 1997) that this equation does not isolate the effects of foreign competition on the wage gap.

The results of the calculation for the 1987/77 period as well as for the 1977/67 period are presented in table 2.1. As indicated in the table, in 1987 the wages of highly educated workers (workers with thirteen or more years of education) exceeded those of less educated workers (workers with twelve years or less) by 50.3 percent, compared to 38.0 percent in 1977. The hypothetical gap in 1987 would have been 48.0 percent if factor trade had been the same as in 1977. Thus, the change in trade between these years (whatever it causes) contributed 2.3 percentage points to the 12.3 percentage point increase (or 18.7 percent) in the increase in wage inequality.

If 1977 factor trade had been the same as in 1967, the gap hypothetically would have been 36.4 percent in contrast to the actual wage gap of 38.0. The interpretation is that the actual change in trade between 1967 and 1977 contributed 1.6 percentage points to the 1977 gap. The actual wage gap fell from 51.0 percent in 1967 to 38.0 in 1977, a decline of 13.0 percentage points. The change in trade reduced the narrowing of the wage gap by 11 percent ($= 1.6/[13.0 + 1.6]$).

In a recent paper, Deardorff (1997) extends the Deardorff-Staiger model beyond just Cobb-Douglas production functions and preferences to cover

---

include such things as changes in domestic relative factor endowments, it is necessary to label as a change in global trading opportunities ". . . something strictly internal to the US" (Leamer 1996a, 22). In short, it seems to me (and, judging by his own research, also to Leamer at a fundamental level) that without making arbitrary and not very reasonable assumptions about price pass-through effects and the meaning of changes in trading opportunities, one cannot adequately study the behavior of U.S. wages by focusing solely on changes in product prices. For an approach to disentangling the effects of changes in technology from changes in trade that is quite different from that followed in Leamer (1996a), see Baldwin and Cain (forthcoming).

17. It should be emphasized that equation (5) is not being used to calculate the effects of such ambiguous terms as "changes in trading opportunities," but simply to tell us what would have happened to the wage gap between two years if the United States had undertaken policies in the later year to stabilize the factor content of trade at its earlier level (assuming both that the changes to U.S. technology, endowments, and preferences that actually occurred between the two years would still have occurred, and that preferences and technology are Cobb-Douglas in form). As emphasized in the next sentence, one cannot attribute the difference between this hypothetical wage gap and the actual current wage gap to some specific factor such as changes in foreign competition. The calculations are helpful, nevertheless, in providing boundary estimates of what the U.S. wage effects would have been if the actual change in net exports had been due entirely to changes in foreign supply-and-demand conditions (and none at all to changes in domestic technology, tastes, or factor supplies) and there were Cobb-Douglas preferences and technology.

Table 2.1   **The Effect of Changes in Trade on the Highly Educated/Less Educated Labor Wage Gap, 1977/1967 and 1987/1977**

	1977 = Year t, 1967 = Year $t-1$	1987 = Year t, 1977 = Year $t-1$
Hypothetical wage gap in year t, holding factor trade at year $t-1$ level	.364	.480
Actual wage gap in year t	.380	.503
Gap in year t attributable to change in trade between year t and year $t-1$	.016	.023

Sources: Data on wages and proportions of workers by education groups and industry are from the March Current Population Surveys. Data on the value of exports and imports are from the seventy-nine industry (the two-digit level of classification) input-output tables published by the Bureau of Economic Analysis (BEA) of the U.S. Department of Commerce. These data are expressed in real terms, using the implicit price deflator for personal consumption expenditures from the National Income and Product Accounts. The Census Bureau's industry classification is concorded to the BEA's input-output industry classification. Employment and price data are from the Output and Employment Database of the Office of Employment Projections, Bureau of Labor Statistics. Estimates of the direct and indirect labor content of exports and imports are based on the BEA's 1977 and 1987 input-output tables.

all CES production functions and preferences.[18] In doing so, he shows that the elasticity of a factor price (suitably normalized) with respect to its endowments is $-1/$(the elasticity of substitution). Therefore (approximating changes in logs by percentage changes), the percentage change in a factor price will be $-1/$(elasticity of substitution) times the change in factor content as a fraction of endowment. Modifying the changes in factor contents as a fraction of endowments in equation (5) by using substitution elasticities of, say, two and five rather than unity implies that the hypothetical wage gap in 1987 would have been 49.2 percent and 49.9 percent, respectively, rather than 48.0 percent, if factor trade had been the same as in 1977. Thus, with these substitution elasticities, the change in trade between these years accounts for only 8.9 percent and 3.2 percent, respectively, of the increase in wage inequality over this period.

The usefulness of such empirical estimates is a matter of judgment. Panagariya (1998) argues that the assumptions underlying the calculations are so stringent that the procedure cannot be considered a reliable guide to measuring the contribution of trade to wage inequality. He points out that empirical studies do not support the assumption that elasticities of substitution in production are the same across industries and, moreover, that there is no evidence of identical constant elasticity of substitution

18. Panagariya (1998) extends the earlier Deardorff-Staiger model in this manner. Krugman (1995) derives a related result. As Panagariya points out, Krugman confines his attention to infinitesimally small changes so that he is able to derive locally a reduced-form elasticity of substitution between skilled and unskilled labor without having to assume that all production and utility functions have identical constant elasticities of substitution.

utility functions across goods. He also notes that the analysis requires the absence of any trade-induced technical changes and any trade-induced changes in factor endowments and tastes. These are important qualifications, but it seems to me that the underlying assumptions are sufficiently reasonable to provide another useful empirical means of roughly assessing the possible importance of increased foreign competition versus other factors in influencing the extent of wage inequality.

2.5   Conclusions

One main conclusion of this paper is that relative factor prices cannot, in general, be inferred from measures of the factor content of trade. In a simple two-factor Heckscher-Ohlin model with two or more goods, the ratio of the relatively abundant factor embodied in net exports to the relatively scarce factor embodied in net imports does measure the relative prices of the two factors, provided trade is balanced. However, this relationship breaks down when there are three or more factors. Measures of changes in the quantities of factors embodied in net exports to the domestic supplies of these factors are not reliable indicators of factor price changes, even in the simple 2×2 Heckscher-Ohlin model.

Another conclusion is that within-industry versus between-industry shifts in the relative factor proportions used in producing traded goods are not adequate indicators of the relative importance of the different exogenous factors affecting relative factor prices. In a general equilibrium model with factor substitution, exogenous changes in factor endowments, tastes, and technology all affect both the proportions of factors used within industries and the proportions of these factors used among industries. There is no unique relationship between the type of exogenous change and the relative importance of these two types of shifts.

As Deardorff and Staiger (1988) show, if technologies and preferences are Cobb-Douglas, factor prices are systematically related to factor endowments. Using the relationships that they derive and U.S. data on factor supplies, relative wages, and the factor content of trade, section 2.4 of this paper estimates that the change in trade between 1977 and 1987 contributed about 19 percent of the increase in wage inequality between these years. Between 1967 and 1977, the change in trade reduced the narrowing of the gap that took place between these years by about 11 percent. Using Deardorff's (1997) extension of the Deardorff-Staiger analysis to cover all constant elasticity of substitution technologies and preferences, it is also shown that the contribution of trade would have been about one-half or one-fifth as large as these figures if the substitution elasticities had been two or five, respectively. It should be stressed not only that the assumptions underlying this analysis are very stringent but that the portion attributable to trade could have been brought about by domestic changes in factor endowments, preferences, and technology as well as by increased foreign competition.

References

Baldwin, Robert E. 1995. The effect of trade and foreign direct investment on employment and relative wages. *OECD Economic Studies* 23 (winter): 7–54.

Baldwin, Robert E., and Glen G. Cain. Forthcoming. Shifts in relative U.S. wages: The role of trade, technology and factor endowments. *Review of Economics and Statistics.*

Berman, Eli, John Bound, and Zvi Griliches. 1994. Changes in the demand for skilled labor within U.S. manufacturing: Evidence from the Annual Survey of Manufactures. *Quarterly Journal of Economics* 109:367–97.

Berman, Eli, Stephen Machin, and John Bound. 1997. Implications of skill-biased technological change: International evidence. NBER Working Paper no. 6166. Cambridge, Mass.: National Bureau of Economic Research, September.

Bhagwati, Jagdish, and Vivek Dehejia. 1994. International trade theory and wages of the unskilled. In *Trade and wages: Leveling wages down?* ed. J. Bhagwati and M. Kosters, 36–75. Washington, D.C.: American Enterprise Institute.

Deardorff, Alan V. 1997. Factor prices and the factor content of trade revisited: What's the use? Research Seminar in International Economics, School of Public Policy. Discussion Paper no. 409. Ann Arbor: University of Michigan.

Deardorff, Alan V., and D. S. Hakura. 1994. Trade and wages: What are the questions? In *Trade and wages: Leveling wages down?* ed. J. Bhagwati and M. Kosters, 76–107. Washington, D.C.: American Enterprise Institute.

Deardorff, Alan V., and Robert W. Staiger. 1988. An interpretation of the factor content of trade. *Journal of International Economics* 24:93–107.

Dixit, Avinash, and Victor Norman. 1980. *Theory of international trade: A dual, general equilibrium approach.* Cambridge: Cambridge University Press.

Helpman, Elhanan, and Paul R. Krugman. 1985. *Market structure and foreign trade: Increasing returns, imperfect competition, and the international economy.* Cambridge: MIT Press.

Katz, Lawrence F., and Kevin Murphy. 1992. Changes in relative wages, 1963–1987: Supply and demand factors. *Quarterly Journal of Economics* 107 (February): 36–78.

Krugman, Paul. 1995. Technology, trade, and factor prices. NBER Working Paper no. 5355. Cambridge, Mass.: National Bureau of Economic Research, November.

Lancaster, Kelvin. 1957. The Heckscher-Ohlin trade model: A geometric treatment. *Economica*, n.s. 24:25–28, 31–32.

Leamer, Edward E. 1994. Trade, wages and revolving door ideas. NBER Working Paper no. 4716. Cambridge, Mass.: National Bureau of Economic Research, April.

———. 1996a. In search of Stolper-Samuelson effects on U.S. wages. NBER Working Paper no. 5427. Cambridge, Mass.: National Bureau of Economic Research, January.

———. 1996b. What's the use of factor contents? NBER Working Paper no. 5448. Cambridge, Mass.: National Bureau of Economic Research, February.

Leontief, Wassily W. 1953. Domestic production and foreign trade: The American capital position re-examined. *Proceeding of the American Philosophical Society* 97:332–49.

Melvin, James R. 1968. Production and trade with two factors and three goods. *American Economic Review* 58 (December): 1249–68.

Murphy, Kevin, and Finis Welch. 1991. The role of international trade in wage differentials. In *Workers and their wages,* ed. M. Kosters, 39–69. Washington, D.C.: American Enterprise Institute.

Panagariya, Arvind. 1998. Trade and wages: The content of the factor content. Paper presented at the International Center of International Economics, College Park Md., University of Maryland, 16 February.

Sachs, Jeffrey D., and Howard J. Shatz. 1994. Trade and jobs in U.S. manufacturing. *Brookings Papers on Economic Activity,* no. 1: 1–83.

Travis, William P. 1964. *The theory of trade and protection.* Cambridge, Mass.: Harvard University Press.

Vanek, J. 1968. The factor proportions theory: The N-factor case. *Kyklos* 21 (4): 749–56.

Comment   Edward E. Leamer

According to Bill Gates's thesaurus, *bob* (the verb) means alternatively to prune or to duck, and *bob* (the noun) is a haircut.

In writing this comment, I have the pleasure to honor two other Bobs: Baldwin, the author of the article, and Lipsey, the Festschrift honoree. As an introduction to this comment, I remind the reader what *Bob* means in international economics. It means careful and painstaking data work. It means getting the theory right. It means deep understanding. It is the opposite of duck. It refers to two distinguished economists who have insisted on a conversation about international economics that is adequately and appropriately informed by data. Because the subject of international economics has wisely become more empirical in the 1990s, now is a fine time to say thanks to our two Bobs for carrying this burden so long and so well.

With that as an introduction, the reader will not find it surprising to learn that there is not a single sentence in this paper with which I disagree (except those few sentences that must have slipped by Baldwin's screen!). Thus I think Bob Baldwin has the theory and the data right. If I could ask for something, it would be for more firmness. This trade and wages debate is very important, and we cannot allow it to be dominated by wrong-headed ideas. I am worried that Bob's light touch may leave the impression that the methods he comments on are not all that bad To help out, here is my one-sentence version of this paper: *Both the between-and-within accounting and the factor content calculations are completely pointless if they are intended to inform us whether trade is having an impact on wages.*

Edward E. Leamer is the Chauncey J. Medberry Professor of Management and professor of economics and statistics at the University of California, Los Angeles, and a research associate of the National Bureau of Economic Research.

Between-and-Within Calculations

Let's first dispose of the between-and-within studies initiated by Berman, Bound, and Griliches (1994). They conclude that it is skill-biased technological change, not trade, that is driving the increase in the premium for skills because of two reasons: (1) The ratio of nonproduction to production workers has been on the rise overall in the United States, even as the ratio of wages has risen. *If trade were the driver, one would expect the input use of the cheaper factor to increase, not to fall.* (2) This shift toward nonproduction workers occurs mostly within sectors, and not much between sectors. *If trade matters, it does so by altering the sector composition of output. Since the big shifts have been within sectors, then it is technology, not trade, that matters.* (Wrong and/or misleading statements are in italics.)

As Bob Baldwin correctly points out, there is nothing about our trade models that allows the conclusion that trade affects only the sectoral composition of employment, and not the within-industry mix of inputs. The basic theoretical logic of this between-and-within calculation is therefore faulty. However, repeating the theory doesn't seem to carry the day. Maybe some data will do the job. Figure 2C.1 illustrates the facts for the apparel sector: rising ratio of nonproduction to production workers and rising rela-

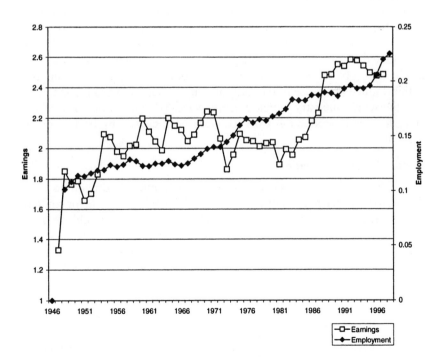

Fig. 2C.1   Apparel sector: ratios of nonproduction to production, employment and earnings

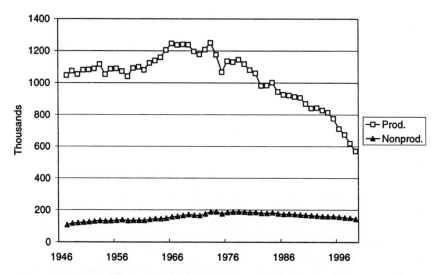

Fig. 2C.2   Production and nonproduction workers in apparel

tive wages. This must be technology, right? Wrong. Figure 2C.2 shows that the rise in the ratio of nonproduction jobs to production jobs in apparel, which began in the early 1970s, is due to a dramatic reduction in production jobs. This coincides with a big increase in imports (not shown). Thus faced with cheap apparel imports from low-wage countries, U.S. employers had three options—lower U.S. wages, raise U.S. productivity, or move the production jobs to Asia. They opted for some of all of these. Thus the within-industry increase in the ratio of nonproduction to production jobs, and the within-industry increase in the wages of nonproduction workers compared with production workers, were both caused by trade, not by technology.

Factor Content Calculations

The factor content calculations are a more difficult dragon to slay. Again, to focus the mind, I display in figure 2C.3 data on the factor content of U.S. trade computed by Leamer (2000). What exactly should we infer from the facts that until the 1980s, the labor embodied in U.S. trade was a very small fraction of the U.S. labor supply, and that in the 1980s, imports of high-school hours as a fraction of U.S. supply rose to almost 8 percent? From numbers like these, Katz and Murphy (1992) report, "Table VII presents the changes in relative labor demand predicted by changes in international trade in manufactures. . . . The table indicates that the effects on relative labor demands of trade were quite moderate until substantial deficits developed in the 1980s. The adverse effects of trade on relative labor demand are concentrated on high school dropouts" (p. 65); and "De-

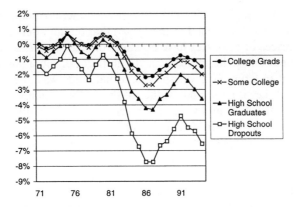

Fig. 2C.3   Hours worked embodied in trade: percent of U.S. hours
Source: Leamer (2000).

mand shifts arising from changes in international change in manufacturing only start to be of quantitative significance with the appearance of large trade deficits in the 1980s" (p. 77). I don't think these conclusions are valid, and I don't think that Bob Baldwin does, either. But Baldwin's paper seems to have been written both by "Bob" and by some alien force that I will call "Bub."

For example, Bob writes, "The conclusion reached is that *only* under special assumptions are such linkages justified" (my italics), but Bub does it anyway: "Section 2.4 . . . presents empirical estimates of how trade may have affected the U.S. wage gap between more educated and less educated workers in recent years that are based on these assumptions." Bob cautions again, "Panagariya (1998) argues that the assumptions underlying the calculations are so stringent that the procedure cannot be considered a reliable guide to measuring the contribution of trade to wage inequality." But Bub replies "Between 1967 and 1977, the change in trade reduced the narrowing of the gap that took place between these years by about 11 percent." Fortunately, Bob gets the final words: "It should be stressed not only that the assumptions underlying this analysis are very stringent but that the portion attributable to trade could have been brought about by domestic changes in factor endowments, preferences, and technology as well as by increased foreign competition."

I think Bob is right and Bub is wrong. I don't mean that Bub is making a technical error. The physicist Neils Bohr would explain to Bub: "You're not making sense. You're just being logical." Likewise, Deardorff and Staiger.

Here is the basic point: The Stolper-Samuelson mapping of product prices into factor prices is the conceptually straightforward and direct setting in which to study how changes in trading opportunities are affecting

U.S. wages. One implication of the Stolper-Samuelson mapping is that events (such as the U.S. deficit in the 1980s) that do not alter technologies or relative prices of tradables have no effect on U.S. wages. Study prices, not quantities. Thus, the increase in the imports of labor inputs in the 1980s evident in figure 2C.3 doesn't mean that trade was affecting wages in the 1980s. Likewise, the small values of the factor contents in the 1970s don't mean that U.S. wages were unaffected by global trading opportunities, or by changes thereto. On the contrary, relative apparel and textile prices declined by 30 percent in the 1970s, and that relative price change, if the theory is correct, must beget wage changes.

While we are on the subject of "small," I remind the reader that there is an active literature in international economics (Trefler 1995; Gabaix 1997) that is attempting to explain why the factor contents are so small, not just for the United States but for most other countries as well. Until we figure out what is the best model for explaining why the factor contents are so small, I think it is very unwise to draw any conclusions from the fact that they are small.

If you want a full meal, not just a taste, visit Leamer (2000).

In conclusion, I am fond of saying that theories are neither true nor false; they are sometimes useful and sometimes misleading. Students in my class who have been studying hypothesis testing in econometrics are completely perplexed by this idea, but they feel better when I tell them that economists are neither right nor wrong—they are sometimes useful, and sometimes misleading.

Thanks, Bob, and thanks, Bob.

References

Berman, Eli, John Bound, and Zvi Griliches. 1994. Changes in the demand for skilled labor within U.S. manufacturing: Evidence from the Annual Survey of Manufactures. *Quarterly Journal of Economics* 109:367–97.

Gabaix, Xavier. 1997. The factor content of trade: A rejection of the Heckscher-Ohlin-Leontief hypothesis. Harvard University Working Paper.

Katz, Lawrence F., and Kevin Murphy. 1992. Changes in relative wages, 1963–1987: Supply and demand factors. *Quarterly Journal of Economics* 107 (February): 36–78.

Leamer, Edward E. 2000. What's the use of factor contents? *Journal of International Economics* 50 (1): 17–50.

Trefler, Daniel. 1995. The case of the missing trade and other HOV mysteries. *American Economic Review* 12:1029–46.

II

Multinational Firms

Multinational Firms
Reconciling Theory and Evidence

James R. Markusen and Keith E. Maskus

3.1 Introduction

An important component of Robert Lipsey's research has involved the study of direct foreign investment and often the relationship between investment and trade. From our point of view, this research is of major importance, and our first task in this paper is to explain why.

The field of international trade developed in the modern era, largely as a study of trade in goods. Mundell (1957) wrote an important article in which he noted that trade in goods and trade in factors were substitutes, perhaps suggesting that there is little point in expanding our theory to include trade in factors: The same equilibrium in terms of commodity prices, factor prices, and welfare can be achieved by trading either goods or factors. Only much later was it noted that Mundell had shown this in the context of an extremely special case, namely a 2×2 Heckscher-Ohlin model with zero trade costs in both goods and factors. Positive analyses showed a wide variety of circumstances in which trade in goods and factors are complements (Markusen 1983; Wong 1986; Markusen and Svensson 1985; Ethier and Svensson 1986; Neary 1995). Normative analyses showed that the effects of policy often depend crucially on what is traded (Brecher and Diaz-Alejandro 1977; Bhagwati and Brecher 1980; Dick 1993).

James R. Markusen is professor of economics at the University of Colorado, Boulder, a research associate of the National Bureau of Economic Research, and a research fellow of the Centre for Economic Policy Research, London. Keith E. Maskus is professor of economics at the University of Colorado, Boulder.

Markusen's portion of this research was funded by a grant from the National Science Foundation through the National Bureau of Economic Research. The authors thank David Carr and Rebecca Neumann for data work and estimation, and Ann Harrison for useful and insightful comments.

Although it had many antecedents (e.g., Kemp 1969; Melvin 1969; Linder 1961), an industrial-organization (IO) approach to trade was developed in the 1980s. This approach incorporated elements of imperfect competition, increasing returns to scale, and product differentiation into general equilibrium trade models. Yet this new theory, however welcome, was largely disjoint from the study of multinational enterprises. Firms in the trade-IO literature are typically single-plant production units with all firm activities in a single location. This is rather odd insofar as most of the firms that fit the general facts and paradigms of the IO approach to trade are indeed multinationals with production plants in several countries. Research on multinationals was certainly produced, but it was often (at best) partial equilibrium in nature and focused on individual firms rather than on explaining the pattern of direct investment in relation to country and industry characteristics.

Robert Lipsey is a distinctive individual in that he apparently ignored this allocation of trade, national firms, and general equilibrium to trade theory, and of multinational firms to the international business studies. Lipsey wrote a number of important articles in which he related the pattern of direct investment by multinational firms to national characteristics and to trade flows. This work presented researchers with a comprehensive and challenging set of stylized facts to explain. His research helped make it clear that multinationals had to be integrated into both trade theory and the empirical analysis of trade and investment flows.

The work by Lipsey that most clearly relates to this paper includes the following. Two early papers with Merle Yahr Weiss examined determinants of foreign production and exports (Lipsey and Weiss 1981, 1984). During the same period Lipsey developed a long coauthorship with Irving Kravis, looking at the determinants of the competitiveness of multinational firms and how these firms affect other variables of interest, such as domestic employment (Kravis and Lipsey 1982, 1988, 1992; Lipsey and Kravis 1987). Single-authored papers on determinants of inward and outward investment and the internationalization of production include Lipsey (1988, 1989, 1993, 1995). A series of other papers was the result of collaboration with Magnus Blomström (Blomström and Lipsey 1989, 1993), in some cases with other coauthors (Blomström, Kravis, and Lipsey 1988; Blomström, Lipsey, and Kulchycky 1988; Blomström, Lipsey, and Ohlsson 1990; Lipsey, Blomström, and Ramstetter 1998). This body of work provides a tremendous volume of empirical evidence on direct investment and trade, which needs to be reconciled with formal theory.

A few attempts to develop a formal general-equilibrium theory of multinational firms developed during the early 1980s. Helpman (1984) had a model in which production involved two activities—one capital intensive and one labor intensive—that could be geographically separated. Markusen (1984) took a rather different approach, assuming the existence of firm-level (as opposed to plant-level) scale economies arising from the joint-input nature of knowledge capital across geographically separated production facilities. Helpman's model captured the notion of vertically integrated firms, but allowed no investments to take place between very similar countries, which is clearly counter to empirical fact. Markusen's model captured the notion of horizontally integrated firms that undertake the same activity in multiple countries, but excluded any motive for vertical specialization. Theoretical refinements of these ideas can be found in Helpman (1985), Horstmann and Markusen (1987, 1992), Brainard (1993a), Markusen (1997), and Markusen and Venables (1998); a survey is found in Markusen (1995).

During the same period in which some of this formal theory was developing, a large body of empirical work developed relating direct investment to country and industry characteristics, much of this by Robert Lipsey alone or with various coauthors as just noted. It quickly became clear that the overwhelming proportion of direct investment occurs among the similar, high-income developed countries, not among dissimilar countries. "North-north" investment dominates "north-south" investment even after correcting for income levels and other determinants. At a superficial level, horizontal, multiplant models fit the data better than do vertical specialization models, which do not predict direct investment among similar countries.

Formal econometric reconciliation or testing of the theories with the evidence was slow in coming. Two important papers by Brainard (1993b, 1997) confirmed the casual observation that similarities rather than differences between countries in terms of size and relative endowments are closely related to the level of direct investment relative to trade. These papers provide additional support to the horizontal view that firm-level scale economies rather than factor intensity differences between activities provide the more important explanation of direct investment. Yet subsequent to 1987, the year of Brainard's data sample, a boom in direct investment to developing countries emerged. This suggested that perhaps it was unmeasured investment barriers that accounted for the low levels of direct investment to these countries. Carr, Markusen, and Maskus (forthcoming) estimate a model that integrates both horizontal and vertical motives for direct investment on 1986–94 panel data and find support for that integrated approach. Complementary work by Ekholm (1995, 1997, 1998a, 1998b) supports the findings of Brainard and of Carr, Markusen, and Maskus, and adds convincing evidence about the importance of intrafirm trade in knowledge-intensive headquarters services. Of relevance to the present study, recent empirical work that focuses on the relationships between direct investment and trade flows (particularly intrafirm), such as whether trade and investment are in some sense complements or substitutes, includes papers by Blonigen (1997, 1998), Swenson (1998), and Smith (1998).

The objective of this paper is to extend this inquiry by decomposing foreign affiliate production data into sales to the host-country market and export sales. We first develop and extend existing theory from Markusen (1997) and Carr, Markusen, and Maskus (forthcoming) to generate separate predictions of how local sales versus export sales should be related to parent-country and host-country characteristics. This approach will attempt to get at the horizontal versus vertical distinction that is not explicitly considered in Carr et al. (forthcoming). These theoretical predictions are then taken to the data.

Results fit well with the theoretical hypotheses. Local sales of foreign affiliates are strongly dependent on market size and trade costs into the host country. The difference in skilled labor abundance between the parent and host country is only weakly related to local affiliate sales in both economic and statistical terms. Export sales are weakly related to market size and to host-country trade costs. They are strongly related to the skilled labor endowment differences of the parent and host countries, and strongly related to an interaction term between skill differences and country size: Exports by affiliates are particularly important when the parent is both small and skilled-labor-abundant (e.g., Sweden, the Netherlands, Switzerland). Both local sales and export sales are strongly negatively related to a host-country investment barrier (cost) index.

The ratio of exports to local sales is positively related to the relative skilled labor abundance of the parent, and negatively related to market size, the host-country investment cost index, and the host-country trade cost index. The findings on trade and investment costs may be due to a substitution phenomenon. If the investment is undertaken to serve the local market, firms will bear the trade and investment costs. If the investment is made to serve the market in the parent or third countries, high local trade and investment costs will induce the firm to look elsewhere.

3.2 The Knowledge-Capital Model

In this section, we outline what we refer to as the *knowledge-capital model* of the multinational enterprise. A formal algebraic development is presented in Markusen (1997), and many of its testable implications are analyzed in Carr et al. (forthcoming).

Assume a two-good, two-factor, two-country world. Refer to the factors as skilled (S) and unskilled (L) labor. Good Y is produced with constant returns to scale by a competitive industry and is unskilled labor intensive. The countries are referred to as h (home) and f (foreign).

Good X is produced with increasing returns by imperfectly competitive, Cournot firms. Production of X requires a firm-level fixed cost—headquarters services such as R&D, management, finance, accounting, marketing and so forth. An X firm may then have one or two plants, and a plant and headquarters may be geographically separated. Headquarters services are a joint input across plants, creating firm-level scale economies, also referred to in the literature as multiplant economies of scale. The idea is that headquarters services (e.g., blueprints) are often knowledge based and can be provided to additional production facilities at low or zero marginal cost. We also assume plant-level fixed costs (scale economies).

Assumptions about the factor intensities of fixed costs are crucial to the story. We assume that headquarters services use skilled labor exclusively. Plant-level fixed costs are a combination of skilled and unskilled labor. Final production occurs with constant costs and requires only unskilled labor. Transport costs between markets use unskilled labor. Finally, we assume that plant production, including both fixed costs and marginal costs, is more skilled labor intensive than Y production, the composite of the rest of the economy. This is not particularly important to any of the results in this paper, but is important in generating certain results concerning the factor price effects of investment liberalization (Markusen 1997). In summary, then, the ranking of activities from most skilled labor intensive to least skilled labor intensive is as follows:

[headquarters only] > [integrated X] > [plant only] > [Y].

This completes the description of the model, and allows us to specify more precisely what is meant by the knowledge-capital approach. There are three defining assumptions:

1. *Transportability or fragmentation.* The services of knowledge-based assets may be fragmented from production and are easily supplied to geographically separate production facilities.
2. *Skilled labor intensity.* Knowledge-based assets are skilled labor intensive relative to final production.
3. *Jointness.* The services of knowledge-based assets are (at least partially) joint (public) inputs into geographically separate production facilities.

The first two properties give rise to vertical multinationals that locate their single plant and headquarters in different countries depending on factor prices and market sizes. The third property gives rise to horizontal multinationals that have plants producing the final goods in multiple countries.

More formally, several types of firms may be active in equilibrium in a free-entry Cournot equilibrium for the model we have just outlined. The term *national firms* refers to single-plant firms with their headquarters and plant in the same country; the term *horizontal multinationals* refers to two-plant firms with their headquarters in one country or the other. *Vertical multinationals* refers to single-plant firms with their headquarters and plant in different countries.

Here we simply outline the results that emerge from this model with respect to what types of firms are active in equilibrium as a function of country characteristics, such as differences in size, relative endowments, and the level of trade costs and total world demand. The interested reader is referred to Markusen (1997) for a fuller development.

Horizontal multinationals tend to arise when the two countries are similar in size and relative endowments, total demand is high, and trade costs are moderate to high. In order to understand the importance of similarity in size, it is perhaps easiest to note that single-plant firms (national or vertical) have an inherent advantage when the countries are of very different size: Put a single plant in the large country, avoiding costly capacity in the small market. Growth in total demand will induce shifts (in some regions of parameter space) from single-plant production, serving the other market by high marginal-cost exports, to high fixed-cost branch plant production.

Vertical multinationals are favored over national firms and horizontal multinationals when the countries have very different relative endowments, especially when the skilled-labor-abundant country is also small. Differences in factor prices encourage fragmentation of activities, such that the headquarters in the skilled-labor-abundant country and differences in size encourage placing the plant in the large country. These two motives reinforce one another when the skilled-labor-abundant country is also small.

These results are interesting, but not very useful to take to the data. We do not have good data on the types of firms existing, and in reality, these pure types are greatly blurred in any case. However, the model can be used to generate results on the sales of affiliates of country i firms in country j. This reduced form gives us direct predictions on observable data, fully endogenizing the trade flows, types of firms that are active, and so forth, without requiring us to identify those items in the data.

Figures 3.1–3.4 present results from simulations using the model from Markusen (1997) and Carr et al. (forthcoming). These diagrams are world Edgeworth boxes, with unskilled labor on the x axis and skilled labor on the y axis. The origin for country i is at the southwest (SW) corner and the origin for country j is at the northeast (NE) corner. For points on the SW-NE diagonal, the countries have the same relative endowments but differ in size. Note for later reference that movements within these Edgeworth boxes are compensated experiments, in that total world factor endowments are constant (and, therefore, world GDP is approximately constant). These diagrams are most useful for developing intuition about two-way data in which we observe production and sales by affiliates of country i firms in country j and vice versa. Thus in any pair (i-to-j and j-to-i) of observations, total GDP and factor endowments are held constant.

Affiliate sales are graphed on the vertical axis of figure 3.1. Affiliate sales

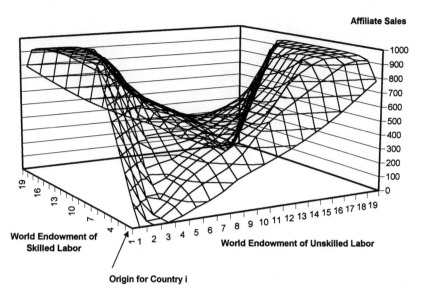

Fig. 3.1   World affiliate sales

appear as a saddle, with an inverted U-shaped curve along the SW-NE diagonal. As noted earlier, horizontal multinationals dominate production when the countries are identical, whereas national firms located in the larger country dominate when the countries are very different in size. In the center of the box, exactly half of world production is affiliate sales, while the other half is the output of the horizontal multinationals' domestic plants.

The highest level of affiliate sales occurs in the NW and SE areas of the Edgeworth box in figure 3.1, where one country is both small and skilled labor abundant.[1] In this case, most firms are vertical multinationals headquartered in the small, skilled-labor-abundant country, so most plants are located in the larger, skilled-labor-scarce country. Output of these plants is classified as "affiliate production," of course, so most (in the limit, all) world X production is affiliate sales.

Figures 3.2, 3.3, and 3.4 show simulation results for affiliate sales in just one direction: affiliates of country i firms producing in country j. Figure 3.2 shows the local sales in country j of affiliates of country i firms. There is again an inverted U-shaped relationship along the SW-NE diagonal. But

1. The locus of points in which countries i and j have equal incomes is much steeper than the NW-SE diagonal of the Edgeworth boxes in figures 3.1–3.4. It runs between columns 8 (north edge) and 12 (south edge). So, for example, country i is smaller than j to the left of this locus.

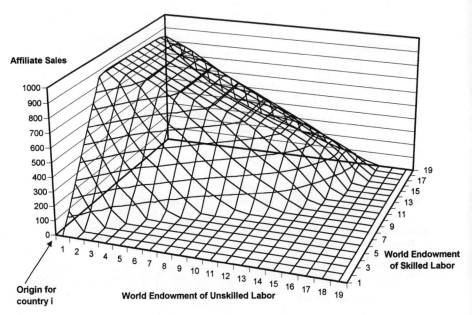

Fig. 3.2   Local sales of affiliates of country *i* firms in country *j*

the highest levels occur when country *i* is both small and skilled labor abundant for the reasons just noted.

Figure 3.3 shows the export sales of affiliates back to the parent country *i*. This diagram is a "mountain," reaching a maximum when country *i* is small and skilled labor abundant, but not too small and not too skilled labor scarce. The not-too-small requirement is obvious, because little output is exported back to a very small country. The not-too-skilled-labor-abundant requirement is less obvious, and it has to do with the assumption that some host-country skilled labor is required in plant-level fixed costs. As country *j* becomes too skilled labor scarce, production there becomes very expensive and national firms in country *j* substitute for vertical firms headquartered in *i* and producing in *j*.

There are clear differences between figures 3.2 and 3.3. Most notably, only local sales occur if the countries are very similar, or if country *i* is very small and very skilled labor abundant. Yet there are some similarities that make it difficult to propose sharply different hypotheses regarding how these two classes of affiliate sales should be related to country characteristics.

Figure 3.4 clarifies this ambiguity a bit by displaying the ratio of affiliate exports back to the parent to local affiliate sales in the host country. This graph suggest that this ratio is most closely related to the skilled labor abundance of the parent in relation to the host country. Relative size

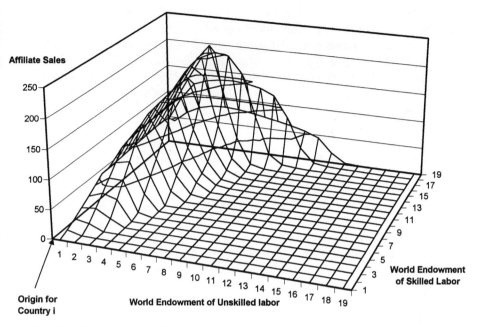

Fig. 3.3 Export sales of affiliates of country *i* firms in country *j*

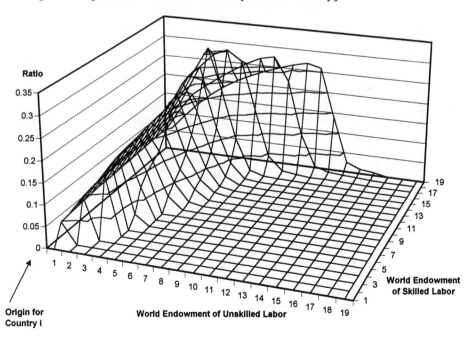

Fig. 3.4 Ratio of export sales to local sales, affiliates of country *i* firms in country *j*

differences play some role, but the ratio clearly is not higher when the parent country i is both small and skilled labor abundant.[2]

These simulation results suggest a number of independent variables that should be used to explain the three dependent variables: local sales by affiliates of country i firms in country j (fig. 3.2), export sales by the same affiliates (fig. 3.3), and the ratio of these two variables (fig. 3.4). Refer to these variables as RSALESL, RSALESE, and RATIOEL (R for *real* in the first two). We now list the right-hand-side variables, adding a discussion of the hypothesized signs and magnitudes using figures 3.1–3.4 and other more obvious intuition. Again, note that these hypotheses are most appropriate to two-way compensated observations as noted earlier. We shall return to this point shortly.

SUMGDP denotes the sum of two countries' real GDPs. This should have a positive coefficient in explaining RSALESL and RSALESE. However, the effect should be stronger on RSALESL; the reason is that growth will, at various points in parameter space, lead to a switch from high marginal-cost single-plant firms to high fixed-cost multiplant firms, increasing local sales more than in proportion to growth in incomes. Accordingly, we hypothesize that RATIOEL should be negatively related to SUMGDP.

GDPDIFF is the difference between the two countries' real GDP levels, and GDPDIFSQ is the squared difference. GDPDIFSQ should be negatively related to all three dependent variables, as suggested by figures 3.2–3.4. Moving along various loci parallel to the SW-NE diagonal, all three dependent variables are higher near the center than at the extremes, although the maximum point generally is not exactly where the two countries are the same size.

SKDIFF denotes the relative skilled labor abundance of the *parent* country relative to that of the host; formally, it is the share of the labor force that is skilled in country i (parent or source) minus the same share in country j (host). SKDIFF should be positively related to both RSALESL and RSALESE. However, it is likely to have a stronger impact on RSALESE than on RSALESL from examination of figures 3.2 and 3.3. Relative endowments and factor price differences are the primary determinants of export sales, whereas local sales are influenced heavily by country sizes as well. Accordingly, we hypothesize that SKDIFF will have a positive sign in the RATIOEL regression, as suggested by figure 3.4.

INVJ denotes an index of investment barriers (costs) into country j, the host country. Higher numbers indicate higher investment costs. This is hypothesized to be negatively related to both RSALESL and RSALESE. However, investments to serve the local market may be less sensitive to

2. Recall that country i is smaller than country j at all points left of a line running from approximately column 8 on the north side of the box to column 12 on the south side.

these costs than are investments to serve export markets, because alternative locations may be selected for the latter; thus we hypothesize that the magnitude of the coefficient in the RSALESL equation should be less than that in the RSALESE equation, and therefore that the sign on INVJ should be negative in the RATIOEL equation as well.

TCJ denotes an index of trade barriers (costs, not including distance or freight) into country j. Higher numbers indicate higher barriers or costs. Such barriers should encourage investments to serve the local market, so the hypothesized sign is positive in the RSALESL equation. The effect should be noticeably less in the RSALESE equation and may be negative, insofar as trade costs raise the costs of imported intermediate inputs. The sign of the coefficient in the RATIOEL equation should thus be negative.

TCI is a similar measure of trade barriers back into the parent country. This has little effect on production for local sales in country j, but is expected to have a negative effect on production for export, insofar as much of that may be going back to the home country. This variable should thus have a negative sign in the RATIOEL equation.

SKDIFF*GDPDIFF is an interactive term. Referring to figures 3.2–3.3, the effect of an increase in SKDIFF should be larger when the parent is smaller (GDPDIFF $<$ 0), and the effect of an increase in GDPI (parent GDP) should be smaller when the parent country i is skilled labor abundant (SKDIFF $>$ 0). Both effects imply that the sign of the coefficient on the interactive term should be negative in the RSALESL and RSALESE regressions. Figure 3.4, however, does not suggest a very sharp hypothesis as to whether it should be positive or negative in the RATIOEL equation. Therefore, we are agnostic about the sign in the RATIOEL equation.

DIST will denote a distance measure between pairs of countries. Theory does not offer us much of a prediction about distance. It may lead to a substitution: producing abroad instead of exporting to a distant country. However, distance raises the transaction costs of investments as well as those of exports. It is possible that distance might affect production for export more negatively than it would production for local sale (which might actually be encouraged), but we are generally agnostic insofar as we do not understand the transactions costs of investing at a long distance.

In addition to examining these hypotheses on two-way data (inward and outward affiliate sales data for the United States), we examine them on U.S. outward data only. The advantage of the latter is that it breaks down affiliate export sales into sales back to the parent country and sales to third countries. Sales back to the U.S. parent may be closely identified with vertical investments such as foreign assembly plants. We should note, however, that the intuition generated by figures 3.1–3.4 may not always be appropriate, insofar as these diagrams are compensated experiments holding the two-country total factor endowment constant. Thus an increase in SKDIFF is an increase in the U.S. skilled labor abundance and a fall in the host-country skilled labor abundance in the simulations. For the U.S. outward data, an increase in SKDIFF is a fall in the host-country skilled labor abundance holding the U.S. endowment constant. Similar comments apply to GDPDIFF, and in the outward regressions we will use GDPJ since it is only the latter variable that changes.

A problematic issue with the outward-only data arises from the fact that the United States (the parent) is always far bigger than the host, although not always skilled labor abundant relative to the host. This restricts observations to an area in the NE section of the Edgeworth boxes in figures 3.2–3.4, which is a considerable difficulty given the nonlinearity and nonmonotonicity of the theoretical predictions over the parameter space of the Edgeworth box. For example, note that increases in SKDIFF could lead to a fall in outward U.S. investment in this region (foreign plants are replaced by U.S. national firms serving the host by exports). Thus we should expect some differences in the U.S. outward-only results versus the two-way results due to the fact that they are somewhat different experiments and because we are constrained to a subregion of parameter space in the outward-only data. Further comment is postponed until we view the results.

3.3   Data Sources and Variable Construction

The data form a panel of cross-country observations over the period 1986–94. We take real sales volume of nonbank manufacturing affiliates in each country to indicate production activity. The U.S. Department of Commerce provides annual data on sales of foreign affiliates of American parent firms and on sales of U.S. affiliates of foreign parent firms. Thus, for each year, the United States serves as both the headquarters country for its firms producing abroad and the affiliate country for foreign firms producing there. There are thirty-six countries in addition to the United States for which we have at least one year of complete data. Annual sales values abroad are converted into millions of 1990 U.S. dollars using an exchange rate adjusted local wholesale price index, with exchange rates and price indexes taken from the *International Financial Statistics* (*IFS*) of the International Monetary Fund.

As just noted, the inward data (U.S. affiliates of foreign parents) list only total exports of the affiliates to all countries. The outward data (foreign affiliates of U.S. parents) break down exports of those affiliates into exports back to the United States and exports to third countries. The latter series is particularly valuable, but constrains the analysis to a subarea of the Edgeworth box in which the parent country (United States) is always very large relative to the host, as has been noted. The inward-outward (two-way) data are thus in some ways much better for examining the theory, but suffer from a clear third-country problem, whereas the theory is developed in a two-country context. Thus, we examine two cases, each of which has a drawback: the inward-outward data using total affiliate export sales to all countries, and outward-only data in which exports can be distinguished between exports back to the parent and exports to third countries.

Real GDP is measured in billions of 1990 U.S. dollars for each country. For this purpose, annual real GDP figures in local currencies were converted into dollars using the market exchange rate. These data are also from the *IFS*.

Skilled labor abundance is defined as the sum of occupational categories 0/1 (professional, technical, and kindred workers) and 2 (administrative workers) in employment in each country, divided by total employment. These figures are compiled from annual surveys reported in the *Yearbook of Labour Statistics* published by the International Labour Organization. In cases in which some annual figures were missing, the skilled labor ratios were taken to equal the period averages for each country. The variable SKDIFF is then simply the difference between the relative skill endowment of the parent country and that of the affiliate country.

The cost of investing in the affiliate country is a simple average of several indexes of impediments to investment throughout the period, reported in the *World Competitiveness Report* of the World Economic Forum. The indexes include restrictions on ability to acquire control in a domestic company, limitations on the ability to employ foreign skilled labor, restraints on negotiating joint ventures, strict controls on hiring and firing practices, market dominance by a small number of enterprises, an absence of fair administration of justice, difficulties in acquiring local bank credit, restrictions on access to local and foreign capital markets, and inadequate protection of intellectual property. These indexes are computed on a scale from 0 to 100, with a higher number indicating higher investment costs.

A trade cost index is taken from the same source and is defined as a measure of national protectionism, or efforts to prevent importation of competitive products. It also runs from 0 to 100, with 100 representing the highest trade costs. All of these indexes are based on extensive surveys of multinational enterprises.

We also incorporate a measure of distance, which is simply the number of kilometers of each country's capital city from Washington, D.C. It is unclear whether this variable captures trade costs or investment costs, since both should rise with distance.

3.4 Results

Tables 3.1–3.3 show results for regression equations on the full inward-outward data set. Table 3.1 gives results for dependent variable RSALESL (local sales in country *j* of affiliates of country *i* firms). Signs are as predicted for *direct* effects, although the two variables involving SKDIFF are

Table 3.1   **Results for Panel Estimation, Inward and Outward Data**

	Dependent variable:	RSALESL (weighted least squares)
	Total observations:	381
	R^2:	0.728
	Adjusted R^2:	0.722

Variable	Parameter Estimate	Sign as Predicted?	T for HO: Parm = 0	Prob > |T|
SUMGDP	10.2937	Yes	9.108	0.0001
GDPDIFSQ	−0.0009	Yes	−7.163	0.0001
SKDIFF	10,531	Yes	0.877	0.3813
GDPDIFF*SKDIFF	−2.6932	Yes	−1.114	0.2658
INVCJ	−633.3970	Yes	−7.119	0.0001
TCJ	366.5574	Yes	6.142	0.0001
TCI	−22.0996	?	−0.195	0.8451
DIST	−1.5326	?	−9.293	0.0001
INTERCEPT	469.22		0.046	0.9631

Table 3.2   **Results for Panel Estimation, Inward and Outward Data**

	Dependent variable:	RSALESE (weighted least squares)
	Total observations:	381
	R^2:	0.486
	Adjusted R^2:	0.473

Variable	Parameter Estimate	Sign as Predicted?	T for HO: Parm = 0	Prob > |T|
SUMGDP	2.9274	Yes	3.971	0.0001
GDPDIFSQ	−0.0003	Yes	−3.504	0.0005
SKDIFF	42,961	Yes	5.523	0.0001
GDPDIFF*SKDIFF	−6.9520	Yes	−4.434	0.0001
INVCJ	−277.2284	Yes	−4.758	0.0001
TCJ	52.1164	?	1.332	0.1836
TCI	65.6274	No	0.892	0.3729
DIST	−0.6398	?	−5.927	0.0001
INTERCEPT	7,501.94		1.127	0.2604

not statistically significant. Country size, investment costs, and trade costs into the host-country market have strong explanatory power. Trade costs back into the parent country (TCI) have little explanatory power, and theory does not hypothesize that it should.

Table 3.2 gives results for dependent variable RSALESE (export sales to all countries by affiliates of country i firms in country j). Signs are as hypothesized except for TCI, which should be negative, at least for exports going back to the home countries (these cannot be broken out in the data, as previously noted). The two terms involving SKDIFF are both larger in magnitude (economic significance) than in the RSALESL regression, and highly statistically significant. The magnitude of the SUMGDP coefficient, on the other hand, is much smaller in the RSALESE regression. These results suggest that market size is a more important determinant of production for local sales while differences in relative endowments are a more important determinant of production for export.

These comparisons can be misleading, however, due to differences in the size of the dependent variables (local sales are larger than export sales in most observations). Table 3.3 therefore uses the ratio of export sales to local sales. Results confirm that market size is more important for local sales (coefficient on SUMGDP is negative) and that skill differences are more important for export sales (coefficient on SKDIFF is positive); thus, the proportion of export sales increases as host country j becomes more unskilled labor abundant (skilled labor scarce).

The coefficients on the INVCJ and TCJ variables in the ratio equation of table 3.3 are negative. This conforms to our intuition about substitutability. Production for local sale, by definition, cannot move to a third country, and thus local sales may be relatively insensitive to these costs. Production for export sale may be more sensitive to investment and trade costs because the firm can choose an alternative location to serve a broader market, as suggested by the negative signs in the ratio equation. TCI is positive in this regression, which is consistent with results in tables 3.1 and 3.2. This outcome is not consistent with our intuition, but note that the significance level is low. Higher parent-country trade costs should discourage foreign production for export back to the parent, but should not affect production for local sale.

Tables 3.4–3.8 present results on the U.S. outward-only sample, allowing

Table 3.3   **Results for Panel Estimation, Inward and Outward Data**

Dependent variable:	RATIOEL (weighted least squares)	
Total observations:	371	
R^2:	0.335	
Adjusted R^2:	0.319	

Variable	Parameter Estimate	Sign as Predicted?	T for HO: Parm = 0	Prob > |T|
SUMGDP	−0.000671	Yes	−4.327	0.0001
GDPDIFSQ	−1.92E-08	Yes	−1.209	0.2273
SKDIFF	3.175373	Yes	3.121	0.0019
GDPDIFF*SKDIFF	−0.000043	?	−0.173	0.8630
INVCJ	−0.043374	Yes	−3.491	0.0005
TCJ	−0.010975	Yes	−1.261	0.2082
TCI	0.014789	No	1.094	0.2749
DIST	0.000055	?	2.446	0.0149
INTERCEPT	6.100586		4.222	0.0001

Table 3.4   **Results for Panel Estimation, U.S. Outward Only**

	Dependent variable:	RSALESL (weighted least squares)
	Total observations:	274
	R^2:	0.773
	Adjusted R^2:	0.766

Variable	Parameter Estimate	Sign as Predicted?	T for HO: Parm = 0	Prob > |T|
GDPJ	20.8423	Yes	10.362	0.0001
GDPDIFSQ	−0.0018	Yes	−8.120	0.0001
SKDIFF	−948,636	?	−11.980	0.0001
GDPDIFF*SKDIFF	174.5818	?	11.905	0.0001
INVCJ	−517.8056	Yes	−6.546	0.0001
TCJ	314.8092	Yes	5.943	0.0001
DIST	−1.2044	?	−7.810	0.0001
INTERCEPT	73,798.00		9.863	0.0001

a breakdown of production for export sale into sales back to the United States (RSALESUS in table 3.5) and sales to third countries (RSALESF in table 3.6). The most dramatic change in these results relative to tables 3.1–3.3 is the reversal in the signs of SKDIFF and GDPDIFF*SKDIFF. This suggests that U.S. outward investment is attracted to more-skilled-labor-abundant countries, for both local production and production for export, with strong statistical significance. The latter result is particularly at odds with the two-way results.

There are two possible explanations, other than simply concluding that inward and outward investments follow different models. First, there is the compensated versus uncompensated issue that we mentioned earlier. In the U.S. outward-only data, an increase in SKDIFF holds U.S. skilled labor abundance constant, effectively lowering world skilled labor abundance. This is a somewhat different experiment than that in the two-way data, which includes not only such uncompensated observations across different countries, but also a great many compensated observation pairs comparing i-to-j and j-to-i affiliate production. The response of affiliate production to an increase in host-country skilled labor abundance (decrease in SKDIFF) should be more positive or less negative than if this change is accompanied by a fall in the parent-country skilled labor abundance, and that is what the results are telling us.

The second possible explanation relates to the fact that the parent country (the United States) is always much larger than the host in the U.S. outward data. How this might affect the results is shown most clearly in figure 3.2. When country i is quite large relative to country j, a (compensated) increase in SKDIFF may produce a fall in RSALESL: Heading toward the north edge of the box, we go over the "hump" and RSALESL

Table 3.5   **Results for Panel Estimation, U.S. Outward Only**

	Dependent variable:	RSALESUS (weighted least squares)
	Total observations:	244
	R^2:	0.358
	Adjusted R^2:	0.336

Variable	Parameter Estimate	Sign as Predicted?	T for HO: Parm = 0	Prob > |T|
GDPJ	2.1956	Yes	1.445	0.1499
GDPDIFSQ	−0.0002	Yes	−1.332	0.1843
SKDIFF	−177,143	No	−3.049	0.0026
GDPDIFF*SKDIFF	33.4368	?	3.088	0.0023
INVCJ	−346.6351	Yes	−5.722	0.0001
TCJ	207.5793	No	5.141	0.0001
DIST	−0.7968	?	−6.635	0.0001
INTERCEPT	20,469		3.616	0.0004

Table 3.6   **Results for Panel Estimation, U.S. Outward Only**

	Dependent variable:	RSALESF (weighted least squares)
	Total observations:	259
	R^2:	0.598
	Adjusted R^2:	0.585

Variable	Parameter Estimate	Sign as Predicted?	T for HO: Parm = 0	Prob > |T|
GDPJ	6.8947	Yes	5.690	0.0001
GDPDIFSQ	−0.0006	Yes	−4.615	0.0001
SKDIFF	−237,383	No	−4.803	0.0001
GDPDIFF*SKDIFF	44.7907	?	4.860	0.0001
INVCJ	−211.3208	Yes	−4.541	0.0001
TCJ	−8.6449	Yes	−0.279	0.7805
DIST	−8.6449	?	−3.001	0.0030
INTERCEPT	29,941.00		6.715	0.0001

start to fall. What is happening in the theory model is that host country j is becoming sufficiently skilled labor scarce that branch plants there are closed and production is concentrated in national firms headquartered in country i. This implies a negative sign on SKDIFF, which is the result we are getting in tables 3.4–3.6. This finding is in fact consistent with results in Zhang and Markusen (1999), which show that the smallest, poorest (skilled-labor-scarce) countries receive a far smaller share of world direct investment than their share of income. The result and associated theory also points out the importance of knowing which part of the box is being examined and of adding more investing countries, as is done in the two-way sample.

Table 3.7 shows results for the ratio of affiliate export sales back to the United States to affiliate sales to the local market, and table 3.8 shows results for the ratio of affiliate sales to third markets to affiliate sales to the local market. Results on market size confirm those in table 3.3, that a larger market shifts a proportion of sales from exports to local sales. The findings also confirm the results on INVCJ and TCJ (TCI was dropped because country i is always the United States). The results on SKDIFF and GDPDIFF*SKDIFF are not consistent with tables 3.4–3.6; however,

Table 3.7   Results for Panel Estimation, U.S. Outward Only

Dependent variable:	RATIOUSL (weighted least squares)
Total observations:	231
R^2:	0.413
Adjusted R^2:	0.392

Variable	Parameter Estimate	Sign as Predicted?	T for HO: Parm = 0	Prob > |T|
GDPJ	−0.000693	Yes	−3.708	0.0003
GDPDIFSQ	−4.12E-08	Yes	−2.134	0.0340
SKDIFF	2.364984	Yes	0.391	0.6963
GDPDIFF*SKDIFF	−0.000186	?	−0.165	0.8689
INVCJ	−0.019319	Yes	−2.831	0.0051
TCJ	−0.004806	Yes	−0.959	0.3387
DIST	0.000087	?	6.225	0.0001
INTERCEPT	1.947083		2.925	0.0038

Table 3.8   Results for Panel Estimation, U.S. Outward Only

Dependent variable:	RATIOFL (weighted least squares)
Total observations:	236
R^2:	0.343
Adjusted R^2:	0.320

Variable	Parameter Estimate	Sign as Predicted?	T for HO: Parm = 0	Prob > |T|
GDPJ	−0.001291	Yes	−3.881	0.0001
GDPDIFSQ	−2.36E-08	Yes	−0.683	0.4953
SKDIFF	29.904477	Yes	2.630	0.0091
GDPDIFF*SKDIFF	−0.005218	?	−2.467	0.0144
INVCJ	−0.045391	Yes	−3.517	0.0005
TCJ	−0.003751	Yes	−0.403	0.6876
DIST	−0.000026	?	−0.841	0.4014
INTERCEPT	3.913419		3.330	0.0010

these point estimates have extremely low statistical significance in table 3.7, while the positive sign on SKDIFF in table 3.3 is highly significant. Both coefficients are statistically significant in table 3.8. Thus, the results suggest that U.S. outward investment is not attracted to low-skilled countries, even investment for production for export back to the United States (table 3.5).

Results on market size and relative endowments must be interpreted carefully, however, since GDP appears in three terms and relative endowments in two terms. Let us write the first four terms of the regression equations as

(1) β_1SUMGPD + β_2GDPDIFSQ + β_3SKDIFF

$$+ \beta_4\text{GDPDIFF} * \text{SKDIFF}.$$

The derivatives of this equation with respect to host-country variables GDPJ and SKLJ are then as follows (an increase in GDPJ is a negative change in GDPDIFF, and an increase in SKLJ is a negative change in SKDIFF):

(2) $\dfrac{\partial \text{RSALES}}{\partial \text{GDPJ}} = \beta_1 - 2\beta_2\text{GDPDIFF} - \beta_4\text{SKDIFF},$

(3) $\dfrac{\partial \text{RSALES}}{\partial \text{SKLJ}} = -\beta_3 - \beta_4\text{GDPDIFF}.$

Table 3.9 computes values of these derivatives at the mean values of SKDIFF and GDPDIFF for the two samples. Table 3.9 gives the absolute change in sales by country i affiliates in j in response to a growth in country j's income and to an increase in country j's skilled labor abundance (decrease in its unskilled labor abundance). Effects of increases in country j's investment and trade cost indexes are also listed. The top panel gives results for the inward-outward estimation, while the lower panel gives estimates for the U.S. outward estimation only. Below the level estimates, an elasticity figure is computed. We do not compute elasticities with respect to INVCJ and TCJ, since these are qualitative indexes.

According to results in the top panel of table 3.9, local sales are elastic with respect to host-country income, with an elasticity of $\varepsilon = 1.6$. Export sales are less elastic, at $\varepsilon = 1.1$. Local sales are very insensitive to the skilled labor ratio in the host country, while export sales have an elasticity with respect to the skilled labor ratio of $\varepsilon = -0.7$. Production for export sales is attracted to less-skilled-labor-abundant (more-skilled-labor-scarce) countries. Comparing local sales to export sales, the former respond more to income, whereas the latter respond more to skilled labor scarcity as suggested by the regression results discussed earlier.

The pattern for the U.S. outward-only data (lower panel of table 3.9) is qualitatively similar to the top panel but quantitatively different. Production

Table 3.9   **Effects of Host-Country Size and Skilled Labor Abundance on Foreign Affiliate Production for Local Sale and Export (derivatives evaluated at the mean of independent variables) ($ millions)**

Effect on:	$1 Billion Increase in Country J's GDP	One Percentage Point Increase in SKLJ[a]	One Point Increase in INVCJ	One Point Increase in TCJ
Local sales of country i affiliates in country j (inward and outward data)	16.7 (1.558)	−12.1 (−0.017)	−633.4	366.6
Export sales of country i affiliates in j to all countries (inward and outward data)	4.7 (1.118)	−189.0 (−0.681)	−277.2	52.1
Local sales of U.S. affiliates in country j (U.S. outward data only)	22.7 (1.044)	280.5 (0.599)	−517.8	314.8
Export sales of U.S. affiliates in country j to United States (U.S. outward data only)	1.3 (0.213)	8.3 (0.064)	−346.6	207.6
Export sales of U.S. affiliates in country j to other countries (U.S. outward data only)	9.0 (0.989)	12.0 (0.061)	−211.3	−8.6

For the last two rows: $\varepsilon w = 0.681$ (GDP column); $\varepsilon w = 0.062$ (SKLJ column).

Note: Numbers in parentheses are elasticity values.

[a] By "One Percentage Point Increase in SKLJ" we mean, for example, an increase from 15 percent to 16 percent, not an increase from 15 percent to 15.15 percent.

for local sale has an elasticity with respect to local market size of about 1.0, while the elasticities of exports back to the United States and to third countries are 0.2 and 1.0, respectively. A weighted average of these two elasticities (εw) yields a figure of 0.68. Thus the elasticity of exports with respect to host-country size is less than that for local sales by an amount similar to the two-way estimates. The elasticity of local sales with respect to the host-country skilled labor ratio is about 0.6, while the average of the two export elasticities is 0.06. Production for export back to the United States or to third countries is insensitive to the host-country skilled labor ratio, at least at the mean of GDPDIFF. Again, the pattern is qualitatively similar to that for the two-way estimate in that the export elasticity with respect to local skilled labor is smaller than that for local sales (i.e., less positive or more negative).

Overall, the results in table 3.9, taking into account interactive effects, clearly confirm that production for local sales is more sensitive to local market size than is production for export. Production for local sales has an elasticity with respect to the host-country skilled labor ratio that is larger than the elasticity for production for export. Production shifts relatively in favor of local sales when the host is more skilled labor abundant and relatively in favor of exports when the host is skilled labor scarce.

There is an interesting quantitative difference between the two-way and U.S. outward estimates of the elasticities with respect to the host-country skilled labor ratio (subject again to the caveats that these are point estimates, evaluated at the mean of GDPDIFF in each sample, and that the means differ in the two samples). While production for export is attracted by host-country unskilled labor abundance in the two-way sample, there is virtually no effect in the U.S. outward sample. We might infer from this that production by U.S. affiliates for export, including that back to the United States, is not primarily attracted to low-skilled countries, contrary to a popular impression of multinationals exporting jobs to low-wage countries. While this may occur in arm's-length outsourcing (e.g., subcontracting), our results suggest that it is not primarily multinationals that are responsible for such a phenomenon. As we have noted, this is consistent with the theoretical assumption that branch-plant production is skilled labor intensive relative to the rest of the host economy. Past a certain level of skilled labor scarcity in the host economy, inward direct investment begins to fall as that country becomes increasingly skilled labor scarce (Zhang and Markusen 1999).

3.5 Summary and Conclusions

Robert Lipsey's work over many years has given us a rich empirical literature that relates the behavior of multinational firms to industry and country characteristics. Theoretical work that endogenizes multinational firms into general equilibrium trade models has developed somewhat more recently, and offers predictions about the relationship between affiliate production and parent-country and host-country characteristics. In particular, the knowledge-capital approach to the multinational enterprise identifies motives for both horizontal and vertical multinational activity and predicts how affiliate activity should be related to variables such as country sizes and relative endowment differences.

This paper draws implications from the theory as to how production for local sales versus production for export sales relates to country characteristics, and then subjects these hypotheses to empirical estimation. Results fit well with the theory in terms of economic and statistical significance. Local (host-country) market size is more important for production for local sales than for production for export sales. Host-country skilled labor scarcity is important for export production relative to production for local sales. Investment and trade-cost barriers in the host country affect production for export more negatively than they do production for local sales.

Some quantitative difference was found in the two-way (inward and outward) sample versus the U.S. outward-only sample with respect to host-country skilled labor scarcity. In the U.S. outward-only sample, host-country skilled labor scarcity (unskilled labor abundance) had little effect on U.S. affiliate production for export sale, whether back to the United States or to third countries. This suggests that U.S. outward investment is not drawn primarily to unskilled-labor-abundant countries, contrary to a common fear that outsourcing by multinationals is resulting in a loss of U.S. unskilled jobs. (Firms could, of course, be outsourcing to unaffiliated subcontractors). In the two-way sample, production for exports is drawn to unskilled-labor-abundant countries. However, the results are qualitatively similar in the two samples insofar as unskilled labor abundance in the host is *relatively* more important for export sales.

References

Bhagwati, Jagdish N., and Richard A. Brecher. 1980. National welfare in an open economy in the presence of foreign-owned factors of production. *Journal of International Economics* 10 (1): 103–15.

Blomström, Magnus, Irving B. Kravis, and Robert E. Lipsey. 1988. Multinational firms and manufacturing exports from developing countries. NBER Working Paper no. 2493. Cambridge, Mass.: National Bureau of Economic Research, January.

Blomström, Magnus, and Robert E. Lipsey. 1989. The export performance of US and Swedish multinationals. *Review of Income and Wealth,* ser. 35, no. 3: 245–64.

———. 1993. The competitiveness of countries and their multinational firms. In *Multinationals in the global political economy,* ed. Lorraine Eden and Evan H. Potter, 129–41. New York: St. Martin's Press.

Blomström, Magnus, Robert E. Lipsey, and Ksenia Kulchycky. 1988. US and Swedish direct investment and exports. In *Trade policy issues and empirical analysis,* ed. Robert E. Baldwin, 259–97. Chicago: University of Chicago Press.

Blomström, Magnus, Robert E. Lipsey, and Lennart Ohlsson. 1990. What do rich countries trade with one another? R&D and the composition of US and Swedish trade. *Banca Nazionale del Lavoro Quarterly Review* 173 (June): 215–35.

Blonigen, Bruce. 1997. Firm-specific assets and the link between exchange rates and foreign direct investment. *American Economic Review* 87 (3): 447–66.

———. 1998. In search of substitution between foreign production and exports. University of Oregon, Department of Economics, Working Paper.

Brainard, S. Lael. 1993a. A simple theory of multinational corporations and trade with a trade-off between proximity and concentration. NBER Working Paper no. 4269. Cambridge, Mass.: National Bureau of Economic Research, February.

———. 1993b. An empirical assessment of the factor proportions explanation of multinationals sales. NBER Working Paper no. 4580. Cambridge, Mass.: National Bureau of Economic Research, December.

———. 1997. An empirical assessment of the proximity-concentration tradeoff between multinational sales and trade. *American Economic Review* 87 (4): 520–44.

Brecher, Richard A., and Carlos F. Diaz-Alejandro. 1977. Tariffs, foreign capital and immiserizing growth. *Journal of International Economics* 7 (4): 317–22.

Carr, David, James R. Markusen, and Keith E. Maskus. Forthcoming. Estimating the knowledge-capital model of the multinational enterprise. *American Economic Review.*

Dick, Andrew R. 1993. Strategic trade policy and welfare: The empirical consequences of foreign ownership. *Journal of International Economics* 35 (3/4): 227–49.

Ekholm, Karolina. 1995. *Multinational production and trade in technological knowledge.* Lund Economic Studies no. 58. University of Lund, Lund, Sweden.

———. 1997. Factor endowments and the pattern of affiliate production by multinational enterprises. CREDIT Working Paper no. 97/19. University of Nottingham, Nottingham, UK.

———. 1998a. Headquarter services and revealed factor abundance. *Review of International Economics* 6 (4): 545–53.

———. 1998b. Proximity advantages, scale economies, and the location of production. In *The geography of multinational firms,* ed. Pontus Braunerhjelm and Karolina Ekholm, 59–76. Boston: Kluwer Academic Publishers.

Ethier, Wilfred, and Lars E. O. Svensson. 1986. Theorems of international trade with factor mobility. *Journal of International Economics* 20 (1/2): 21–42.

Helpman, Elhanan. 1984. A simple theory of trade with multinational corporations. *Journal of Political Economy* 92 (3): 451–71.

———. 1985. Multinational corporations and trade structure. *Review of Economic Studies* 52 (3): 443–58.

Horstmann, Ignatius J., and James R. Markusen. 1987. Strategic investments and the development of multinationals. *International Economic Review* 28 (1): 109–21.

———. 1992. Endogenous market structures in international trade. *Journal of International Economics* 32 (1/2): 109–29.

Kemp, Murray C. 1969. *The pure theory of international trade and investment.* New York: Prentice Hall.

Kravis, Irving B., and Robert E. Lipsey. 1982. The location of overseas production and production for export by US multinational firms. *Journal of International Economics* 12 (3/4): 210–23.

————. 1988. The effect of multinational firms' foreign operations on their domestic employment. NBER Working Paper no. 2760. Cambridge, Mass.: National Bureau of Economic Research, December.

————. 1992. Sources of competitiveness of the United States and of its multinational firms. *Review of Economics and Statistics* 74 (2): 193–201.

Linder, Staffan B. 1961. *An essay on trade and transformation.* Uppsala, Sweden: Almqvist and Wiksells.

Lipsey, Robert E. 1988. Changing patterns of international investment in and by the United States. In *The United States and the world economy,* ed. Martin Feldstein, 475–545. Chicago: University of Chicago Press.

————. 1989. The internationalization of production. NBER Working Paper no. 2923. Cambridge, Mass.: National Bureau of Economic Research, April.

————. 1993. Foreign direct investment in the United States: Changes over three decades. In *Foreign direct investment,* ed. Kenneth A. Froot, 113–70. Chicago: University of Chicago Press.

————. 1995. Outward direct investment and the U.S. economy. In *The effects of taxation on multinational corporations,* ed. M. Feldstein, J. R. Hines, Jr., and R. Glenn Hubbard, 7–33. Chicago: University of Chicago Press.

Lipsey, Robert E., Magnus Blomström, and Eric Ramstetter. 1998. Internationalized production in world output. In *Geography and ownership as bases for economic accounting,* ed. Robert E. Baldwin, Robert E. Lipsey, and J. David Richardson, 83–135. Chicago: University of Chicago Press.

Lipsey, Robert E., and Irving B. Kravis. 1987. The competitiveness and comparative advantage of U.S. multinationals 1957–1984. *Banca Nazionale del Lavoro Quarterly Review* 161 (June): 147–65.

Lipsey, Robert E., and Merle Yahr Weiss. 1981. Foreign production and exports in manufacturing industries. *Review of Economics and Statistics* 63 (4): 488–94.

————. 1984. Foreign production and exports of individual firms. *Review of Economics and Statistics* 66 (2): 304–8.

Markusen, James R. 1983. Factor movements and commodity trade as complements. *Journal of International Economics* 13 (3/4): 341–56.

————. 1984. Multinationals, multi-plant economies, and the gains from trade. *Journal of International Economics* 16 (3/4): 205–26.

————. 1995. The boundaries of multinational firms and the theory of international trade. *Journal of Economic Perspectives* 9 (2): 169–89.

————. 1997. Trade versus investment liberalization. NBER Working Paper no. 6231. Cambridge, Mass.: National Bureau of Economic Research, October.

Markusen, James R., and Lars E. O. Svensson. 1985. Trade in goods and factors with international differences in technology. *International Economic Review* 26 (1): 175–92.

Markusen, James R., and Anthony J. Venables. 1998. Multinational firms and the new trade theory. *Journal of International Economics* 46 (2): 183–203.

Melvin, James R. 1969. Increasing returns to scale as a determinant of trade. *Canadian Journal of Economics* 3 (3): 389–402.

Mundell, Robert. 1957. International trade and factor mobility. *American Economic Review* 47 (3): 321–35.

Neary, J. Peter. 1995. Factor mobility and international trade. *Canadian Journal of Economics* 28 (November, special iss.): S4–S23.

Smith, Pamela J. 1998. Patent rights and bilateral exchange: A cross-country analysis of US exports, FDI, and licensing. University of Minnesota Working Paper.

Swenson, Debra. 1998. The tradeoff between trade and foreign investment. University of California, Davis, Working Paper.

Wong, Kar-Yui. 1986. Are international trade and factor mobility substitutes? *Journal of International Economics* 21 (1/2): 25–44.
Zhang, Kevin H., and James R. Markusen. 1999. Vertical multinationals and host-country characteristics. *Journal of Development Economics* 59 (2): 233–52.

Comment   Ann E. Harrison

I'd like to begin by saying how much I welcome the opportunity to contribute to this conference in honor of Robert Lipsey. One of my greatest joys in being affiliated with the NBER (and there have been many) has been the opportunity to get to know him. One outcome has been a recent paper that we coauthored on the impact of multinational activity on host-country wages, where we found that multinational corporations (MNCs) pay a wage premium vis-à-vis domestic enterprises equal to around 10 percent (Aitken, Harrison, and Lipsey 1997).

It is also a great pleasure to be able to discuss Jim Markusen and Keith Maskus's paper. This paper is very appropriate for the conference: The authors are applying some very interesting ideas to real data.

Let me begin by highlighting two reasons this is timely: (1) It provides a concise but illuminating review of the previous literature on direct investment and multinational activity, focusing in particular on Bob Lipsey's voluminous contributions to that literature. (2) It provides a nice review of some of Jim Markusen's research, focusing on some of his key ideas and presenting graphical representations of his theoretical results.

This paper measures the importance of two different motives for multinational activity: exploiting differences in endowments (which leads to vertical MNC activity, with skill-intensive activities such as R&D done at home, and labor-intensive activities such as assembly done abroad) versus exploiting certain firm-specific assets or ideas that can be shared across units. The latter motive for MNCs is likely to lead firms to establish similar units across countries, leading to horizontal FDI. The question is, How can we distinguish between these two motives in the data?

The authors are able to identify empirically the importance of these two motives through clever use of U.S. data on inward and outward MNC activity: MNCs that locate facilities abroad for reexport are likely to be doing so in order to take advantage of differences in factor endowments. Take, for example, *maquiladoras* in northern Mexico who exploit cheap labor and reexport all their final production back to the United States. MNCs who expand horizontally and set up similar facilities at home and

Ann E. Harrison is professor at Columbia Business School and a faculty research fellow of the National Bureau of Economic Research.

abroad do so to exploit their knowledge (which can be shared across multiple facilities) and are less sensitive to differences in endowments.

Another attractive feature of this paper is that it is the only research of which I am aware that directly tests the implications of general equilibrium models of FDI on actual data. Clearly, this research agenda could provide much scope for future papers. I have several suggestions for future research.

First, it is easy to understand the motive for a vertical MNC and how to identify the motive empirically: MNC activity should be correlated with differences in endowments. I have a difficult time, however, trying to understand how we test for the alternative hypothesis: How do we capture the horizontal motive empirically? Based on the theory, the authors argue that horizontal MNC activity is more likely between countries of similar size with similar endowments. It is difficult for me to understand why there should be any MNC activity at all in this case—why don't countries just trade? The answer must be that high tariffs or transport costs make it difficult to trade and therefore lead to horizontal MNC. So I find the authors' results on protection a better measure of the importance of horizontal MNC activity than the variable that they use (GDP size) to provide support for horizontal MNC activity. I suspect that GDP size is important because it reflects opportunities to take advantage of protected domestic markets, rather than scale-induced horizontal expansion. One nice empirical result in the paper is that tariff-jumping is clearly a motive for horizontal MNC activity but not for vertical MNC activity.

Another reason for horizontal MNC activity could be market imperfections that make it difficult to exploit intangible assets through arm's-length licensing, such as poor contract enforcement. This is the so-called internalization hypothesis, which can be captured through variables such as R&D-to-sales ratios. The authors do include measures of protection and transport costs, but not measures of R&D intensity.

This brings me to my next point: In future research, it would be interesting to compare the results in the current paper with results using disaggregated manufacturing data. The authors have made excellent use of country-level data on MNC activity both into and out of the United States, but my intuition tells me that the motive for MNC activity within a country will vary quite a bit by subsector. Let's take, for example, the sales of U.S. affiliates in Mexico:

At the border, U.S. *maquiladoras* are assembling garments for reexport to the United States. This is clearly based on differences in endowments and is of the vertical MNC type.

The big three U.S. auto makers, at least before NAFTA, were completely driven to produce in Mexico because of prohibitive tariffs and quotas.

So FDI in autos was of the horizontal type, becoming more vertical only at the end of the sample period.

Colgate Palmolive has a huge operation in Mexico. This seems to be based on the desire to exploit firm-specific assets by relocating there. This is horizontal MNC activity based on intangible assets and correlated with home R&D intensity.

If we add all three types of affiliate sales together for the empirical work, my fear is that these different effects become muddled and it becomes very difficult to distinguish between the different motives for foreign direct investment. The aggregation problem could explain why it is difficult to get consistent results across different specifications. The variable SKLDIF in some cases captures endowment differences, and in other cases captures the fact that there is less direct investment between less similar countries (i.e., we get horizontal FDI).

I have some other, minor, comments. In the real world, there are more than two factors. How do the authors account for natural-resource intensive reasons for moving? Why do the authors use weighted least squares? It would also be useful to know the weights used in the estimation. Since the authors have a panel over time and across countries, they could also try using a fixed-effects approach. I wonder how the importance of exchange rate fluctuations are taken into account. A large share of Japanese MNC activity into the United States was driven by the desire to hedge against a strong yen and a fluctuating exchange rate. Do the authors include time dummies to account for this?

The authors use a cost-of-investing index, which measures the barriers to FDI and is consistently negatively correlated with affiliate activity. This index includes a lot of independent factors such as restrictions on majority controls, labor market restrictions on hiring and firing, entry barriers through existing oligopolies, and inadequate protection of intellectual property. It would be very interesting to be able to measure the independent effects of these separate policies. This again would be easier to do with more disaggregate data, which would increase sample size and allow the authors to add more right-hand-size variables.

Let me conclude by saying how much I have enjoyed reading and thinking about the results in this paper.

Reference

Aitken, B., A. Harrison and R. Lipsey. 1997. Spillovers, foreign investment, and export behavior. *Journal of International Economics* 43 (1/2): 103–32.

4

Determinants and Effects of Multinational Growth
The Swedish Case Revisited

Birgitta Swedenborg

4.1 Introduction

The enormous growth of international direct investment and multinational corporations (MNCs) in the postwar period has raised challenging issues for international trade theory and practical policy alike. Robert Lipsey has contributed more than anyone else to our empirical knowledge of many of these issues, particularly our understanding of the relationship between international production and trade. Therefore, it seems fitting to devote this paper in a volume honoring Robert Lipsey to the relationship between MNC growth and trade.[1]

A seemingly perennial question in the debate over MNCs has been whether international production by MNCs reduces trade. Certainly, investing countries have been concerned that foreign production by home-country firms replaces exports and thereby exports jobs.[2] Much of the theory on international investment, too, implies a negative relationship in that it focuses on the choice between exports and foreign production in serving foreign markets. The prevalent view, however, is both too partial and too

Birgitta Swedenborg is research director at the Center for Business and Policy Studies in Stockholm, Sweden.

The author is indebted to Jörgen Nilsson at the Research Institute of Industrial Economics (IUI) for computer assistance. She also thanks Bruce Blonigen, Karolina Ekholm, Robert Lipsey, Erik Mellander, and Roger Svensson for helpful comments.

1. It is also fitting because Robert Lipsey has been a constant source of support and inspiration in my own earlier work in this area.

2. Analysis of this question goes back at least to reports by Reddaway (in collaboration with Perkins, Potter, and Taylor, 1967, and with Potter and Taylor, 1968) for the United Kingdom, and to the studies by Hufbauer and Adler (1968) and Lipsey and Weiss (1969, 1972) for the United States, while recent examples include the OECD (1995), Barrell and Pain (1997), and Blomström, Fors, and Lipsey (1997).

static. Reduced exports of some products need not mean reduced exports overall. Multinational production may mainly be a way by which home-country firms can grow larger by specializing production in different countries in accordance with the competitive advantage of each. Therefore, a more relevant question is how international production affects the patterns of specialization and employment in different countries. A related question is what, in a world of internationally mobile firms, determines the competitive advantages of countries as production locations. Both questions are of considerable policy interest today in many countries that are dependent on increasingly footloose MNCs, and that worry about their ability to attract or retain production by these companies. Sweden is such a country.

The purpose of this paper is to explore these issues by analyzing the determinants and effects of foreign investment by Sweden. Over the last decades, foreign production by Swedish firms has grown dramatically. What lies behind this growth and how has it affected exports from and specialization patterns in Sweden? What can it tell us about the competitive advantage of firms and of Sweden as a production location?

Sweden is a small country on the periphery of Europe. Nevertheless, it offers an interesting and natural case study, both because it is, relative to the size of its economy, a very large foreign investor, and because it is the only country other than the United States for which there exist continuous and detailed (firm-level) data on the international operations of its MNCs in the manufacturing sector. The data now cover the thirty-year period from 1965 to 1994.[3]

There are two main motivations for the present study. The first is that no one has yet analyzed the entire thirty-year period for which there is now data.[4] Much has changed in this period and the factors that explained the pattern of foreign production and exports in the earlier part of the period may not be the same as those that explain it in the later part. More importantly, the added time dimension in the data set allows us to study the dynamics of change. Previous analyses have been mainly cross-sectional, and differences between firms (or industries) have been interpreted as indicating the nature of the relationship over time between, for example, exports and foreign production. Yet, the relevance of cross-sectional evidence for making inferences about relationships that are es-

---

3. The data have been collected by the Research Institute of Industrial Economics (IUI) in Stockholm. I was responsible for the design of these surveys and the collection of data in the first four censuses covering 1965, 1970, 1974, 1978, and 1986.

4. My earlier analyses of the same or related issues covered the period 1965–78 and, in less detail, through 1986 (Swedenborg 1979, 1982, 1985, 1991) and Swedenborg, Johansson-Grahn, and Kinnwall 1988). Newer data include 1990 and 1994. The fact that most of this earlier analysis is not available in English provides further motivation for the present study. Recent analyses (in English) of Swedish direct investment do not fully exploit the time dimension of the data set. See, e.g., the recent contributions in Andersson, Fredriksson, and Svensson (1996), Svensson (1996b), and Braunerhjelm and Ekholm (1998).

sentially dynamic in nature is highly uncertain. The observed relationship may mainly reflect inherent differences between firms rather than a relationship that applies to all firms over time. Using firm data over several years allows us to actually analyze changes over time. Specifically, in an analysis that combines cross-sectional and longitudinal data, firm-specific fixed effects can be held constant and the relationship between variables that change over time can be distinguished. Here, we will study changes over a thirty-year period, something that has not been done before.

The second motivation for the present study is that the important question of the "effect" of foreign production on home-country exports and, indirectly, the pattern of employment, remains controversial. Different studies on Swedish data have reached different results. Earlier studies have shown either no effect on exports or modest net complementarity between foreign production and exports, while more recent ones have found considerable net substitutability. Renewed analysis can clarify whether these differences are due to differences in model specification and methods or in the time periods analyzed.

The policy issues underlying an analysis of the effects of international investment are different today from what they were in the 1970s. In those days, the issue in many investing countries was whether they should try to restrict foreign investment by home-country firms—assuming that could be done. Sweden, for example, retained controls on foreign direct investment up until the mid-1980s, when the final vestiges of its foreign-exchange regulations from 1939 were dismantled. Today, such controls are no longer on the political agenda. Instead, the policy issue is related to the determinants of a country's competitive advantage as a production location and whether the home country can attract or retain the kind of production that it would like. If high-skill production, R&D, and, ultimately, corporate headquarters are moved out of the country, it may signal problems that the home country may want to address through policy.

This paper is organized as follows: Section 4.2 briefly describes the importance of Swedish MNCs in the Swedish economy. Section 4.3 goes on to analyze the determinants of foreign production by Swedish manufacturing firms and the effects on parent-company exports over the period from 1965 to 1994. Section 4.4 discusses the effects on the firm's overall competitiveness and implications for changes in the pattern of specialization in the home country. Section 4.5 contains concluding remarks.

4.2 The Role of Swedish MNCs in the Swedish Economy, 1965–94

Relative to its size, the Swedish manufacturing industry is among the most multinational in the world. The ratio of employment in foreign manufacturing affiliates to total employment in Swedish manufacturing was 44 percent in 1994. In 1960, the ratio was 12 percent. The corresponding

Table 4.1   The Role of Swedish MNCs in the Swedish Economy (percent)

	1965	1994
Employment relative to Swedish manufacturing		
Manufacturing affiliates abroad	16	44
Swedish parents	35	40

	1965–1994
Employment change	
Total manufacturing in Sweden	−36
Swedish parents	−25
Manufacturing affiliates abroad	181
All affiliates abroad (including sales affiliates)	210

figure for U.S. firms was 25 percent at its peak in 1977, after which it declined slightly (Lipsey 1995).

A small number of Swedish companies accounts for the growing internationalization of Swedish manufacturing. Only some 130 corporations had manufacturing affiliates abroad in 1994. The number of companies has always been small, but the population of parent companies has, of course, changed through mergers, acquisitions, divestitures, and the disappearance of old and the entry of new MNCs. Nevertheless, Swedish MNCs have consistently made up a large part of Swedish manufacturing. In 1994 they accounted for some 40 percent of Swedish manufacturing employment, some 55 percent of total Swedish exports, and as much as 90 percent of industrial R&D. In other words, they are on average very large, very export oriented, and very R&D intensive.

Throughout the period 1965–94 MNCs as a group have shown higher employment growth in Sweden than has the rest of the Swedish manufacturing industry, which, in the period of stagnant or falling manufacturing employment since the mid-1970s, has meant that they have reduced their employment relatively less than other firms. Employment in their foreign manufacturing affiliates increased steadily up to 1990 but dropped off from 1990 to 1994, with the onset of the economic crisis in Sweden in the early 1990s and a downturn in major markets. For the whole thirty-year period an employment decline in the Swedish manufacturing industry by 36 percent and in Swedish parents by 25 percent contrasts with manufacturing-affiliate employment growth of 181 percent and total foreign-employment growth (including sales affiliates) of 210 percent. Table 4.1 summarizes these developments.

Figure 4.1 gives a snapshot of the relentless internationalization of the MNCs themselves. Foreign production has steadily grown as a share of their total sales, exporting from Sweden has roughly held its share, and sales in the home market have shrunk to just over 10 percent of total sales in 1994.

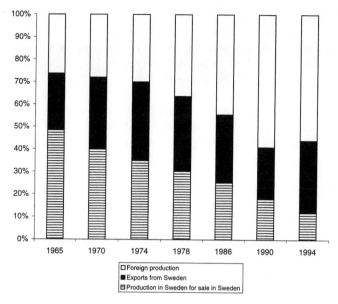

Fig. 4.1   The internationalization of Swedish MNCs 1965–94: total company sales divided into home production for home sale, exports, and foreign production (percent)

Note: Foreign production includes affiliate exports to Sweden. In order to get total sales in the home market, exports from affiliates back to Sweden must be added to "production in Sweden for sales in Sweden." Affiliate exports to Sweden was around 4 percent of total company sales in 1994.

4.3   Determinants and Effects of Foreign Production by Swedish MNCs

An important reason for Sweden's historical position as a large (net) foreign investor can be found in the small size of its home market and in the country's traditional dependence on being able to sell in foreign markets. For Swedish firms, foreign production has been an alternative to exports in serving foreign markets. Historically, only a negligible fraction of foreign output has been exported back to the home market. This is in contrast to foreign production by MNCs from countries such as the United States and Britain, for whom exports back to their large home markets have been more important. The close relationship between exports and foreign production for Swedish firms is also reflected in their geographical patterns. Foreign manufacturing is concentrated among the industrial countries (some 90 percent), and within these, in Western Europe, specifically the European Union (EU; more than 60 percent), which corresponds roughly to the geographical pattern of Swedish exports.

But what is the nature of the competitive advantage of Swedish MNCs in foreign markets, and what has determined whether they serve these markets through exports or foreign production?

Modern theory sees the competitive advantage of MNCs as based on a firm-specific asset such as superior knowledge, which, once produced, can be used at little or no additional cost throughout the firm and regardless of location. (The original references are Hymer 1976; Kindleberger 1969; Johnson 1970; Caves 1971. See, e.g., Markusen 1995 for a recent statement.) Such an asset may be the result of investment in R&D or marketing, or it may be the result of learning by doing. It is specific to the firm but mobile within the firm and across national borders. It gives rise to economies of firm size or to multiplant economies of scale. It also implies imperfect competition. In this view, the size and growth of firms are determined to a large extent by their firm-specific knowledge advantage (Demsetz 1988).

The choice between exports and foreign production, on the other hand, depends on comparative production costs in different locations, trade barriers, and transportation costs. Comparative production costs may reflect differences in relative factor prices. Lower wages in a foreign country, for example, might induce firms to locate their more labor-intensive activities in that country. Comparative production costs may also depend on the ability to exploit economies of scale at the plant level when locating production in a particular country. When both scale economies and transportation costs are important, for example, the MNC will have fewer plants and will tend to locate them in large countries to minimize transportation costs. A country's competitive advantage as a production location, then, may depend on relative factor prices, the size of its market, and the distance to other markets. Tariff and nontariff barriers to trade tend, of course, to favor local production.

The previous explanation of a country's competitive advantage is an eclectic mixture drawn from different trade theories that actually give different predictions. According to the factor-proportions theory of trade, dissimilarity in relative factor prices and factor endowments determines specialization and trade. According to the imperfect-competition theory of trade, similarities in relative factor endowments encourage intraindustry trade in differentiated products. In the latter, the location of production is instead determined by the ability to exploit scale economies and by trading costs (Dunning 1977; Helpman and Krugman 1985). These theories are not mutually exclusive, however, since a country's output may consist of both homogeneous products, for which differences in factor proportions are important, and differentiated products, for which they are not. Each theory may, therefore, be relevant to explaining a part of a country's production and trade (Lancaster 1980; Dixit and Norman 1980; Brainard 1993).

Clearly, exports and foreign production are determined simultaneously, and largely by the same set of factors. Both are affected positively by the MNC's firm-specific competitive advantage, and both are affected in opposite directions by factors affecting locational choice. The latter explains the presumption in trade theory that the relationship between the two is one of substitution. (Markusen [1998] describes a model in which they may be complements, however.) Yet, if exports and foreign production are determined simultaneously, how can one speak of the "effect" of foreign production on exports? What is generally intended here is the effect on exports compared to a situation in which an increase in foreign production is not allowed because of a policy restricting foreign investment. In this setting, foreign production becomes a policy variable. It is, of course, a hypothetical situation and defining the counterfactual is not easy. The latter has plagued most analyses of the effects of foreign production on exports (see Lipsey 1995 for an overview). In an econometric analysis the problem can be reduced by estimating the effect of foreign production by two-stage least squares regression analysis (2SLS), whereby foreign production becomes exogenous in the second stage of analysis (see Swedenborg 1979).

Although the basic relationship between foreign production and exports of a particular tradable good is generally one of substitution, the partial effect of foreign production on the firm's total exports is uncertain a priori and must be determined empirically. For a single-product firm the effect is negative or zero, depending on the extent to which exporting could have taken place in the alternative situation when foreign production is restricted. For example, if trade barriers are prohibitive, or if in the absence of foreign production by home-country firms production by other firms would have filled the void, the effect would be zero. For a multiproduct firm, which is either vertically or horizontally integrated, the effect depends on two opposite influences. One is the potentially negative effect on exports of substitute products. The other is the potentially positive effect on exports of complementary products, which may be either inputs in foreign production or products that are complementary in final use. Since most, if not all, MNCs are multiproduct firms, the net effect on exports depends on the strength of substitution relative to complementarity effects (for a formal model, see Swedenborg 1979).

On a priori grounds, a case could be made that foreign production by MNCs has allowed increased specialization between countries in accordance with the competitive advantage of each and thereby has contributed to increased output through a more efficient allocation of resources worldwide. Arguably, impediments to both international trade and to the firm managing operations in many different countries have declined due to a lowering of tariff levels and to lower costs of transportation and communication. This should have allowed MNCs to increasingly locate production so as to minimize production costs and/or trading costs. It should have allowed the MNC to bring its firm-specific asset (whether based on superior technological, marketing, or managerial know-how) to bear in countries that may lack such know-how but that have a competitive advantage as a production location.

What are the implications for the home country? The increased mobility of international firms means that production abroad becomes a more ready substitute for home production by the firm. If the home country does not have a competitive advantage as a production location for part of the firm's output, or if exports are hindered by trade barriers, the firm can increase production by moving abroad. Total output of the firm's particular (differentiated) products is thereby greater than it otherwise would have been. The firm is larger than it otherwise would have been. The effect on home-country exports depends on whether this allows the firm (or other home-country firms) to specialize in accordance with home-country competitive advantage. A positive net effect on the investing firm's exports is one indication of increased specialization. Another may be increased investment in, for example, R&D in the home country, which is made possible by larger overall firm size. The effect, it must be emphasized, is always evaluated relative to the hypothetical situation in which foreign production is not allowed to increase.

4.3.1   Empirical Analysis: Total Foreign Production and Exports of MNCs

Let us now turn to an empirical analysis of the determinants and effects of foreign production by Swedish firms. We want to explain both total foreign production and exports, and foreign production in and exports to individual countries. We also want to estimate, by 2SLS, the partial effect of foreign production on exports from Sweden. In doing so, we distinguish between products that may be substitutes for and those that may be complements to foreign production. The relationships we want to estimate for the firm's overall foreign production and exports are

$$(1) \quad \ln(SQ)_{it} = a_0 + a_i Z_i + a_t DT_t + b_1 \ln R\&D_{it} + b_2 \ln LS_{it}$$
$$+ b_3 \ln(K/L)_{it} + b_4 NR_i + b_5 \ln YR_{it} + e_{it},$$

$$(2) \quad \ln(SX)_{it} = a_0 + a_i Z_i + a_t DT_t + b_1 \ln R\&D_{it} + b_2 \ln LS_{it}$$
$$+ b_3 \ln(K/L)_{it} + b_4 NR_i + b_5 (pSQ)_{it} + e_{it},$$

$$(2a) \quad \ln(SXS)_{it} = a_0 + a_i Z_i + a_t DT_t + b_1 \ln R\&D_{it} + b_2 \ln LS_{it}$$
$$+ b_3 \ln(K/L)_{it} + b_4 NR_i + b_5 (pSQ)_{it} + e_{it},$$

$$(2b) \quad \ln(SXC)_{it} = a_0 + a_i Z_i + a_t DT_t + b_1 \ln R\&D_{it} + b_2 \ln LS_{it}$$
$$+ b_3 \ln(K/L)_{it} + b_4 NR_i + b_5 (pSQ)_{it} + e_{it}.$$

Subscript i refers to firm i, subscript t to year t. The dependent variables are the net (local) sales value of foreign production (SQ), defined as manufacturing-affiliate sales abroad less imports from parents, and of exports from Sweden (SX). Total exports are divided into exports to nonaffiliates

(SXS), which we expect may be noncomplementary to (or substitutes for) foreign production, and exports to affiliates (SXC), which we expect may be complementary to foreign production. These expectations can, of course, be questioned. Exports to manufacturing affiliates include both products that are used as inputs by the affiliates and products that are merely resold. While the former should be complementary to foreign output, the latter need not be. Similarly, exports to nonaffiliates may contain a mixture. The empirical analysis will reveal whether these definitions correspond to the theoretical concepts. Definitions of all variables are given in the appendix.

The firm's overall exports and foreign production are expected to depend on specific characteristics both of the firm and of the industry in which it operates. Research and development expenditures (R&D) measure the firm's firm-specific asset. Physical-capital intensity (K/L) and the skill level of labor (LS) in the firm's domestic production are industry characteristics that may affect the cost of home (relative to foreign) production and reveal whether factor proportions affect the location of production. A dummy variable (NR) for two natural-resource-based industries (metals and forest products), in which Sweden has a comparative advantage, is also included. These industries have historically been located near the natural resource and are, moreover, characterized by scale economies. For both these reasons, NR is expected to bias the firm toward exporting. So far, the explanatory variables are the conventional ones in this kind of analysis. A less conventional one is the age of the firm's oldest foreign manufacturing affiliate (YR). This firm-specific variable is included to take into account dynamic-historical factors, specifically that it takes time to grow large abroad. It may also reflect the effect of accumulated knowledge in the affiliate based on learning by doing, which, too, is an effect of time. Since this variable should have a direct effect on foreign production only—not on exports—it is used as an instrumental variable to allow 2SLS estimation of the effect of foreign production. The predicted value of SQ (pSQ) is obtained from the first stage and inserted as an explanatory variable in the exports regressions in the second stage.

We introduce a dummy variable for each firm (Z) in order to control for the effect of inherent characteristics of firms that stay constant over time, and a dummy variable for time (DT) to control similarly for the effect of time—for example, specific occurrences at time t or a general time trend that affects all firms the same way. The firm dummy allows us to hold each firm constant and analyze the relationship between the independent and dependent variables over time. For this to be meaningful we impose the condition that the firm is represented in the data in at least three of the six years for which we have data. That reduces the data set, since it eliminates firms that have dropped out as MNCs after a relatively short period or that are relatively recent entrants.

In order to make a comparison between the results of cross-sectional analysis and analysis of panel data we present regressions first without controlling for firm fixed effects (Z), and then with such a control. The former pools all cross-sectional observations; the latter pools only those that have manufacturing affiliates abroad in at least three of the census years.

Table 4.2 reports the results. Panel A shows the results when firm-specific fixed effects are not controlled for, and panel B, when they are.[5] First, we note—in panel A—that R&D expenditures have the expected positive effect on both foreign production and exports. The age of foreign operations has the expected positive effect on foreign production, which underlines the importance of taking into account dynamic-historical factors in cross-sectional analysis. Natural-resource intensity (NR) has a strong positive effect on total exports, while the other factor-proportion variables (K/L, LS) have no effect on either exports or foreign production. The lack of significance for physical-capital intensity is consistent with other studies that show that Sweden has lost its earlier comparative advantage in capital-intensive production (Lundberg 1992; Leamer and Lundborg 1997). What remains may be captured by the NR variable, since these resource-based industries are also very capital intensive. The insignificance of the skilled-labor measure is perhaps more surprising, since Sweden has been shown to have a comparative advantage in skill-intensive production at least through the early 1980s (Lundberg 1992). According to Leamer and Lundborg (1997), however, such an advantage was substantially eroded by the late 1980s.

The effect of foreign production on exports is seen to be weak and insignificant in the substitute-exports equation and strongly positive in the complementary-exports equation. The net effect is a surprisingly strong positive effect on total exports. It is surprising because exports to nonaffiliates are so much larger than exports to manufacturing affiliates, and the effect on the former could therefore have been expected to carry through more strongly. (The mean value of the former is almost five times the size of that of the latter.)

Panel B in table 4.2 shows what happens when we hold each firm constant and examine the relationship between the variables over time. First of all we note that the same firm and industry characteristics remain significant determinants of foreign production and exports; but both the size of the coefficients and their significance are much reduced when firm fixed effects are controlled for. Thus, the role of these characteristics in cross-sectional analysis is, to a large extent, to differentiate between firms with inherent differences rather than to reflect their impact over time. This is

---

5. In earlier analysis (Swedenborg 1979, 1982) the dependent variables were in ratio form and controlled for the firm's size in the home market. Use of the absolute value of the dependent variables, as in table 4.1, corresponds more closely to theoretical relationships and is easier to interpret. The use of a dummy variable for each firm makes it less necessary to normalize for firm size. The results, in any case, turn out to be quite similar.

Table 4.2   **Determinants and Effects of Total Foreign Production and Exports by Swedish MNCs 1965–94 (OLS and 2SLS; log form)**

Independent Variables	Dependent Variables			
	SQ_i	SX_i	SXS_i	SXC_i
A. Pooled Cross-Sections				
Constant	3.85***	4.46***	4.80***	−0.32
	(5.80)	(7.00)	(6.81)	(−0.34)
$R\&D_i$	0.56***	0.47***	0.55***	0.09
	(22.21)	(8.96)	(9.60)	(1.18)
LS_i	−0.02	0.06	0.02	0.08
	(−0.10)	(0.32)	(0.10)	(0.31)
K/L_i	0.13*	0.08	0.09	−0.08
	(1.83)	(1.25)	(1.34)	(−0.96)
NR_i	0.38	1.92***	2.01***	1.22***
	(1.55)	(9.08)	(8.61)	(3.94)
YR_i	0.67***			
	(12.18)			
DT^a				
pSQ_i		0.21***	0.10	0.76***
		(3.03)	(1.29)	(7.60)
N	672	587	587	587
R^2	0.67	0.74	0.70	0.57
F	128.24***	151.30***	127.19***	71.35***
B. Panel Data with Firm Fixed Effects				
Constant	4.72***	7.28***	7.95***	0.49
	(6.65)	(10.81)	(9.73)	(0.34)
$R\&D_i$	0.21***	0.13***	0.13***	0.05
	(3.97)	(3.32)	(2.76)	(0.65)
LS_i	−0.07	0.06	−0.02	0.22
	(−0.36)	(0.48)	(−0.11)	(0.79)
K/L_i	0.06	0.10	0.10	0.21
	(0.48)	(1.35)	(1.11)	(1.26)
NR_i	0.40	0.83***	0.88**	0.58
	(0.83)	(2.58)	(2.26)	(0.85)
YR_i	0.61***			
	(7.21)			
DT_t^a				
Z_i^a				
pSQ_i		−0.03	−0.16	0.75***
		(−0.39)	(−1.44)	(3.94)
N	404	370	370	370
R^2	0.88	0.94	0.92	0.82
F	29.38***	57.38***	40.88***	15.75***

Note: Summary of appendix tables 4A.1 and 4A.2. All variables are natural logarithms. R^2 is corrected for degrees of freedom. Numbers in parentheses are *t*-values. Only firms for which there are data in at least three years are included in the regressions in panel B. (Variables are defined in the appendix.)

[a]Time dummies included in both panels, firm dummies only in panel B, but not shown here. The time dummies are significantly positive and increasing in the SQ and SX equations in panel B. The firm dummies are overwhelmingly significant.

*Denotes significant at the 10 percent level.

**Denotes significant at the 5 percent level.

***Denotes significant at the 1 percent level.

not unexpected, but it does caution against interpreting coefficients estimated on cross-sectional data as indicating the effect of changes over time.

The dummy variables (not shown) contribute to the high explanatory values of the equations, but they also reveal our ignorance. The time dummies are quite significant and their coefficients are positive and increasing over time. All firms' foreign production and exports (but not complementary exports) increase over time in a way that cannot be explained by the other variables.[6] The firm dummies (overwhelmingly significant) reveal that firm-specific attributes that have not been measured play a significant role. This is hardly surprising, since R&D spending is only one possible source of a firm-specific asset. Managerial, production, and marketing know-how, brand names, and so forth, are not necessarily related to R&D.

The partial effect of foreign production on total exports is now insignificant. The coefficient for substitute exports is negative but insignificant, while the coefficient for complementary exports is strongly positive and significant. The results are consistent with our expectations regarding exports to both nonaffiliates and affiliates and lend some credence to the terminology adopted. Since the estimated coefficients are elasticities, the coefficient on complementary exports shows that a 1 percent increase in foreign production is associated with a 0.75 percent increase in complementary exports. Because complementary exports is such a small part of total parent exports, this effect is drowned in the total.

When it comes to the effect of foreign production on exports we are, of course, interested only in the dynamics of change. We want to know how exports change over time as a result of an increase in foreign production. Here, cross-sectional analysis yields ambiguous results, while analysis of panel data where interfirm differences are held constant—as in panel B of table 4.2—allows us to distinguish the effect we are interested in. This is worth emphasizing, since most previous analyses of this relationship have not made this use of the longitudinal dimension of the data. (The exceptions are Swedenborg 1982, 1991, for a shorter time span.)[7]

The high explanatory value of the regressions and the significance of the instrumental variable YR in the foreign-production equation should improve the precision with which the effect of foreign production is esti-

6. When the firm dummies were not included (table 4.2, panel A) the time dummies were significant only in the SX equation and only for two extreme years. One was an export boom (1974), the other an economic crisis (1990).

7. Blonigen (2000) uses product-level time-series data on Japanese production in and exports to the United States. His motive is to try to ascertain the substitution relationship that most theory predicts should exist between production abroad and exports of a given product, but that more-aggregated analyses fail to find. He succeeds in this. However, he does not seem to be interested in the effects of foreign production on exports in the sense that we are here, since he does not control for other variables that may simultaneously affect these variables. Nor does he take into account the firm's exports of other products, except those that are inputs in foreign production, to obtain a net effect comparable to that which has been estimated in more aggregated studies.

mated in the export equation by 2SLS. This should reduce the concern expressed by Blomström, Lipsey, and Kulchycky (1988) that the results from using 2SLS are uncertain because a low explanatory power means that much of the relevant variation in the affiliates' production is neglected in the second-stage estimation. Although 2SLS is the theoretically correct method for estimating this simultaneous relationship, these authors' reservation makes them prefer estimation by ordinary least squares (OLS).

In order to check what difference the choice of estimation method makes, the same regressions as in table 4.2, panel B, were estimated by OLS. The results suggest that OLS estimation tends to overestimate the positive effect of foreign production on exports compared to 2SLS estimation.[8]

The estimated effect of foreign production on overall exports is remarkably consistent with results obtained for earlier years (Swedenborg 1982, 1991). Previous analysis (when based on pooled cross-sectional data) has also shown a strong positive effect on complementary exports, a weak negative effect on substitute exports, and an insignificant net effect. Even the sizes of the coefficients are very similar in similar specifications of the regression equations. For example, the coefficient for the effect of foreign production on complementary exports obtained on panel data through 1986 (and with 30 percent fewer parent companies than in table 4.2, panel B) was 0.70 compared to 0.75 in table 4.2.

In general, one would expect to find an increasingly negative relationship between foreign production and exports over time. The growth and maturing of foreign affiliates could be expected to lead to a diminished dependence on imports from parents. Furthermore, the fact that growth in foreign production to such a large extent has been through acquisitions of existing firms, which have a lower propensity to import from the Swedish company, would tend in the same direction (Swedenborg, Johansson-Grahn, and Kinnwall 1988; Andersson, Fredriksson, and Svensson 1996). A tendency toward a more negative effect on exports over time may account for the negative time trend in the complementary-exports estimation, which shows that such exports do not grow over time in the same way as other exports. This trend is not statistically significant, however.

Before drawing any definite conclusions regarding the effects of foreign production on parent exports we should analyze the same relationship for individual countries. Presumably, it is in individual countries of production where the main effect occurs—provided, of course, that affiliate exports to

8. OLS estimation yields the following coefficients (t-values in parentheses): for SX 0.06 (1.82), for SXS 0.00 (0.08), and for SXC 0.51 (7.54). Assuming that SQ is indeed endogenous, the 2SLS estimator should be consistent while the OLS estimator should not.

Ideally, one would like to test whether YR is a valid instrument, i.e., whether YR is exogenous. This is not possible, however, since equation (2) is exactly identified. In order to test for exogeneity the equation would have to be overidentified.

third countries are not a major influence. An analysis across countries can also reveal what country characteristics determine the volume of exports and foreign production, and possibly the choice between these methods of serving foreign markets as well.

4.3.2 Foreign Production in and Exports to Individual Countries

For an analysis across countries we add country characteristics as explanatory variables. The country's gross domestic product (GDP) is a measure of market size. It is a demand characteristic and as such should positively affect total sales in a foreign market. It could also have a positive effect on foreign production when scale economies at the plant level are important, and when trading costs—both trade barriers and possibly information and transaction costs generally—make it advantageous to produce near the final market. A large market allows the firm to take advantage of economies of scale and, given trading costs, means that production may be located in the large market even though this country may not be the lowest cost producer.

Per capita income (GDPcap) is also a demand characteristic (reflecting income elasticity) but it may also be a cost variable (reflecting the skill level in the country). Its influence is therefore ambiguous. In practice, it is highly correlated with a third variable, w_{ij}/w_{is} which is a measure of the wage in the foreign country relative to that of Sweden. The age variable (YR) now refers to the age of the oldest manufacturing affiliate in a country.

The equations to be estimated are now

$$(3) \quad \ln(\mathrm{SQ})_{ijt} = a_0 + a_i Z_i + a_j \mathrm{DC}_j + a_t \mathrm{DT}_t + b_1 \ln \mathrm{R\&D}_{it} + b_2 \ln \mathrm{LS}_{it}$$
$$+ \ b_3 \ln(K/L)_{it} + b_4 \ln \mathrm{NR}_i + b_5 \ln \mathrm{YR}_{ijt} + b_6 \ln \mathrm{GDP}_{jt}$$
$$+ \ b_7 \ln \mathrm{GDPcap}_{jt} + b_8 \ln(w_{ij}/w_{is})_t + e_{ijt},$$

$$(4) \quad \ln(\mathrm{SX})_{ijt} = a_0 + a_i Z_i + a_j \mathrm{DC}_j + a_t \mathrm{DT}_t + b_1 \ln \mathrm{R\&D}_{it} + b_2 \ln \mathrm{LS}_{it}$$
$$+ \ b_3 \ln(K/L)_{it} + b_4 \ln \mathrm{NR}_i + b_5 \ln \mathrm{YR}_{ijt} + b_6 \ln \mathrm{GDP}_{jt}$$
$$+ \ b_7 \ln \mathrm{GDPcap}_{jt} + b_8 \ln(w_{ij}/w_{is})_t + b_9 \ln(\mathrm{pSQ})_{ijt}$$
$$+ \ e_{ijt},$$

$$(4a) \quad \ln(\mathrm{SXS})_{ijt} = a_0 + a_i Z_i + a_j \mathrm{DC}_j + a_t \mathrm{DT}_t + b_1 \ln \mathrm{R\&D}_{it}$$
$$+ \ b_2 \ln \mathrm{LS}_{it} + b_3 \ln(K/L)_{it} + b_4 \ln \mathrm{NR}_i + b_5 \ln \mathrm{YR}_{ijt}$$
$$+ \ b_6 \ln \mathrm{GDP}_{jt} + b_7 \ln \mathrm{GDPcap}_{jt} + b_8 \ln(w_{ij}/w_{is})_t$$
$$+ \ b_9 \ln(\mathrm{pSQ})_{ijt} + e_{ijt},$$

(4b) $\ln(\mathrm{SXC})_{ijt} = a_0 + a_i Z_i + a_j \mathrm{DC}_j + a_t \mathrm{DT}_t + b_1 \ln \mathrm{R\&D}_{it}$

$$+ b_2 \ln \mathrm{LS}_{it} + b_3 \ln(K/L)_{it} + b_4 \ln \mathrm{NR}_i + b_5 \ln \mathrm{YR}_{ijt}$$

$$+ b_6 \ln \mathrm{GDP}_{jt} + b_7 \ln \mathrm{GDPcap}_{jt} + b_8 \ln(w_{ij}/w_{is})_t$$

$$+ b_9 \ln(\mathrm{pSQ})_{ijt} + e_{ijt},$$

where subscript j refers to country j. Important omitted variables are those that would unambiguously affect foreign production and exports in opposite directions, such as transportation costs and a country's trade policy. High barriers to trade would reduce exports and encourage foreign production. Their omission might mean that we tend to overestimate the negative relationship between exports and foreign production. A country dummy (DC) is introduced to control for the effect of omitted country characteristics.

Table 4.3 reports the influence of country characteristics on production for local sales in and exports to individual countries when firm-specific fixed effects at the parent-company level are controlled for. Panel A shows the results when country-specific fixed effects are not controlled for, and panel B, when they are. The influence of parent characteristics is not shown, since these are of less interest in an analysis across countries, which tends to give more weight to firms that produce in many countries than to firms that may be larger but produce in only a few.

First, we note—in panel A—that the length of time that the firm has produced in a country (YR) has a strong positive effect on the size of foreign production, confirming the earlier finding. Second, market size has a strong positive effect on foreign production and a much weaker positive effect on substitute exports. It also has a strong negative effect on complementary exports. The latter is of less interest since the demand for complementary exports is a derived demand. It should perhaps be pointed out that the inclusion of the estimated value of foreign production (pSQ) in the exports equations does not account for these results, since its inclusion does not alter the influence of any of the other independent variables.

The fact that market size has a stronger positive effect on foreign production than on exports suggests that trading costs and market considerations are important and that they affect the location of production. If trading costs were low, firms would produce in the country with the lowest production costs and export to all other markets. Market size would not affect how the firm chooses to serve a foreign market. A large market also allows firms to take advantage of scale economies in production. These interpretations are consistent with the proximity-concentration hypothesis, which postulates that there is a trade-off between achieving proximity to customers and concentrating production to achieve scale economies. Thus, both Brainard (1997) and Ekholm (1998) find that scale economies

Table 4.3 **Determinants and Effects of Swedish MNC Foreign Production in and Exports to Different Countries 1965–94 (OLS and 2SLS; log form)**

Independent Variables	Dependent Variables			
	SQ_{ij}	SX_{ij}	SXS_{ij}	SXC_{ij}
A. Panel Data with Firm Fixed Effects				
Constant	−6.30***	−21.01***	−34.94***	3.17
	(5.40)	(−8.32)	(−11.13)	(1.25)
YR_{ij}	0.45***			
	(11.68)			
GDP_j	0.52***	0.03	0.32***	−0.82***
	(17.70)	(0.27)	(2.43)	(−7.57)
$GDPcap_j$	0.12	2.09***	2.60***	0.30*
	(1.51)	(12.91)	(12.93)	(1.78)
w_{ij}/w_{is}	0.19*	0.60***	0.57**	0.69***
	(1.90)	(2.92)	(2.23)	(3.35)
DT^a				
Z_i^a				
pSQ_{ij}		0.47***	−0.24	1.83***
		(2.76)	(−1.15)	(10.73)
N	1,644	1,652	1,652	1,652
R^2	0.58	0.45	0.43	0.37
F	24.34***	15.35***	14.01***	11.24***
B. Panel Data with Firm and Country Fixed Effects				
Constant	1.64	33.04***	17.95	−2.08
	(0.24)	(2.69)	(1.09)	(−0.15)
YR_i	0.40***			
	(10.81)			
GDP_j	−0.79	−4.82***	−4.53***	0.83
	(−1.46)	(−4.98)	(−3.48)	(0.74)
$GDPcap_j$	2.03***	6.27***	7.04***	−2.78**
	(3.31)	(5.60)	(4.67)	(−2.15)
w_{ij}/w_{is}	−0.03	0.29	0.06	1.03***
	(−0.28)	(1.59)	(0.26)	(4.91)
DT^a				
Z_i^a				
DC_j^a				
pSQ_{ij}		0.07	−0.66***	2.02***
		(0.45)	(−2.98)	(10.60)
N	1,644	1,652	1,652	1,652
R^2	0.62	0.61	0.52	0.41
F	22.01***	21.09***	15.04***	9.79***

Note: Summary of appendix tables 4A.3 and 4A.4. All variables are natural logarithms. R^2 is corrected for degrees of freedom. Numbers in parentheses are *t*-values; *t*-values < 1 are not shown. Only firms for which there are data in at least three years are included in the regressions. (Variables are defined in the appendix.)

[a]Firm characteristics and dummy variables not shown here. Time and firm dummies included in both tables, country dummies included only in panel B. Time dummies are significantly negative in panel A and mostly insignificant in panel B. Firm and country dummies are quite significant.

*Denotes significant at the 10 percent level.

**Denotes significant at the 5 percent level.

***Denotes significant at the 1 percent level.

negatively affect the firm's propensity to supply a particular market through local production, which confirms an earlier finding for Swedish firms (Swedenborg 1982), while trade barriers and market size have the opposite effect.

By contrast, per capita income in a country has a strong positive effect on exports but not on foreign production. A higher relative wage in a country, which is highly correlated with per capita income, does have a positive effect on foreign production, but it is a weaker effect than that on exports. High-income countries thus seem to be important markets in general for Swedish firms. We can also conclude that lower wages for unskilled workers is not a motive for foreign production by Swedish firms.[9]

The estimated net effect on exports of foreign production in individual countries is surprisingly positive. The coefficient for total exports indicates that a 1 percent increase in foreign production in a country leads to a 0.47 percent increase in exports to the same country! This seems too good to be true. Behind this effect is a weak negative effect on substitute exports and a very strong positive effect on complementary exports. Since substitute exports to countries where firms have manufacturing affiliates is only 70 percent larger than complementary exports on average (compared to almost five times larger in overall exports), the effect on complementary exports carries through strongly.[10]

In order to isolate the effect of variables that change over time, a country fixed effect is introduced in the regressions summarized in table 4.3, panel B. A country dummy controls for country characteristics that affect all firms in a country but stay constant over time. It also captures the effect of omitted variables. Transportation costs (distance), traditional commercial ties, and possibly the country's trade policy are examples.

The inclusion of country dummies does not improve the overall efficiency of the estimate of foreign production and complementary exports according to the F-test. It does, however, raise the F-value in the other exports equations. It also changes some results. The country dummies take over the role of market size in the foreign-production equation and make the influence of market size on exports significantly negative. Why market growth should have a negative effect on exports is hard to see, however.

---

9. This appears to contradict Brainard's (1997) finding that the higher GDP per worker is in the United States relative to abroad, the higher the propensity to supply the foreign market through exports rather than through local production. Brainard's result suggests that factor-proportion differences stimulate exports relative to affiliate production, while the results here point in the opposite direction. However, it is not clear what we should make of that. As Brainard herself notes, her results do not allow her to reject a model with only country and industry fixed effects.

10. Sometimes total exports or, more frequently, exports to affiliates (SXC) in a particular country are zero. Since the log of zero is not defined, zero values have been set equal to one. This method does give a heavy weight to these observations. However, it seemed preferable to excluding the observations altogether.

Since the country dummies also make the growth of per capita income more significantly positive, one possible explanation is that, holding unique country characteristics constant, the growth of GDP and of GDPcap are correlated. Still, we can conclude that income growth in foreign markets is an important explanation of the growth of both foreign production and exports.

The most important change is that the effect of foreign production on substitute exports is now significantly negative, yielding a zero effect on total exports. The reason for this change is puzzling. The omission of country characteristics such as trade barriers should have implied a tendency to overestimate the negative relationship between exports and foreign production—not to underestimate it. Here, the dummy variables are truly measures of our ignorance. They apparently capture several unique characteristics of each country, including the importance of each market to Swedish firms.

The continued strong, positive effect on complementary exports also seems excessive. How can we explain a coefficient that says that a 1 percent increase in foreign production leads to an increase in complementary exports of almost 2 percent? One possible explanation is the definition of "complementary exports." As mentioned earlier, these are defined as parent exports to manufacturing affiliates of intermediate products used both as inputs and as final products for resale by the affiliate. The affiliate's import of inputs cannot increase more than in proportion to output growth; imports of final products can.

One possibility, then, is that the parent's exports of final products are greatly stimulated by the local production of a manufacturing affiliate. Alternatively, a larger share of parent exports is channelled through the manufacturing affiliate, which also serves as a sales company. It is hard to believe the latter to be an important factor generally. For one thing, imports of intermediate products make up some 60 percent of total affiliate imports from parents, and this share has increased over the period. For another, Swedish MNCs have a very large network of foreign sales affiliates and more often than not in countries where they also have manufacturing. Employment in pure sales affiliates abroad amounts to as much as a third of employment in manufacturing affiliates, and the country distribution of that employment corresponds to that of manufacturing affiliates. Nevertheless, it seems likely that such a rechanneling of complementary final products to manufacturing affiliates for resale is part of the explanation.[11]

11. It is not due to exports to third markets. Otherwise, a third possibility might have been that part of the affiliates' imports from parents are reexported as final goods to third markets. However, this has been allowed for in the definition of complementary exports for sale in country *j*, where affiliate imports from the parent is multiplied by the ratio of net local sales to net total sales by manufacturing affiliates. This is a somewhat excessive correction, since

As before, controlling for fixed effects should yield the most reliable estimate of the partial effect of foreign production on exports over time. Therefore, we are again led to conclude that the net effect of foreign production is probably close to zero. Behind this net effect is a changed composition of parent exports, away from the kind of products that are produced abroad and toward products that are complementary to foreign production.[12]

These results are broadly consistent with previous findings in similar studies, both for Sweden and for the United States. Most econometric evidence points to either no effect or a positive effect of foreign production on total parent exports (Lipsey and Weiss 1981, 1984; Blomström, Lipsey, and Kulchycky 1988). Lipsey (1995) surveys the long line of empirical studies of the effect of foreign production on exports. Blomström and Kokko (1994) survey the evidence for Sweden in more detail.

The notable exceptions to this general agreement are Svensson's studies (1993, 1996a, 1996b), using the same data on Swedish MNCs as in the present analysis but limited to the period 1974–90. The extent and significance of his divergent results have been exaggerated, however, since in part his results are consistent with the ones reported here. Using different definitions of "substitute" and "complementary" exports, he also finds that affiliate production for local sales has a negative effect on parent exports of final goods and a positive effect on exports of intermediate products to the country of production, and that the net effect, though negative, is insignificant. The difference is that, in addition, he finds that affiliate exports to third countries has a highly significant and much larger negative effect on parent exports to those countries. His analysis differs from the one here in that he includes countries where foreign production is zero, which in itself may be motivated. Unfortunately, this forces him to omit all MNCs with affiliates in fewer than six countries; that means that all small and medium-sized MNCs are omitted, because data on exports to countries where these firms do not have manufacturing affiliates are unavailable before 1990. Thus, the gain in being able to include countries where firms have no manufacturing has to be weighed against the loss from excluding a substantial proportion of Swedish MNCs from the analysis. That may explain some of Svensson's divergent results.[13] The main

---

it assumes that imports from parents of final products for resale also are exported. Still, the estimated effect of foreign production on complementary exports is hardly affected by whether this correction is made.

12. Again, we might compare with OLS estimation. This yields the following coefficients (with t-values in parentheses) for SQ: on SX 0.14 (3.18), on SXS -0.11 (-1.85), and on SXC 0.89 (18.62). Although they are in no way unreasonable, the net effect on total exports is again more positive than in 2SLS estimation.

13. A further reason for his divergent results, as Lipsey (1995) points out, is probably his formulation of the equations. Exports and foreign production are normalized for the global sales of the firm, which virtually guarantees a negative effect on exports. If increased foreign

reason for the large negative effect on parent exports to third countries, however, is probably the measure he uses for affiliate exports to third countries. Since information on affiliate exports to individual countries is lacking in the data, the analysis is confined to the EU and the country distribution of these exports within the EU is simply assumed (Svensson 1996a, 82–83). That is not a particularly reliable basis for an analysis of this relationship. In any case, the results reported previously in table 4.2 refer to the effects on the overall exports from parent companies and therefore incorporate possible displacement of parent exports to third countries.

The broad consistency of results, while reassuring, is remarkable for several reasons. Different studies have tested different formulations of the problem, used different methods and data, and looked at different time periods. However, the consistency achieved in the present analysis of a much longer time period comes only through using a more discerning specification of the model. The cross-sectional model—in tables 4.2, panel A, and 4.3, panel A—shows a much more positive relationship between foreign production and exports than has been found in earlier analyses. It is only after controlling for interfirm differences to look at changes over time—in tables 4.2, panel B, and 4.3, panel B—that we again find a negligible effect on overall exports.

To conclude, using panel data and separating out the partial relationship between variables over time, the analysis here has reaffirmed earlier results that have shown that there is no net substitution between foreign production and exports. Thus, empirical analysis again contradicts the common theoretical presumption of a negative relationship between foreign production and exports. The reason, we have argued, is that this presumption is not necessarily valid when firms produce many products and are able to adapt their output mix to changing conditions in different countries and over time. We also find evidence of such adaptation. Foreign production leads to a significant shift in the pattern of specialization in the home country, away from the kinds of products that are produced abroad and toward products that are complementary to foreign production. These changes are offsetting so that the net effect on total exports is zero.

Furthermore, the analysis has confirmed that a firm-specific asset such

---

production leads to an increase in global sales with little effect on parent exports, as most analyses suggest, the ratio of exports to global sales will necessarily fall as the ratio of foreign production to global sales increases.

As mentioned in an earlier footnote, the relationships analyzed in the present study have also been estimated in ratio form, where the dependent variable is normalized for the firm's size in the home market. This normalization is not subject to the same criticism. Also, the results with respect to the effects of foreign production on exports are consistent with the ones obtained for the variables in absolute form. The ratio form yields the following coefficients for the effect of the propensity to produce abroad (t-values in parentheses) for the model in table 4.1, panel B: on "substitute" exports −0.5 (0.62), on "complementary" exports 0.56 (3.58), and on total exports 0.01 (0.17). Adjusted R^2 is 0.69 in the foreign production equation and 0.78 in the exports equation.

as that based on R&D spending is an important source of firm-specific competitive advantage, but that other firm-specific attributes that we cannot measure also play a significant role. It has also reaffirmed the importance of taking history into account in cross-sectional analysis, in that it matters how long the firm has been producing abroad.

When it comes to identifying the determinants of the competitive advantages of countries as production locations, the results show that the size of a country's market affects the volume of local production. This suggests that trading or transaction costs in combination with scale economies at the plant level play an important role in determining how a foreign market is served, which is consistent with earlier analyses based on the proximity-concentration hypothesis. The results also show, however, that unique country characteristics that we have not measured play an even more important role. A high and growing per capita income greatly stimulates exports to a country as well as local production. Swedish firms both export to and produce in high-income (and high-wage) countries—that is, countries that are very similar to Sweden. This, in turn, can explain why relative factor proportions in production, such as physical-capital intensity and human-capital intensity, do not affect either exports or foreign production. Together these findings suggest that the new, imperfect-competition theory of international trade and production is more relevant in explaining the pattern of production and trade by Swedish MNCs than is the factor-proportions theory of trade.

4.4 Effects of Increased Firm Size

The absence of net substitution between foreign production and exports means that foreign production is a net addition to the overall sales of the MNCs. By producing abroad, MNCs increase their foreign market shares. They also grow much larger than they otherwise could have. This has, of course, been a motive for foreign expansion, but it also has important implications for the competitive position of MNCs and also for the home country.

Increased firm size allows firms to take advantage of economies of firm size. They can invest more in activities that increase the firm's overall competitiveness, since the cost of such investment can be spread over much larger sales. Examples of such fixed costs are R&D, advertising, a widespread and specialized distribution and service network through sales affiliates in other countries, and more specialized headquarter services. The investments benefit the entire company, regardless of where production is located. Some of it, like knowledge, has the characteristic of a public good within the firm.

How important are such effects? Foreign production by Swedish MNCs constituted almost 60 percent of total corporate sales (cf. fig. 4.1). If all of

Table 4.4   R&D Intensity According to Different Measures 1965–94 for Swedish
                   MNCs (percent)

	1965	1974	1986	1994
Total R&D/total MNC sales	2.08	2.08	3.83	4.65
Total R&D/Swedish parent sales	2.59	2.93	6.71	9.72
Swedish R&D/Swedish parent sales	2.37	2.51	5.83	7.32

Note: Figures refer to all MNCs in each year. The corresponding figures for continuing firms,
i.e., firms that are represented in the data in the whole period, are much higher. For them,
the first measure of R&D intensity was 6.69 percent in 1994; the second measure was
13.04 percent.

this is a net addition to MNC output, Swedish MNCs are two and a half
times bigger than they would have been in the absence of foreign production; but the effects may be much larger than that. The regression estimates
apply to marginal changes in foreign production, not to an all-or-nothing
change. It is impossible to know what these companies would have been
today if they had not become multinational.

Investment in R&D can illustrate the point. The Swedish manufacturing
industry ranks among the most R&D-intensive in the world (OECD 1995).
Most of that is accounted for by Swedish MNCs (more than 90 percent).
This is a reflection of the fact that most corporate R&D is still located in
Sweden (75 percent in 1994, higher in earlier years), while much of the
production that finances it is located abroad.

Table 4.4 shows the R&D intensity in Swedish MNCs measured in three
different ways. The first measures total R&D relative to total sales; the
second shows total R&D relative to Swedish parent sales; and the third
shows Swedish R&D relative to Swedish parent sales. Regardless of how
it is measured, R&D intensity has grown over the period shown. The overall R&D intensity—the first measure—shows what the company's total
operations can support. But the results of that R&D are available in full
to the Swedish part of the company. Therefore, it is the second measure
that should be the basis for the competitiveness of the Swedish operations.
That, clearly, is much higher than it could have been without foreign operations. Higher R&D, in turn, has a positive effect on Swedish exports
(table 4.2).

The conclusion we can draw is this. Multinational production by home-
country firms does affect the pattern of specialization in the home country
and in the following way. It leads to increased specialization in (exports
of) R&D-intensive products. This is true regardless of where R&D activities are located. Since most R&D is located in the home country, it probably also leads to increased specialization in R&D itself. The location of
R&D in the home country is due to the fact that R&D was historically
performed near the main production facility. In order to retain R&D ac-

tivities in the home country as the production base increasingly shifts to other countries, however, the home country has to prove that it has a competitive advantage in R&D. Its supply of scientists and engineers, the quality of its educational institutions, and its ability to attract foreign specialists are all part of what constitutes such an advantage.[14] In Sweden today, leading MNCs are questioning whether Sweden can live up to these competitive attributes.

4.5 Summary and Conclusions

The growth of MNCs has made it necessary to distinguish between the competitive advantage of firms and the competitive advantage of countries. Since the late 1960s, Swedish exports have failed to keep up with the growth of world exports and the Swedish share of OECD value added has been lagging (Blomström and Lipsey 1989; Andersson, Fredriksson, and Svensson 1996; Leamer and Lundborg 1997). However, the deteriorating competitive position of Sweden in export markets does not have a counterpart in a deteriorating competitive position of Swedish firms. They have, in fact, increased their foreign market shares and they have done so by expanding production abroad. The sheer size of that expansion makes it clear that domestic production could never have been an alternative way to realize such growth.

Increased foreign market shares through multinational production have not come at the expense of production at home. The analysis reported here has found that the enormous growth of foreign production by Swedish firms in the thirty-year period 1965–94 has not, in itself, had a negative effect on parent-company exports. A weak negative effect on exports to nonaffiliates—"substitute exports"—has been offset by a strong positive effect on exports to manufacturing affiliates—"complementary exports." These effects, as emphasized throughout, are defined relative to a hypothetical alternative situation in which foreign production had been restricted by policy.

Our results broadly confirm previous findings in similar analyses, both for Sweden and the United States; but there is a difference. In earlier studies this dynamic relationship between exports and foreign production has been inferred from cross-sectional analysis. Here, the longitudinal dimension of cross-sectional data for individual firms has been used to analyze the partial effect of foreign production on exports for all firms over time.

---

14. Fors (1998) analyzes the reasons Swedish MNCs locate R&D activities abroad. He concludes that the main reason is the need to adapt products and processes to conditions in the foreign market. However, he finds that an additional motive seems to be to carry out R&D in countries that are specialized technologically in the industry in which the firm operates, presumably to benefit from technological spillovers in that environment.

This allows us to draw the conclusion with much greater confidence. We can also note that coefficients estimated on cross-sectional data, in general, tend to overestimate the relationship between variables over time.

Our analysis also allows us to reject Svensson's (1996a) partly contrary findings for Sweden. Svensson claims that the reason he is able to find substitution is his taking into account affiliate exports to third countries, and exports to countries in which firms do not have manufacturing affiliates. We can reject that explanation, since we find no net substitution for the firm's overall exports, which, of course, include effects in all countries. Instead, we suspect that the reasons for his divergent findings are certain methodological weaknesses.

What are the implications of MNC growth for the home country—for Sweden? The most important effect comes from the effect of larger firm size on the ability of MNCs to invest more in R&D, in specialized head-quarter services, and in a more widespread distribution network abroad—all of which benefit the Swedish part of the MNCs. This means increased specialization in R&D-intensive output in Sweden and, as long as R&D is located mainly at home, in R&D production itself. Although hard to measure, it seems likely that the location of both R&D and headquarter services can result in valuable spillover effects for the home country as well.

Thus, Sweden has benefited and still benefits from being home to large MNCs. The pattern of specialization in Sweden, however, is also determined by Sweden's comparative advantage as a production location. Sweden is at a disadvantage in having a small home market, since trading costs and market factors make firms prefer production near the final market. Important markets and countries of production for Swedish firms, our results show, are high-income countries with similar or higher skill levels than Sweden's.

The growth of foreign production may, of course, in itself signal that Sweden is becoming a less attractive location of production for its increasingly global firms. Is there any indication that this might be the case? One such indication is that Sweden seems to be losing its competitive advantage in skill-intensive and technologically advanced production. Sweden has lagged behind other OECD countries in real income and productivity growth over this period. In 1970 Sweden ranked third in real income per capita among the OECD countries; after a gradual decline over most of the period, followed by a sharp drop in the early 1990s, Sweden ranked sixteenth in 1994. Leamer and Lundborg (1997) argue that part of the reason is that Sweden has not kept up with other countries in the accumulation of physical and human capital, which in turn may be due to the low after-tax return on such investment in the egalitarian Swedish welfare state.

Another, more recent, indication is the exodus of corporate headquarters from Sweden in the late 1990s. International mergers involving large

Swedish MNCs *as equals* have consistently meant locating corporate head-quarters outside Sweden, mainly, it seems, for tax reasons.[15]

If Sweden's productivity continues to lag behind, as many analyses predict it will in the absence of structural reforms of its welfare state (Lindbeck et al. 1994; Freeman, Topel, and Swedenborg 1997), it bodes ill for Sweden's ability to remain a home base for its global companies. Swedish MNCs have adapted to rising productivity in other countries by raising the capital and skill intensity in their foreign affiliates relative to that at home (Swedenborg 1991). If this continues, there is a serious risk that production by Swedish MNCs in Sweden will become specialized in less skill-intensive and technologically advanced production than in some of their foreign affiliates. If, in addition, R&D and headquarter services move abroad, the current benefits of being home to successful Swedish MNCs will disappear. Negative effects of an eroding competitive advantage in such production would have occurred in the absence of MNCs. However, the adjustment to such a change may occur more rapidly and more completely through the internal adaptation of MNCs. Also, the benefits lost are much greater for a country that has been home for large MNCs. Therefore, the policy issue Sweden confronts in the years ahead is what, if anything, it should do to remain an attractive base for its global companies.

Appendix

List of Variables

Dependent Variables

SQ_i Foreign manufacturing affiliates' net sales abroad; i.e., affiliate sales minus imports from Swedish parent i

SX_i Parent i's exports from Sweden

SXS_i "Substitute" or "noncomplementary exports"; i.e., $SX - SXC$

SXC_i "Complementary" exports, measured as parent exports to manufacturing affiliates

SQ_{ij} Affiliate net local sales in country j; i.e., affiliate sales minus imports from Swedish parents by affiliate weighted by (net sales/gross sales), where the weight is necessary to account for the fact that imports from Swedish parent are also exported from country j

---

15. It started with ASEA-BrownBovery's locating in 1986 in Zürich. In the late 1990s it seems to have become endemic. Pharmacia-Upjohn in 1995 located in London (and subsequently moved to the United States); MeritaNordbanken and Stora-Enso in 1998 both located in Helsinki; Astra-Zeneca in late 1998 will locate in London; and Ericsson, in 1998, without a merger, decided to move part of its corporate headquarters to London. Other companies are expected to follow.

SX_{ij} Parent i's exports to country j
SXC_{ij} "Complementary" exports to country j; i.e., parent exports to manufacturing affiliates (net sales/gross sales)
pSQ Predicted value of SQ

Independent Variables

$R\&D_i$ Total company-sponsored expenditures for research and development

LS_i Labor skill measure (wages and salaries per employee in Sweden)

K/L_i Capital intensity (book value of property, plant, and equipment per employee in Swedish parent)

NR Natural-resource intensity (dummy variable for the paper and pulp industry and the iron and steel industry)

YR_i Age of the oldest manufacturing affiliate by decade; i.e., t minus year of establishment, using only the first three digits

YR_{ij} Age of the oldest manufacturing affiliate in country j

w_{ij}/w_{is} Average wage in affiliate in country j relative to average wage in Swedish parent

GDP_j Real gross domestic product expressed in purchasing-power-parity-adjusted U.S. dollars from Penn World Tables

$GDPcap_j$ Real GDP per capita from Penn World Tables

Other Dummy Variables

DT_t Dummy variable for time t
Z_i Dummy variable for firm i
DC_j Dummy variable for country j

$t = 1, \ldots, 7$ (1965, 1970, 1974, 1978, 1986, 1990, 1994)
$i = 1, \ldots, n$
$j = 1, \ldots, m$ (excl. Sweden); S = Sweden

Data Sources

All variables are from the IUI data base on Swedish MNCs except GDP and GDP per capita, which are from Penn World Tables.

Table 4A.1 **Company Regressions with Cross-Sections Pooled over the Period 1965–94 (OLS and 2SLS)**

Independent Variables	Dependent Variables			
	SQ_i	SX_i	SXS_i	SXC_i
Constant	3.85***	4.46***	4.80***	−0.32
	(5.80)	(7.00)	(6.81)	(−0.34)
$R\&D_i$	0.56***	0.47***	0.55***	0.09
	(22.21)	(8.96)	(9.60)	(1.18)
LS_i	−0.02	0.06	0.02	0.08
	(−0.10)	(0.32)	(0.10)	(0.31)
K/L_i	0.13*	0.08	0.09	−0.08
	(1.83)	(1.25)	(1.34)	(−0.96)
NR_i	0.38	1.92***	2.01***	1.22***
	(1.55)	(9.08)	(8.61)	(3.94)
YR_i	0.67***			
	(12.18)			
DT70	−0.23	0.15	0.07	0.23
	(−1.02)	(0.80)	(0.35)	(0.85)
DT74	0.19	0.40**	0.42**	0.22
	(0.85)	(2.17)	(2.05)	(0.83)
DT78	0.06	−0.06	−0.09	0.03
	(0.26)	(−0.31)	(−0.40)	(0.10)
DT86	0.04	0.05	0.06	0.05
	(0.17)	(0.26)	(0.27)	(0.17)
DT90	0.18	−0.44**	−0.49**	0.03
	(0.70)	(−2.06)	(−2.11)	(0.08)
DT94	0.19	−0.28	−0.33	0.02
	(0.71)	(−1.25)	(−1.33)	(0.05)
pSQ_i		0.21***	0.10	0.76***
		(3.03)	(1.29)	(7.60)
N	672	587	587	587
R^2	0.67	0.74	0.70	0.57
F	128.24***	151.30***	127.19***	71.35***

Note: R^2 is corrected for degrees of freedom. Numbers in parentheses are t-values.
*Denotes significance at the 10 percent level.
**Denotes significance at the 5 percent level.
***Denotes significance at the 1 percent level.

Table 4A.2   **Company Regressions: Panel Data with Firm Fixed Effects, 1965–94 (OLS and 2SLS)**

Independent Variables	Dependent Variables			
	SQ_i	SX_i	SXS_i	SXC_i
Constant	4.72***	7.28***	7.95***	0.49
	(6.65)	(10.81)	(9.73)	(0.34)
$R\&D_i$	0.21***	0.13***	0.13***	0.05
	(3.97)	(3.32)	(2.76)	(0.65)
LS_i	−0.07	0.06	−0.02	0.22
	(−0.36)	(0.48)	(−0.11)	(0.79)
K/L_i	0.06	0.10	0.10	0.21
	(0.48)	(1.35)	(1.11)	(1.26)
NR_i	0.40	0.83***	0.88**	0.58
	(0.83)	(2.58)	(2.26)	(0.85)
YR_i	0.61***			
	(7.21)			
DT70	0.30*	0.48***	0.49***	0.18
	(1.75)	(4.17)	(3.48)	(0.72)
DT74	0.56***	0.75***	0.86***	0.09
	(3.33)	(5.78)	(5.49)	(0.34)
DT78	0.86***	0.75***	0.98***	−0.33
	(4.11)	(4.35)	(4.65)	(−0.89)
DT86	1.07***	0.93***	1.24***	−0.65
	(4.56)	(4.51)	(4.93)	(−1.47)
DT90	1.53***	0.96***	1.34***	−0.79
	(5.49)	(3.70)	(4.27)	(−1.43)
DT94	1.78***	1.26***	1.64***	−0.78
	(5.69)	(4.24)	(4.55)	(−1.24)
Z_i [a]				
pSQ_i		−0.03	−0.16	0.75***
		(−0.39)	(−1.44)	(3.94)
N	404	370	370	370
R^2	0.88	0.94	0.92	0.81
F	29.38***	57.38***	40.88***	15.75***

Note: Only firms that are present in at least three years are included. A total of 98 companies meet this criterion. R^2 is corrected for degrees of freedom. Numbers in parentheses are t-values.

[a] Firm dummies are overwhelmingly significant.

*Denotes significance at the 10 percent level.

**Denotes significance at the 5 percent level.

***Denotes significance at the 1 percent level.

Table 4A.3   **Country Regressions: Panel Data with Firm Fixed Effects, 1965–94 (OLS and 2SLS)**

Independent Variables	Dependent Variables			
	SQ_{ij}	SX_{ij}	SXS_{ij}	SXC_{ij}
Constant	−6.30***	−21.01***	−34.94***	3.17
	(5.40)	(−8.32)	(−11.13)	(1.25)
$R\&D_i$	−0.08	−0.01	−0.16	−0.01
	(−1.24)	(−0.08)	(−1.01)	(−0.06)
LS_i	0.06	2.02***	2.20***	1.52***
	(0.27)	(4.90)	(4.28)	(3.68)
K/L_i	0.02	−0.11	−0.18*	−0.10
	(0.51)	(−1.38)	(−1.79)	(−1.20)
NR_i	0.19	1.46*	−1.82*	−0.26
	(0.49)	(1.91)	(−1.91)	(−0.34)
YR_{ij}	0.45***			
	(11.68)			
GDP_j	0.52***	0.03	0.32***	−0.82***
	(17.70)	(0.27)	(2.43)	(−7.57)
$GDPcap_j$	0.12	2.09***	2.60***	0.30*
	(1.51)	(12.91)	(12.93)	(1.88)
w_{ij}/w_{is}	0.19*	0.60***	0.57**	0.69***
	(1.90)	(2.92)	(2.23)	(3.35)
DT70	0.17	−0.74***	−0.97***	−0.44
	(1.14)	(−2.47)	(−2.61)	(−1.47)
DT74	−0.10	−1.11***	−0.87**	−0.71**
	(−0.67)	(−3.59)	(−2.27)	(−2.29)
DT78	−0.04	−1.89***	−1.16***	−1.21***
	(−0.22)	(−5.17)	(−2.55)	(−3.32)
DT86	0.33*	−2.79***	−1.73***	−2.48***
	(1.78)	(−7.31)	(−3.65)	(−6.49)
DT90	0.66***	−4.63***	−3.12***	−3.41***
	(3.05)	(−10.40)	(−5.64)	(−7.64)
DT94	0.61**	−5.16***	−3.44***	−3.41***
	(2.41)	(−9.90)	(−5.30)	(−6.51)
Z_i^a				
pSQ_{ij}		0.47***	−0.24	1.83***
		(2.76)	(−1.15)	(10.73)
N	1,644	1,652	1,652	1,652
R^2	0.58	0.45	0.43	0.37
F	24.34***	15.35***	14.01***	11.24***

Note: Only firms that are present in at least three years are included. A total of 98 parent companies meet this criterion. R^2 is corrected for degrees of freedom. Numbers in parentheses are t-values.

[a] Firm dummies are overwhelmingly significant.

*Denotes significance at the 10 percent level.

**Denotes significance at the 5 percent level.

***Denotes significance at the 1 percent level.

Table 4A.4   **Country Regressions with Fixed Effects for Firms, Time, and Countries, 1965–94 (OLS and 2SLS)**

Independent Variables	Dependent Variables			
	SQ_{ij}	SX_{ij}	SXS_{ij}	SXC_{ij}
Constant	1.64	33.04***	17.95	−2.08
	(0.24)	(2.69)	(1.09)	(−0.15)
$R\&D_i$	−0.07	0.03	−0.11	0.00
	(−1.18)	(0.25)	(−0.74)	(0.03)
LS_i	−0.18	1.48***	1.52***	1.94***
	(0.92)	(4.13)	(3.14)	(4.68)
K/L_i	0.02	−0.09	−0.13	−0.06
	(0.60)	(−1.29)	(−1.31)	(−0.76)
NR	0.06	0.84	−2.68***	−0.40
	(0.16)	(1.28)	(−3.05)	(−0.53)
YR_i	0.40***			
	(10.81)			
GDP_j	−0.79	−4.82***	−4.53***	0.83
	(−1.46)	(−4.98)	(−3.48)	(0.74)
$GDPcap_j$	2.03***	6.27***	7.04***	−2.78**
	(3.31)	(5.60)	(4.67)	(−2.15)
w_{ij}/w_{is}	−0.03	0.29	0.06	1.03***
	(−0.28)	(1.59)	(0.26)	(4.91)
DT70	0.25	0.16	−0.08	−0.44
	(1.48)	(0.52)	(−0.21)	(−1.25)
DT74	−0.02	0.08	0.30	−0.59
	(−0.08)	(0.20)	(0.58)	(−1.32)
DT78	0.18	−0.16	0.61	−1.31**
	(0.67)	(−0.34)	(0.94)	(−2.37)
DT86	0.61*	−0.35	0.72	−2.66***
	(1.90)	(−0.61)	(0.91)	(−3.93)
DT90	1.00***	−1.51**	−0.04	−3.73***
	(2.69)	(−2.20)	(−0.05)	(−4.70)
DT94	1.00**	−2.10***	−0.34	−3.95***
	(2.48)	(−2.82)	(−0.34)	(−4.59)
$Z_i{}^a$				
$DC_j{}^a$				
pSQ_{ij}		0.07	−0.66***	2.02***
		(0.45)	(−2.98)	(10.60)
N	1,644	1,652	1,652	1,652
R^2	0.62	0.61	0.52	0.41
F	22.01***	21.09***	15.04***	9.79***

Note: Only firms that are present in at least three years are included. A total of 98 companies meet this criterion. R^2 is corrected for degrees of freedom. Numbers in parentheses are t-values.

[a] Dummy variables are overwhelmingly significant.

*Denotes significance at the 10 percent level.

**Denotes significance at the 5 percent level.

***Denotes significance at the 1 percent level.

References

Andersson, T., T. Fredriksson, and R. Svensson. 1996. *Multinational restructuring, internationalization and small economies: The Swedish case.* London: Routledge.

Barrell, R., and N. Pain. 1997. Foreign direct investment, technological change, and economic growth within Europe. *Economic Journal* 107 (445): 1770–86.

Blomström, M., G. Fors, and R. E. Lipsey. 1997. Foreign direct investment and employment: Home country experience in the United States and Sweden. *Economic Journal* 107 (445): 1787–97.

Blomström, M., and A. O. Kokko. 1994. Home-country effects of foreign direct investment: Sweden. In *Canadian-based multinationals,* ed. S. Globerman, 341–64. Calgary: University of Calgary Press.

Blomström, M., and R. E. Lipsey. 1989. The export performance of U.S. and Swedish multinationals. *Review of Income and Wealth* 35 (3): 245–64.

Blomström, M., R. E. Lipsey, and K. Kulchycky. 1988. U.S. and Swedish direct investment and exports. In *Trade policy issues and empirical analysis,* ed. R. E. Baldwin, 259–97. Chicago: University of Chicago Press.

Blonigen, B. A. 2000. In search of substitution between foreign production and exports. *Journal of International Economics,* forthcoming.

Brainard, L. S. 1993. A simple theory of multinational corporations and trade with a trade-off between proximity and concentration. NBER Working Paper no. 4269. Cambridge, Mass.: National Bureau of Economic Research.

———. 1997. An empirical assessment of the proximity-concentration trade-off between multinational sales and trade. *American Economic Review* 87:520–44.

Braunerhjelm, P., and K. Ekholm, eds. 1998. *The geography of multinational firms.* Boston: Kluwer Academic.

Caves, R. E. 1971. International corporations: The industrial economics of foreign investment. *Economica* 38 (February): 1–27.

Demsetz, H. 1988. *Ownership, control, and the firm.* The organization of economic activity, vol. 1. Oxford: Basil Blackwell.

Dixit, A. K., and V. Norman. 1980. *Theory of international trade: A dual, general equilibrium approach.* Cambridge: Cambridge University Press.

Dunning, J. H. 1977. Trade, location of economic activity and the MNE: A search for an eclectic approach. In *The international allocation of economic activity,* ed. B. Ohlin, P.O. Hesselborn, and P. M. Wijkman, 395–418. London: Macmillan.

Ekholm, K. 1998. Proximity advantages, scale economies, and the location of production. In *The geography of multinational firms,* ed. P. Braunerhjelm and K. Ekholm, 59–76. Boston: Kluwer Academic.

Fors, G. 1998. Locating R&D abroad: The role of adaptation and knowledge-seeking. In *The geography of multinational firms,* ed. P. Braunerhjelm and K. Ekholm, 117–34. Boston: Kluwer Academic.

Freeman, R., R. Topel, and B. Swedenborg, eds. 1997. *The welfare state in transition: Reforming the Swedish model.* Chicago: University of Chicago Press.

Helpman, E., and P. R. Krugman. 1985. *Market structure and foreign trade.* Cambridge, Mass.: MIT Press.

Hufbauer, G. C., and F. M. Adler. 1968. *Overseas manufacturing investment and the balance of payments.* U.S. Department of the Treasury Tax Policy Research Study no. 1. Washington D.C.: Department of the Treasury.

Hymer, S. H. 1976. *The international operations of national firms: A study of direct foreign investment.* Cambridge, Mass.: MIT Press.

Johnson, H. 1970. The efficiency and welfare implications of the international corporation. In *The international corporation,* ed. C. P. Kindleberger. Cambridge, Mass.: MIT Press.

Kindleberger, C. P. 1969. *American business abroad: Six lectures on direct investment.* New Haven, Conn.: Yale University Press.

Lancaster, K. 1980. Intra-industry trade under perfect monopolistic competition. *Journal of International Economics* 10:151–75.

Leamer, E. E., and P. Lundborg. 1997. A Heckscher-Ohlin view of Sweden in the global marketplace. In *The welfare state in transition: Reforming the Swedish model,* ed. R. B. Freeman, R. Topel, and B. Swedenborg, 399–464. Chicago: University of Chicago Press.

Lindbeck, A., P. Molander, T. Persson, O. Petersson, A. Sandmo, B. Swedenborg, and N. Thygesen. 1994. *Turning Sweden around.* Cambridge, Mass.: MIT Press.

Lipsey, R. E. 1995. Outward direct investment and the U.S. economy. In *The effects of taxation on multinational corporations,* ed. M. Feldstein, J. R. Hines, Jr., and R. G. Hubbard, 7–33. Chicago: University of Chicago Press.

Lipsey, R. E., and M. Y. Weiss. 1969. The relation of U.S. manufacturing abroad to U.S. exports: A framework for analysis. *1969 Proceedings of the Business and Economic Statistics Section, American Statistical Association,* pp. 497–509.

———. 1972. Analyzing direct investment and trade at the company level. *1972 Proceedings of the Business and Economic Statistics Section, American Statistical Association,* pp. 11–20.

———. 1981. Foreign production and exports in manufacturing industries. *Review of Economics and Statistics* 63 (4): 488–94.

———. 1984. Foreign production and exports of individual firms. *Review of Economics and Statistics* 66 (2): 304–8.

Lundberg, L. 1992. The structure of Swedish international trade and specialization: "Old" and "new" explanations. *Weltwirtschaftliches Archiv* 128 (2): 266–87.

Markusen, J. R. 1995. The boundaries of multinational enterprises and the theory of international trade. *Journal of Economic Perspectives* 9 (2): 169–89.

———. 1998. Multinational enterprises and the theories of trade and location. In *The geography of multinational firms,* ed. P. Braunerhjelm and K. Ekholm, 9–32. Boston: Kluwer Academic.

Organization for Economic Cooperation and Development (OECD). 1995. *Foreign direct investment, trade and employment.* Paris: OECD.

Reddaway, W. B., in collaboration with J. O. N. Perkins, S. J. Potter, and C. T. Taylor. 1967. Effects of U.K. direct investment overseas: An interim report. Cambridge University, Department of Applied Economics, Occasional Paper no. 12.

Reddaway, W. B., in collaboration with S. J. Potter and C. T. Taylor. 1968. Effects of U.K. direct investment overseas: Final report. Cambridge University, Department of Applied Economics, Occasional Paper no. 15.

Svensson, R. 1993. *Production in foreign affiliates: Effects on home country exports and modes of entry.* Stockholm: Industriens Utredningsinstitut.

———. 1996a. *Foreign activities of Swedish multinational corporations.* Ph.D. diss. Uppsala University, Uppsala, Sweden.

———. 1996b. Effects of overseas production on home-country exports: Evidence based on Swedish multinationals. *Weltwirtschaftliches Archiv* 132 (2): 304–29.

Swedenborg, B. 1979. *The multinational operations of Swedish firms: An analysis of determinants and effects.* Stockholm: Industriens Utredningsinstitut.

———. 1982. *Svensk industri i utlandet: En analys av drivkrafter och effekter.* Stockholm: Industriens Utredningsinstitut.

———. 1985. Sweden. In *Multinational enterprises, economic structure, and international competitiveness,* ed. J. Dunning, 217–48. London: Wiley.

———. 1991. Svenska multinationella företag och produktiviteten. In *Internation-*

alisering och Produktivitet. Expertrapport nr 8 till Produktivitetsdelegationen (Expert Report no. 8 to the Commission on Productivity). Stockholm: Allmänna Förlaget.
Swedenborg, B., G. Johansson-Grahn, and M. Kinnwall. 1988. *Den svenska industrins utlandsinvesteringar 1960–1986.* Stockholm: Industriens Utredningsinstitut.

Comment   Bruce A. Blonigen

This paper is a fitting tribute to Robert Lipsey's substantial contributions on foreign direct investment (FDI) and multinational corporations (MNCs). The literature on FDI and MNCs owes a large debt to Lipsey's pioneering work in this area. Furthermore, it is an honor to provide comments on a paper written by Birgitta Swedenborg, who has been so instrumental in developing and analyzing the rich data we now have on Swedish multinational firms.

One of the important issues concerning MNCs that Robert Lipsey has addressed (in numerous articles with various coauthors) is the effect of FDI by MNCs on the parent (or home) country. As Swedenborg points out, this has been a particularly important policy concern in Sweden's history, and, of course, this is an important policy issue for many countries as we witness the increasing globalization of the world economy. These policy issues have led to important work estimating the net effect of MNCs locating production abroad on exports from the home country.

This is not a straightforward exercise for a variety of reasons. The primary difficulty is endogeneity concerns. The MNC's decision to service a foreign market through exports or foreign production is obviously simultaneous, with a variety of observed and unobserved "other" factors determining how much the MNC exports and how much it produces in the foreign market. This makes it difficult to identify the independent effect of foreign production (or affiliate net sales) on exports. Furthermore, the literature is not in agreement about how to properly specify an export equation, much less an equation explaining foreign-affiliate net sales. Finally, there are the typical data measurement issues to contend with.

Swedenborg's paper confronts these estimation issues in a reasonable way and gives us new estimates of the relationship between foreign production and exports using data on Swedish MNCs from 1965 to 1994. There are three significant contributions of Swedenborg's analysis. First, she controls for endogeneity by estimating the export equations with two-stage least squares (2SLS). Second, the panel nature of the data allows her to

Bruce A. Blonigen is associate professor of economics at the University of Oregon and a faculty research fellow of the National Bureau of Economic Research.

control for firm fixed effects, destination-country fixed effects, and time fixed effects. Finally, she separately estimates the effect of foreign net sales on exports by MNCs to their affiliates versus its effect on exports to non-affiliates, yielding more information about what is driving the overall net effect. The overall conclusion one draws is the following: While there is a strong complementarity relationship between exports of MNCs to their affiliates and MNC net sales abroad (presumably through exports of inputs from the parent to the affiliates), the overall net effect is zero when one properly controls for these statistical concerns. This finding contrasts with many previous studies of cross-sectional data that find overall net complementarity using OLS.

Swedenborg's analysis also points to future refinements and extensions. First, her work gives us evidence that endogeneity bias is quite important for these data, and strongly suggests that this issue should be examined further in future work. Swedenborg uses YR (the age of the firm's oldest manufacturing affiliate) as an instrument to identify the effect of foreign net sales on exports. The YR variable is a significant explanatory variable for foreign net sales and, as Swedenborg reports in footnote 7, the 2SLS estimates suggest the OLS estimates are biased upward. While this is an indication that YR is potentially an appropriate instrument, it is neither certain that this is the case, nor that we know how well this instrument controls for endogeneity compared to some alternative set of instruments that could be employed.

Swedenborg's YR variable is a creative instrument choice because it is likely to proxy well for an MNC's FDI experience in the foreign market. This FDI experience arguably decreases a firm's cost of operating in the foreign market and should correlate with more affiliate sales, which Swedenborg finds it does. However, an appropriate instrument needs to be uncorrelated with the error term in the export equations, and it is not clear that YR would satisfy this requirement. In particular, FDI experience in a foreign market may also mean the firm is more familiar with local input sources, which would affect the export equations if greater experience means affiliates substitute more local inputs for imported home-country inputs. This would likely affect the SXC (parent exports to foreign affiliates) equation the most, and this is precisely where Swedenborg finds large complementarity effects—in fact, implausibly large complementarity effects when she examines data at the destination-country level in table 4.3. Remaining endogeneity bias in the SXC equation is obviously important, since the implausibly high complementarity effect for the SXC equation seems to be responsible for netting out the substitution effect of the SXS equation in table 4.3, panel B. In other words, it is plausible that YR is not an appropriately exogenous instrument, particularly for the SXC equation, and that this is masking the true net relationship between foreign sales and exports, which may be one of net substitution.

While it is easy to call for better instruments, it can be difficult to devise more appropriate ones. However, it should be noted that Grubert and Mutti (1991) used tax-policy changes across countries to instrument for foreign-affiliate production in MNC export equations estimated from a panel of U.S. MNCs. As with this paper, they find that 2SLS estimation reduces the net effect of foreign production on exports from being one of complementarity to a statistically insignificant one. Swedenborg also notes that Sweden maintained controls on foreign direct investment until the 1980s. This type of country policy may be observable and quantifiable in some manner, and thus useful as an instrument. The point is that there are likely a number of alternative instrument sets that could be constructed and an examination of this would likely be a fruitful avenue for research, given the results to date of both this paper and that of Grubert and Mutti (1991).

Swedenborg is to be commended for exploiting the panel nature of the data to control for a variety of time-invariant "fixed" effects. A priori one would expect there to be significant firm-specific and destination-country-specific unobserved factors that affect exports, and particularly, foreign production. For example, theory suggests that firm-specific assets (often ones difficult to observe) are the main reason we observe MNCs. Controlling for these effects is quite important, as we can see from the differences between estimates in table 4.2 panels A and B, and between table 4.3 panels A and B. In fact, as with the endogeneity issues, her estimates show there is a substantial bias from pooled (or cross-section) OLS toward finding net complementarity, when one does not control for these fixed cross-sectional effects.

As Swedenborg notes, the data in this paper represent the longest time series to date of Swedish MNCs and the dynamic aspects of the data are quite interesting and worthy of future work. The extent to which Swedenborg exploits the time-series dimension of the data is to control for cross-sectional fixed effects, which yields estimates that are identified from the within-firm time-series dimension of the data. However, figure 4.1 suggests there may be more substantial dynamic considerations connected with the relationship between foreign production and exports than can be obtained from a point estimate derived from the entire period of the data. In particular, figure 4.1 portrays a very interesting look at overall Swedish MNC activity from 1965 through 1994. From 1965 to 1974 there were modest increases in both the share of exports and the share of foreign production in MNC sales. From 1978 to 1990, the share of foreign production almost doubles, while the share of exports falls by almost a third. Finally, from 1990 to 1994 foreign production falls off some, as the share of exports increases back to historical levels.

While information on all years from 1965 through 1994 would presumably be more revealing, this information suggests that the relationship between foreign production and exports changes and evolves over time. That is, there may be structural breaks in this relationship. Does the relationship change in a systematic way that would suggest a life cycle of an MNC's decisions on how to service a foreign market? For example, to what extent do new foreign affiliates switch from importing inputs from the home parent to eventual sourcing from local inputs, and how long does this process take? In other words, does the strong complementarity effect from parents' exporting inputs to foreign affiliates decrease over time, so that we may eventually have a net substitution relationship? These questions suggest that there may be substantial differences between the short-run effect of affiliate sales on exports from the long-run effect, and hence, these issues invite future research.

The possibility of structural breaks, as suggested by data in figure 4.1, also points toward a resolution of differences between Swedenborg's study and Svensson's work (1993, 1996a, 1996b). Svensson's studies generally find net substitution using the same database of Swedish MNCs from 1978 to 1990, while Swedenborg's study finds no net substitution for the period from 1965 to 1994. Swedenborg argues that methodological concerns with Svensson's studies are the source of the difference. However, figure 4.1 suggests that the period of the data may also be a source of the discrepancy. Again, figure 4.1 shows that the share of foreign production to MNC sales almost doubles, while the share of exports falls by almost a third from 1978 to 1990. It seems quite plausible that Swedenborg's methodology would also estimate net substitution over this period of the data.

In summary, my interpretation of this study and previous studies of the relationship between foreign sales and exports is that the net relationship is still very much an open question. I'm not convinced that we can rule out that foreign production involves some net substitution of parent firms' exports—at least for some nontrivial lengths of time, if not overall. The reasons are the following. Swedenborg's paper has shown that controlling for unobserved cross-sectional fixed effects and endogeneity has a very significant impact on the estimated relationship, from one of complementarity to one of no net effect. In addition, there are future refinements (discussed previously) that may translate into a substantially different relationship between foreign production and exports. Finally, while Swedenborg finds there is no net substitution from 1965 to 1994, her own figure 4.1 and previous studies by Svensson suggest that for certain periods, such as with Swedish MNCs from 1978 to 1990, there may be significant net substitution.

Swedenborg's study is a significant contribution toward understanding the future work economists need to undertake in order to develop a fuller understanding of the relationship between foreign production and exports. This policy issue will no doubt continue to be an important one in the future, as we continue our pursuit to understand the increasing globalization of the world economy.

References

Grubert, Harry, and John Mutti. 1991. Taxes, tariffs and transfer pricing in multinational corporate decision making. *Review of Economics and Statistics* 73: 285–93.

Svensson, Roger. 1993. *Production in foreign affiliates: Effects on home country exports and modes of entry.* Stockholm: Industriens Utredningsinstitut.

———. 1996a. *Foreign activities of Swedish multinational corporations.* Ph.D. diss. Uppsala University, Uppsala, Sweden.

———. 1996b. Effects of overseas production on home-country exports: Evidence based on Swedish multinationals. *Weltwirtschaftliches Archiv* 132 (2): 304–29.

5

Home-Country Effects of FDI
Foreign Production
and Structural Change
in Home-Country Operations

Gunnar Fors and Ari Kokko

5.1 Introduction

The home-country effects of foreign direct investment (FDI) have been hotly debated for many years, but the topic has received renewed attention over the past decade. One important reason is the development of the regional integration processes in Europe and the Americas. The reduction of regional trade and investment barriers has created new, large markets and removed restrictions on where plants can be located. The resulting increase in competition and the relocation of industry are expected to improve efficiency and welfare in the integrating region as a whole. However, it is not obvious that the benefits will be distributed equally among the participating countries, or between members of the integration agreement and outsiders. The worry in the home countries of multinational corporations (MNCs)—in particular, those home countries that are large net outward investors—is that investment and production abroad may replace home-country exports, employment, or investment.

The debate on the home-country effects of FDI has a longer history in Sweden than in most other countries, with the exception of the United States. The concern about home-country effects is easy to understand when it is noted that Sweden is a significant outward investor, while inward investment has, until recently, been much more limited. For instance, the outflows of Swedish FDI between 1981 and 1990 were more than five times

Gunnar Fors is head of division at the Swedish National Board of Trade, a government agency under the foreign ministry, Stockholm. Ari Kokko is professor of international business at Abo Akademi University, Turku, Finland, and holds a position at the European Institute of Japanese Studies, Stockholm.
Financial support from the Marianne and Marcus Wallenberg Foundation and HSFR of Sweden is gratefully acknowledged.

larger than the inflows (OECD 1993), and the stock of outward FDI was more than two and one-half times that of inward FDI in the mid-1990s (Braunerhjelm et al. 1996). Moreover, Swedish multinational corporations account for more than half of aggregate Swedish investment and employment in the manufacturing sector, and undertake more than 90 percent of manufacturing R&D. This means that any effects of outward investment are likely to be felt throughout the Swedish economy.

A disproportionately large share of the academic research on home-country effects has also focused on Sweden. Sweden is one of the few countries, besides the United States, where detailed information on the foreign operations of national firms has been collected systematically for a long period of time. The Research Institute of Industrial Economics (IUI) in Stockholm has conducted detailed surveys on the foreign operations of Swedish MNCs about every fourth year since the mid-1960s. These surveys, covering the years 1965, 1970, 1974, 1978, 1986, 1990, and 1994, include all Swedish MNCs in manufacturing with at least fifty employees and at least one majority-owned affiliate abroad. This data set has provided unique opportunities to follow three decades of the internationalization of Swedish industry, both at an aggregate level and at the firm level.

The studies analyzing the impact of FDI on the Swedish economy have, with a few recent exceptions, concluded that the relationship between foreign investment and home-country exports or employment is one of mild complementarity. Similarly, most studies of U.S. investment abroad have suggested a weak positive relationship (or no relationship) between FDI and home-country exports. These findings have reduced the worry that FDI has grown at the expense of investment or job creation in Sweden. However, they do not mean that the impact of FDI on Sweden is negligible. One reason is that investment abroad may be an essential survival strategy for firms in industries with large fixed costs and global competition. Although it is impossible to demonstrate convincingly what would have happened if Swedish firms had not been allowed to engage in FDI, it is safe to assume that many of them would have been smaller and less competitive in sectors where large investments in R&D and marketing are needed. Another reason is that FDI is likely to change the character of home-country production. The studies of the impact of FDI on aggregate home-country employment or exports fail to show that the structure and content of the home country's exports change as firms establish production abroad. Instead of exporting finished products to foreign customers, the MNCs' parent companies will increasingly focus on exporting intermediate inputs to their foreign affiliates.

The purpose of this paper is to add to the existing studies of home-country effects by focusing on the structural changes in home-country production that follow from FDI. Using detailed firm- and plant-level data from a sample of Swedish MNCs for the period 1986–94, we will try to demonstrate the great degree of change that continuously takes place within each MNC. We will also illustrate the direction of some of the structural changes that are in progress and show that the effects of FDI at the plant level are significantly different from those at more aggregate levels. This paper differs from earlier studies using the IUI database in its emphasis on the changes taking place in the home-country operations of the MNCs. This is possible because the IUI data have been complemented by a detailed plant-level database on the home-country operations of the largest Swedish MNCs, provided by Statistics Sweden.

The remainder of the paper is organized as follows. Section 5.2 summarizes the findings of some earlier studies of the production interactions between the foreign and domestic operations of MNCs. The impact of FDI on home-country exports has been the main issue in the earlier literature, but some studies focusing on home-country employment and domestic production structure are also discussed. Section 5.3 introduces the database and describes the changes in the operations of the sample companies between 1986 and 1994, with special emphasis on the great extent of structural change that has taken place within the MNCs. Section 5.4 looks at the relation between foreign production and domestic employment in a simple regression framework, and section 5.5 concludes the paper.

5.2 FDI and Home-Country Exports and Employment

Although the academic research on the home-country effects of FDI has addressed a wide variety of issues—ranging from environment and income distribution to taxation and economic policy (for recent surveys see Caves 1996; Dunning 1993; Industry Commission 1996)—it is clear that questions concerning the impact of outward investment on home-country exports, production, and employment have dominated the agenda. Only a few formal theoretical models of the determinants of foreign and domestic production are available (e.g., Brainard 1993; Markusen 1995), but the number of empirical studies is large. The empirical literature includes both detailed business-oriented analyses and more aggregated econometric studies for several countries at different points in time. This yields a large variation in methodology and results, although some broad generalizations appear to be possible. The more business-oriented authors have typically attempted to examine what would have happened in specific cases if investment abroad had not been possible, whereas econometric studies have tried to detect the overall relationship between FDI and home-country exports in larger samples of firms or industries.

Jordan and Vahlne (1981) provide an example of a Swedish business-oriented analysis of FDI and home-country exports. They aim to compare the domestic employment effects of foreign direct investment with alternative ways to exploit the competitive advantages of a sample of Swedish firms. The alternatives considered are exports from Sweden, licensing, and minority joint ventures, and the analysis attempts to take into account several factors that may influence Swedish exports and employment in the midterm. These include estimates of the market shares that can be captured under the alternative strategies, differences in the ability to face and solve customer problems in the relevant markets, flows of royalties and license payments (which influence the possibilities to undertake R&D), and differences in related product sales under the alternative strategies.

Jordan and Vahlne's overall conclusion is that foreign direct investment has positive effects on Swedish exports and employment, because the establishment of foreign affiliates typically leads to large increases in the foreign market shares and in exports of intermediate products to affiliates. The driving force is the existence (or fear) of various types of trade barriers that would limit the market shares if export were the only available alternative. Foreign production is judged, by Jordan and Vahlne, to be particularly beneficial for low-technology products with high transportation costs. However, the results rest on very specific assumptions about export survival rates, that is, the fractions of the affiliates' market share that could have been served by home exports. In some cases, for standardized products, the assumed survival rates are as low as 2 to 8 percent. A related government research report (Sweden 1981) examines a larger sample of firms and reaches similar results, with the summary conclusion that FDI has been a necessary strategy for the survival and international competitiveness of Swedish firms. Foreign direct investment has been complementary to Swedish exports and employment, because the alternatives would have resulted in much lower foreign market shares for Swedish firms.

It is obvious that the assumptions about export survival rates are of central importance for the outcome, and it is therefore interesting to compare Jordan and Vahlne's (1981) estimates with other estimates. To begin with, it can be noted that many other business-oriented case studies have also been based on very low survival rates. For instance, Stobaugh and associates (1972), who study nine U.S. firms, assume that their entire foreign markets would have been lost within five years in the absence of FDI. A problem with these studies is that the estimates of survival rates are often based on surveys and interviews with company officials, who naturally are interested in "portraying their foreign activities in as favourable a light as possible vis-à-vis their impact on the domestic economy" (Frank and Freeman 1978, 9).

An alternative is provided by Frank and Freeman (1978), who set up a model for the U.S. economy in which survival rates are explicitly calculated from data on costs and revenues. The model yields estimates of survival rates ranging between 20 and 40 percent, depending on industry. However, they rule out shifts in market size that are "occasioned by the establishment of a foreign subsidiary" (p. 35), which means that their figures are probably on the high side: The establishment of an affiliate may lead both to shifts in the demand curve and to increases in market shares. They also calculate a short-run "break-even" survival rate for the U.S. economy in 1970, which would lead to equally large export displacement and export stimulus from FDI. This break-even estimate is 11 percent (p. 62): Foreign direct investment will stimulate domestic exports if the surviving market shares are smaller, but will reduce exports if it is larger. Using their own best estimates of survival rates, Frank and Freeman conclude that foreign direct investment has substituted for U.S. exports and that the net employment effect of FDI is an annual loss of between 120,000 and 160,000 jobs (p. 62). It should be noted that the generality of these results is also uncertain, since the period under examination may not be representative—this was the peak of the U.S. firms' internationalization process.

The problem of assessing survival rates does not usually come up in the econometric studies, which typically employ regression analysis to determine the relation between exports and various firm, industry, and country characteristics. Controlling for as many other determinants as possible, the focus is on the partial effect of foreign direct investment (measured, e.g., as the stock of foreign assets or the value of foreign production). A negative coefficient for FDI implies that foreign production substitutes for exports, whereas a positive sign suggests that complementarity—the stimulus to home exports of intermediate and other related products—is more important in the aggregate. It can be noted that most U.S. studies of this type (e.g., U.S. Tariff Commission 1973; Horst 1974; Bergsten, Horst, and Moran 1978; Kravis and Lipsey 1988; Blomström, Lipsey, and Kulchycky 1988; Lipsey and Weiss 1981, 1984), as well as studies focusing on France, Japan, Canada, and the United Kingdom (e.g., Mucchielli and Saucier 1997; Buigues and Jacquemin 1994; Industry Commission 1996; Reddaway et al. 1968) conclude that the complementarities have tended to outweigh the substitution effects. However, it is also interesting to note that much of the research in both the United States and France was sparked by reports claiming that outward FDI had contributed to significant job losses, amounting to perhaps 900,000 jobs in the United States in the late 1960s (Ruttenberg 1971), and several million jobs in France in the 1990s (Arthuis 1993).

It is likely that there are significant differences between the competitive advantages of Swedish MNCs and multinationals from other home countries, and it may not be possible to generalize results across countries. A number of studies have therefore focused on the Swedish FDI-trade relationship. The most comprehensive of these are presented in Swedenborg (1979, 1982), Blomström, Lipsey, and Kulchycky (1988), and Svensson (1996). The studies are all based on a detailed data set on Swedish multinationals collected by the IUI in Stockholm, but there are significant differences in methodology and results. The major innovation in both of Swedenborg's studies is that she bases her analysis on two-stage least squares (2SLS) estimations, in order to avoid the bias that comes about because both foreign production and exports may be affected by the same omitted variables. The first stage estimates the size of foreign production as a function of various firm, industry, and host-country characteristics, and the second stage estimates exports from the Swedish parent company with the first-stage fitted values of foreign production as one of the independent variables. In Swedenborg (1979), the focus is on a sample of some 100 Swedish manufacturing MNCs with more than 300 foreign affiliates in 1974. Her findings suggest that there was no significant overall effect of foreign production on the exports of Swedish parents that year, but that the aggregate results hide two significant, but opposite, effects. Foreign production seems to substitute for some exports to sales affiliates and non-affiliated customers in the host country, but there is a concurrent (larger) positive effect on the exports of goods (both intermediates and finished products) to producing affiliates. Swedenborg (1982) adds observations for three more years (1965, 1970, and 1978), with very similar results. The effect on total export is still not statistically significant, but there is a clear pattern when complementary and substituting exports are examined separately. A one dollar increase in foreign production is found to result in a twelve cent increase in exports to producing affiliates, but only a two cent fall in exports to other customers in the host country—that is, a net export stimulus of ten cents. Birgitta Swedenborg's contribution to this volume, which examines Swedish FDI during the period 1965–94 in a panel data analysis, largely confirms these conclusions.

Blomström, Lipsey, and Kulchycky (1988) argue that Swedenborg's results are uncertain because her first-stage estimations have low explanatory power, so that much of the relevant variation in the affiliates' production is neglected in the second stage. They examine Swedish exports and foreign direct investment for ten aggregate industry groups in 1978, as well as changes between 1970 and 1978, in a conventional ordinary least squares (OLS) framework. By focusing on changes in the variables, they hope to eliminate the impact of the omitted variables that simultaneously affect foreign production and exports, but not those that affect changes in production or exports. Moreover, they look at total Swedish exports in each industry, rather than at only the parent corporations' exports. This means that they may capture some instances in which the affiliates' activities have substituted for other firms' exports, as well as cases in which FDI has facilitated other Swedish firms' exports to the host market. The latter situation may occur if foreign production familiarizes the host country with Swedish products, or if the affiliates transfer information about the host country's business environment back to Sweden.

Yet, the findings in Blomström, Lipsey, and Kulchycky (1988) differ little from those presented by Swedenborg (1979, 1982). They find no signs of substitution between Swedish exports and foreign production for any of the industries included—if anything, the authors find a larger complementary effect—and no evidence that large foreign production in a country reduces the country's subsequent imports from Sweden. Blomström, Fors, and Lipsey (1997), examining the connection between home employment and foreign production, also find a positive relation, which is interpreted as an indication of complementarity. Swedish MNCs with large foreign production also tend to have large domestic employment, controlling for the size of domestic output. The proposed reason is that MNCs with more foreign activities need additional supervisory, management, marketing, and R&D personnel in the parent company.[1]

A recent study by Svensson (1996), using unpublished data from later surveys of Swedish direct investment abroad, challenges the results of the earlier research. Svensson argues that it is necessary to account for the foreign affiliates' exports to third countries because they are likely to substitute directly for parent exports. Doing this, he finds that there now appears to be substitution between Swedish investment abroad and exports from Sweden. Braunerhjelm and Oxelheim (1998) address the discrepancy between Svensson (1996) and earlier studies by suggesting that the impact of FDI may vary depending on industry characteristics. They argue that FDI and exports should be complements in industries that rely on immobile natural resources (Heckscher-Ohlin industries), but that they may be substitutes in industries relying on technology, brand names, and other intangible assets that are not fixed to the home country (Schumpeter industries)—in particular, if the economic environment in the home country is less attractive than that in the host countries. They also find some empirical support for this hypothesis by examining the relationship between domestic and foreign investment in a regression framework. Their conclusion is that industry differences are likely to be important, and that more studies based on disaggregated data are needed to formulate efficient economic policies.

Although some of the recent studies have found signs of a substitutive relationship between FDI and home-country operations, they all note that the quantitative impact remains relatively small. It is therefore not unfair to summarize the debate on production interactions by noting that, in the aggregate, Swedish FDI does not appear to have any dramatic effect on Swedish investment, production, or exports. However, this assessment neglects the structural changes in the home country that come about because FDI influences the composition of home-country exports. The next section turns to an empirical investigation of these structural changes.

---

1. However, it should be noted that the same relationship could indicate that the MNCs with large foreign production have decided to concentrate relatively labor intensive production processes in Sweden.

5.3   Structural Change in Large Swedish MNCs 1986–1994

The data used in this paper are drawn from a plant-level database on the home-country operations of the thirty largest Swedish multinational conglomerates from 1986 to 1994, provided by Statistics Sweden, and from the database on the foreign operations of Swedish MNCs collected by the IUI. We were forced to drop several of the thirty firms provided by the Statistics Sweden database because they were not included in the IUI database (which excludes holding companies and firms that are active primarily in services), and the sample used in the subsequent analysis covers seventeen MNCs. Although the number of firms is relatively small, it should be noted that they hold a significant share of Swedish FDI. In 1994, they accounted for 57 percent of the domestic employment and 60 percent of the foreign employment of all the MNCs included in the IUI database.

Figures 5.1–5.3 show how the structure of home and foreign operations in the seventeen MNCs has changed between 1986 and 1994. Figure 5.1 depicts the changes in total employment. While domestic employment declined markedly, from more than 230,000 in 1986 to less than 170,000 in 1994, employment in foreign affiliates increased over the same period, from 267,000 to 312,000. The number of domestic plants fell from 229 to 169, while the number of foreign affiliates grew from 304 to 378. However, there was a marked difference in the development of employment in for-

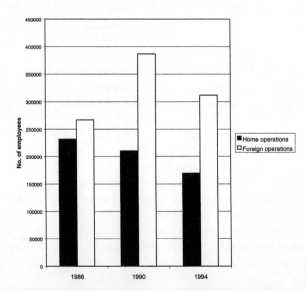

Fig. 5.1   Employment in domestic and foreign operations 1986–94, seventeen Swedish MNCs
Source: IUI and Statistics Sweden.

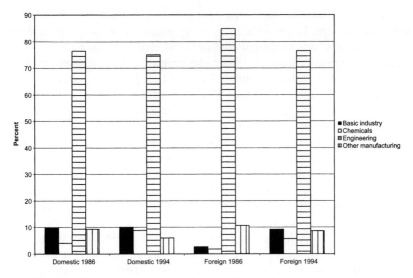

Fig. 5.2   Distribution of employment in domestic and foreign operations across broad industry groups 1986–94, seventeen Swedish MNCs
Source: IUI and Statistics Sweden.

eign affiliates between the two subperiods 1986–90 and 1990–94. Foreign employment increased by 44 percent between 1986 and 1990, when the economy was booming and Swedish MNCs were making very large profits, but fell by 20 percent between 1990 and 1994, when a deep financial crisis led to a severe recession.

Apart from the rapid internationalization process, which raised the foreign share of the MNCs' aggregate employment from 54 percent to 65 percent, there were also some important changes in the industry distribution of employment at home and abroad, and in the geographical distribution of foreign employment. Figure 5.2 illustrates the changes in employment across the four broad industry groups: basic industries, chemicals, engineering, and other manufacturing. The changes in the industry structure of domestic operations between 1986 and 1994 appear relatively limited, although the end points hide significant differences between the two subperiods. Engineering industries contracted and basic industries expanded rapidly during the 1986–90 period, but a reversal of the trend between 1990 and 1994 nearly restored the initial employment shares (although total employment had fallen by more than a quarter, as shown in fig. 5.1). The changes in foreign operations were similar, but their development between 1990 and 1994 was not strong enough to neutralize the fall in the share of engineering and the increase in basic industries between 1986 and 1994. However, in absolute terms, engineering employment in foreign operations actually grew during this period.

Figure 5.3 illustrates the changes in the geographical distribution of foreign employment. In absolute terms, employment grew in all four regions, with the largest absolute increases in the twelve European Union (EU) countries. In relative terms, however, the largest increases took place in the rest of Europe, which is dominated by the European Free Trade Agreement (EFTA) countries. Between 1986 and 1994, the share of this region grew from about 4 percent to nearly 8 percent of the foreign employment of the seventeen MNCs in the sample. The share of the twelve EU countries fell from 54 percent to 52 percent over the same period, in spite of a large absolute increase. There were also significant differences between the two subperiods in all regions except for the rest of Europe. Large employment increases between 1986 and 1990, amounting to about 40 percent in North American Free Trade Agreement (NAFTA) countries and the EU, turned into contractions of 16–18 percent between 1990 and 1994.

Table 5.1 adds further statistics to describe the changes that have taken place over the eight-year period. The table compares capital intensity and labor productivity in the domestic and foreign operations of the sample corporations. Physical-capital intensity (measured as the book value of capital per employee, in constant 1990 prices) more than doubled in both domestic and foreign operations between 1986 and 1994. Value added per employee in Swedish operations (in constant 1990 prices) increased by about 64 percent over the same period, while the corresponding increase in foreign operations was about 10 percentage points lower. Consequently, the gap in labor productivity between domestic and foreign operations increased somewhat over this period. The table also highlights the differences among regions regarding capital intensity and labor productivity.

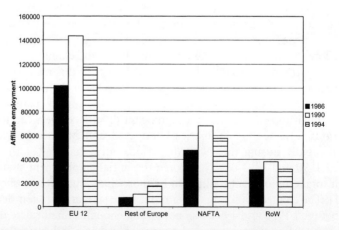

Fig. 5.3   Geographical distribution of foreign employment 1986–94, seventeen Swedish MNCs
Source: IUI database.

Table 5.1   **Capital Intensity and Labor Productivity at Home and Abroad**

	1986	1990	1994
Capital Intensity (K/L, million SEK)			
Home operations	0.246	0.360	0.496
Foreign operations	0.143	0.190	0.318
EU 12	0.157	0.265	0.428
Other Europe	0.184	0.310	0.236
NAFTA	0.189	0.177	0.226
Other	0.085	0.123	0.188
Labor Productivity (VA/L, million SEK)			
Home operations	0.310	0.334	0.507
Foreign operations	0.258	0.258	0.397
EU 12	0.242	0.309	0.445
Other Europe	0.232	0.358	0.318
NAFTA	0.274	0.225	0.322
Other	0.159	0.156	0.264

Source: IUI and Statistics Sweden.

The gap between domestic operations and affiliates in Europe is significantly smaller than implied by the aggregate figures for foreign operations. In fact, in 1990, affiliates in other Europe exhibited higher average labor productivity than the MNCs' Swedish plants. The fluctuation in the relative positions of the regions are to some extent related to changes in exchange rates, but changes in the industry distribution of affiliates are presumably also important.

The differences between the two subperiods regarding total employment and the distribution of employment across industries and regions suggest that both the determinants and the consequences of the internationalization of industry may be quite complex. Both country- and industry-specific determinants of investment appear to be important, and it is clear that these may change significantly over time. The resulting changes in the structure of domestic and foreign production can be quite significant, as suggested by the large changes in the amount and industry distribution of employment in this sample of MNCs.

5.3.1   Plant and Employment Dynamics

Although the figures presented previously suggest a reasonably large degree of change in the operations of Swedish MNCs, they underestimate the degree of change taking place within the corporations. The reason is that the comparisons of aggregate employment and industry distributions of employment reflect only the net changes that have taken place. For instance, the relatively moderate reduction of aggregate employment in Swedish plants between 1986 and 1990 is the sum of much larger job losses in some firms and industries and job creation in others. Figures 5.4–5.6

summarize some information on the changes that have taken place at the plant level. Figure 5.4 gives a rough picture of the dynamics in the population of plants owned by the seventeen MNCs at home and abroad. The figure shows the number of surviving, disappearing, and new plants for 1986, 1990, and 1994. More than half of the 229 Swedish plants that existed in 1986 had disappeared from the sample by 1990, as a result of closures or sales to other firms. (Unfortunately, we have not been able to determine exactly what has happened to the plants dropping out of the sample.) This corresponds to an average death rate for plants of about 12 percent per year, which is roughly similar to that for small and medium-sized enterprises. Simultaneously, the seventeen MNCs established 105 new plants in Sweden. The changes in the population of foreign plants were almost as large. Of the 304 foreign affiliates existing in 1986, 119 had disappeared by 1990, while 205 new affiliates had been established over the same period. The development between 1990 and 1994 was similar, with the exception that the number of new Swedish plants was much lower than the number of disappearing plants, reflecting the contraction in home operations.

Considering the industry distribution of disappearing and new plants in Sweden, there is no doubt that the largest changes occurred in chemicals and in other manufacturing. The number of Swedish plants in both these

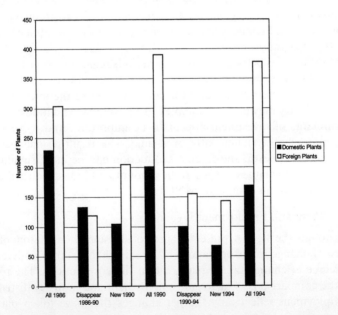

Fig. 5.4   Plant dynamics: changes in the population of domestic and foreign plants 1986–94, seventeen Swedish MNCs
Source: IUI and Statistics Sweden.

industry groups was reduced by more than half. However, the changes were notable even in basic industry, although the total number of Swedish plants fell by only one (from 26 to 25) between 1986 and 1994. Our sample includes 36 plants that disappeared and 35 that were created during the period. It should be noted that this underestimates the true number of changes, since we do not capture plants that emerged and disappeared between 1986 and 1990 or between 1990 and 1994. The largest changes in foreign operations were found in basic industry and chemicals, where the number of affiliates increased from 11–12 to 28. The dramatic changes in the population of affiliates in the engineering industry are also notable. The total number of affiliates grew by 18 (the difference between 215 new and 197 disappearing plants) for a total increase from 239 to 257.

The changes in number of jobs are not quite as dramatic as the changes in number of plants, reflecting the fact that both disappearing and new plants are small relative to the surviving ones. Yet job losses and job creation in Swedish plants corresponded to one-third to one-fourth of total employment in 1986 and 1990, with somewhat higher numbers for the foreign affiliates.

It is clear that this dramatic dynamism reflects a much larger potential for structural change than the aggregate data indicate. As noted in the previous section, few studies have been able to examine the dynamism within MNCs in detail because of the lack of suitable data. This study is plagued by the same problem, but figures 5.5 and 5.6 roughly illustrate some of the changes.

Figure 5.5 shows the average labor productivity of surviving, disappearing, and new plants. This is an interesting measure, since it may reflect the skill and capital intensity of the underlying production process. The pattern implied by (for example) the product life-cycle theory is one in which technical progress leads to higher skill and capital intensity both at home and abroad, presumably to the benefit of both the home and the host countries. However, various market characteristics, such as government intervention or cost conditions, might lead to other results. For instance, one of the main concerns regarding the effects of FDI in Sweden in recent years is that foreign production may lead to the export of attractive capital- or skill-intensive jobs. The data presented in figure 5.5 generally do not provide any strong support to such worries, although the development between 1990 and 1994 is somewhat confusing. The pattern for the subperiod 1986–90, however, is one that could be expected. A comparison of 1986 productivity between those plants that survived until 1990 and those that had disappeared by 1990 reveal that the former exhibited higher labor productivity. In other words, plant closures contributed to the rise in average productivity in the MNCs.

However, the comparison between those Swedish plants that survived and those that disappeared between 1990 and 1994 suggests a somewhat

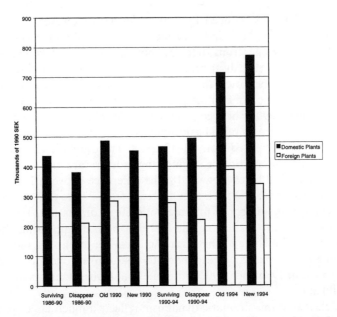

Fig. 5.5   Average labor productivity (VA/L) of surviving, disappearing, and new plants 1986–94, seventeen Swedish MNCs
Source: IUI and Statistics Sweden.

peculiar pattern. The plants that had disappeared by 1994 had higher labor productivity in 1990 than those that survived until 1994. One possible explanation could be that some operations with relatively high value added per worker were moved from Sweden to foreign affiliates of Swedish MNCs during this period.

Figure 5.6 summarizes changes in employment at home and abroad for the twelve industry categories in which Swedish MNCs had both domestic and foreign activities during the period under study. The industries are chosen at the three- and four-digit levels. The most interesting observation is probably that domestic and foreign employment changed in the opposite directions in most (eight of twelve) of the industry categories.

It is worth noting that the pattern of production relocations illustrated by figure 5.6 does not conform to any simple theoretical prediction. There does not appear to be any strong support for Braunerhjelm and Oxelheim's (1998) hypothesis that FDI and exports should be complements in industries based on Swedish raw materials, but should be substitutes in industries with R&D and technology as the competitive assets. The largest job gains have occurred in telecommunications equipment, whereas the largest job losses are found in the automobile industry. Both are among the most R&D-intensive industries in Sweden, with R&D expenditures exceeding 20 percent of value added in 1989. Paper and pulp, and metal products,

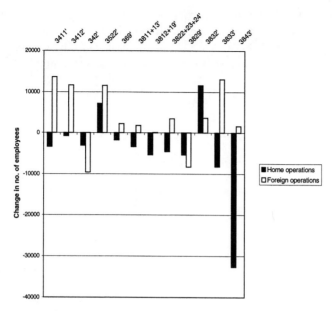

Fig. 5.6   Changes in domestic and foreign employment, three- and four-digit industries 1986–94, seventeen Swedish MNCs
Source: IUI and Statistics Sweden.
Note: Industry categories are as follows (n.e.c. = not elsewhere classified):

3411	Pulp, paper, and paperboard
3412	Containers and boxes of paper and paperboard
342	Printing and publishing
3522	Pharmaceuticals
369	Nonmetallic products n.e.c.
3811+13	Fabricated metal products: hand tools and structural metal products
3812+19	Furnitures and other fabricated metal products n.e.c.
3822+23+24	Agricultural, metal, and woodworking, and special industrial machinery
3829	Machinery n.e.c.
3832	Radio, television, and telecommunications equipment
3833	Electrical appliances
3843	Motor vehicles

are among the industries in which foreign employment has increased while domestic employment has fallen. These industries are presumably more dependent on Swedish natural resources than are other sectors. The four industries in which Swedish and foreign employment have changed in the same direction include printing and publishing, which is the least R&D intensive of the sectors, as well as pharmaceuticals, which is the most R&D intensive. This confusing pattern may be related to the short and relatively turbulent time period under study, but it also corroborates the need for future research in this area. It is possible that a richer data set, including disaggregated information on R&D, labor quality, and exports and imports, would have presented a clearer picture. Considering the complex decision-making process underlying location decisions, it is obvious that research focusing on formal theoretical modeling of the issues at hand will also be valuable. However, the next section will examine the relation between foreign production and domestic employment in a simple regression framework that may allow us to say something more about the character of the structural changes taking place in home operations.

5.4   How Does Foreign Production Affect Parent Employment?

With detailed plant-level data on the domestic and foreign operations of MNCs, it should be possible to examine the relationship between foreign and domestic production in closer detail than most earlier studies have done. In this section, we will therefore present some simple descriptive equations on disaggregated data, following Blomström, Fors, and Lipsey (1997), to examine the relationship between foreign production and domestic employment, given the level of domestic production. For this purpose, we have pooled the observations for 1986, 1990, and 1994, and defined two dependent variables, $PEMPL_{ij}$ and $PEMPL_{ijk}$, to measure employment in Sweden. The subscript i identifies the MNC, the subscript j identifies the time period, and the subscript k denotes the industry. As discussed earlier, each MNC includes several individual firms that are not necessarily involved in the same industry. The explanatory variables measure domestic and foreign production, as proxied by the parent firm's net sales, PNS (sales − imports from the foreign affiliates) and the affiliates' net sales, ANS (sales − imports from the parent's Swedish plants). Subscripts $i, j,$ and k denote the MNC, time period, and industry. The relationship we will estimate in an OLS framework is

(1) $PEMPL_{ij} = a + b*PNS_{ij} + c*ANS_{ij} +$ time dummies

$+$ MNC dummies.

Table 5.2 summarizes the results of some of the regression results. In equation (2a), the dependent variable is aggregate domestic employment for each MNC, $PEMPL_{ij}$. The explanatory variables are the parents' net sales (PNS_{ij}) and the affiliates' aggregate net sales (ANS_{ij}) plus company and time dummies. The negative estimated coefficient for ANS is contrary to that found in Blomström, Fors, and Lipsey (1997), and indicates that the MNCs with the largest production abroad have relatively low employment in Sweden, controlling for the level of Swedish production. In other words, more foreign output means fewer employees at home for a given value of home output. This effect could be a reflection of the structural changes in MNC operations discussed in the previous section. Foreign production would have a negative impact on domestic employment if the more labor-intensive portions of the largest MNCs' operations were relo-

Table 5.2   Regression Analysis: The Relationship between Domestic Employment and Foreign Production in Swedish MNCs

Dependent Variable	(2a) $PEMPL_{ij}$	(2b) $PEMPL_{ijk}$
Constant	1,262.68	−2,616.79
PNS_{ij}	0.46 (3.70)***	
PNS_{ijk}		0.0007 (28.39)***
ANS_{ij}	−0.39 (−2.65)**	
ANS_{ijk}		0.08 (3.58)***
TD 1986	1,782.88 (1.10)	1,543.20 (4.94)***
TD 1990	2,119.57 (1.62)	1,264.37 (3.93)***
Company dummies	Incl.	Incl.
Adjusted R^2	0.92	0.89
F-value	31.63	91.98
N	51	225

cated to their foreign affiliates, while the more skill- or capital-intensive operations were kept in Sweden. This result can be considered as a rough summary of the unclear picture presented by figure 5.6, which illustrated the changes in domestic and foreign employment in twelve disaggregated industries.[2]

To examine whether the negative coefficient in equation (2a) is related to the industry distribution of the operations of the MNCs, we have identified the domestic employment variable by the relevant industry in equation (2b), so that the dependent variable there is $PEMP_{ijk}$. The explanatory variables PNS_{ijk} and ANS_{ijk} are also identified by the industry of operations. In addition, we have included company and time dummies. This raises the number of observations from 51 to 225. Here, results are similar to those in Blomström, Fors, and Lipsey (1997). The positive and significant coefficient of the variable ANS_{ijk} indicates that the firms with large foreign operations in a specific industry also tend to have high levels of employment in Sweden in the same industry, taking into account the level of Swedish production. The positive coefficient for ANS in Blomström, Fors, and Lipsey (1997) was interpreted to mean that the largest MNCs needed additional supervisory, marketing, and R&D personnel in Sweden to man-

2. However, it should be noted that this explanation is not perfectly consistent with the findings from figure 5.5, where we noted that the plants surviving between 1990 and 1994 exhibited lower labor productivity than those disappearing from the sample between those two years.

age their foreign operations, and it is possible that the same mechanism works here as well. At this less-aggregated level, there is no evidence of any relocation of more labor-intensive operations to foreign affiliates.

The differences between the results in equations (2a) and (2b) provide an interesting and complementary piece of information to the ongoing debate on the relation between domestic and foreign production. For the MNCs in the sample and the period under study, it appears that larger foreign production is related to lower domestic employment for a given amount of domestic output. This probably reflects structural changes within the MNCs, which involve a relocation of the more labor-intensive operations to foreign affiliates. Once the industry distribution of operations is controlled for, there appears to be a positive relation between foreign production and domestic employment. The positive impact on domestic employment is probably related to the various activities undertaken at home to coordinate and support the operations of foreign affiliates.

5.5 Concluding Remarks

This paper has surveyed some of the literature on the relationship between FDI and the home-country operations of MNCs, and has tried to highlight the effects of outward FDI on economic structure in the home country. Much of the existing literature on production interactions between the domestic and foreign operations of MNCs has examined what happens to home-country exports and employment as a result of outward FDI. Although the results of earlier studies vary somewhat, there appears to be a consensus that the quantitative effects are not dramatic. The reduced exports of finished products from the home country to independent foreign customers are balanced by increases in exports of intermediate products to the foreign affiliates. However, the structural changes—the transformation that occurs when the parent company becomes increasingly specialized in the production of intermediate goods—have not been discussed in great detail. Drawing from a database covering seventeen of the largest Swedish MNCs, we have therefore attempted to provide a rough picture of how internationalization is connected with structural changes in the home-country operations of the MNCs.

The main finding of this study is that the changes taking place within the MNCs are larger than has been recognized in most earlier studies. Looking at the population of plants owned by the MNCs, we found annual turnover rates of about 10 percent for the period 1986–94. In most of the industries in which the seventeen MNCs in our sample had operations both in Sweden and abroad, the domestic and foreign employment changed in opposite directions. However, in this largely exploratory paper, we were not able to identify any simple pattern in these relocations of production, although the regression exercise in section 5.4 suggested that home-country operations were becoming relatively less labor-intensive as a result of the structural changes. One reason for the weak conclusions is the lack of formal models to explain the determinants of the MNCs' location decisions. The production pattern that can be discerned at any given point in time reflects current conditions as well as past decisions, which means that empirical analysis is not likely to be sufficient for distinguishing the main determinants of MNC behavior. Fortunately, an increasing amount of theoretical work presently focuses on problems where international trade, investment, and location decisions are interconnected.

Another area that has not been discussed in this paper is the welfare consequences of the ongoing structural changes within the MNCs. Since the MNCs' location choices are based on profit maximization, it can be assumed that their decisions reveal that there are private gains to be made from specialization. It is not equally obvious what the net effects are for Sweden. One reason is that there are differences in international market structure, which means that some industries can charge higher prices and generate larger profits than others. Certain types of production may also be connected with positive external effects and spillovers. The aggregate impact of FDI on the home country may be beneficial if production processes with high profits and positive externalities are retained at home, but effects are likely to be less advantageous, or even negative, if these are among the activities that are moved to foreign affiliates. However, there is no generally accepted notion of which industries are most beneficial, which kinds of externalities are relevant, how important they are in quantitative terms, and how they compare with the gains from specialization. If the structural changes within the MNCs turn out to follow some systematic pattern, it is clear that the welfare consequences should also be subject to analysis.

References

Arthuis, J. 1993. *Délocalisations hors du territoire national des activités industrielles et de service.* Rapport du Sénat no. 337, Paris.

Bergsten, F., T. Horst, and T. Moran. 1978. *American multinationals and American interests.* Washington, D.C.: Brookings.

Blomström, M., G. Fors, and R. E. Lipsey. 1997. Foreign direct investment and employment: Home country experience in the United States and Sweden. *Economic Journal* 107:787–97.

Blomström, M., R. E. Lipsey, and K. Kulchycky. 1988. U.S. and Swedish direct investment and exports. In *Trade policy issues and empirical analysis,* ed. R. Baldwin, 259–99. Chicago: University of Chicago Press.

Brainard, L. 1993. A simple theory of multinational corporations and trade with a trade-off between proximity and concentration. NBER Working Paper no. 4269. Cambridge, Mass.: National Bureau of Economic Research.

Braunerhjelm, P., K. Ekholm, L. Grundberg, and P. Karpaty. 1996. Swedish multinational corporations: Recent trends in foreign activities. IUI Working Paper no. 462. Stockholm: Research Institute of Industrial Economics.

Braunerhjelm, P., and L. Oxelheim. 1998. Does foreign direct investment replace home country investment? Paper presented at symposium, New Issues in Trade and Location. 28–30 August, Lund, Sweden.

Buigues, P., and A. Jacquemin. 1994. Foreign direct investment and exports to the European Community. In *Does ownership matter? Japanese multinationals in Europe,* ed. M. Mason and D. Encarnation, 163–99. Oxford: Oxford University Press.

Caves, R. E. 1996. *Multinational enterprise and economic analysis.* Cambridge, UK: Cambridge University Press.

Dunning, J. H. 1993. *Multinational enterprises and the global economy.* Wokingham, U.K.: Addison-Wesley.

Frank, R. H., and R. T. Freeman. 1978. *Distributional consequences of direct foreign investment.* New York: Academic Press.

Horst, T. 1974. American exports and foreign direct investments. Discussion Paper no. 362. Boston: Harvard Institute of Economic Research.

Industry Commission. 1996. *Implications for Australia of firms locating offshore.* Belconnen, ACT: Industry Commission.

Jordan, J. L., and J. E. Vahlne. 1981. Domestic employment effects of direct investment abroad by two Swedish multinationals. Multinational Enterprises Programme. Working Paper no. 13. Geneva: International Labour Office.

Kravis, I., and R. E. Lipsey. 1988. The effect of multinational firms' foreign operations on their domestic employment. NBER Working Paper no. 2760. Cambridge, Mass.: National Bureau of Economic Research.

Lipsey, R. E., and M. Y. Weiss. 1981. Foreign production and exports in manufacturing industries. *Review of Economics and Statistics* 63:488–94.

———. 1984. Foreign production and exports of individual firms. *Review of Economics and Statistics* 66:304–8.

Markusen, J. 1995. The boundaries of multinational enterprises and the theory of international trade. *Journal of Economic Perspectives* 9:169–89.

Mucchielli, J.-L., and P. Saucier. 1997. European industrial relocations in low-wage countries: Policy and theory debates. In *Multinational firms and international relocation,* ed. P. J. Buckley and J.-L. Mucchielli, 5–33. Cheltenham, UK: Edward Elgar.

Organization for Economic Cooperation and Development (OECD). 1993. *OECD reviews on foreign direct investment: Sweden.* Paris: OECD.

Reddaway, W. B., in collaboration with S. J. Potter and C. T. Taylor. 1968. *Effects of U.K. direct investment overseas: Final report.* Cambridge: Cambridge University Press.

Ruttenberg, S. 1971. *Needed! A constructive foreign trade policy.* Washington, D.C.: AFL-CIO.

Stobaugh, R. B., and associates. 1972. *U.S. multinational enterprises and the U.S. economy.* Boston: Harvard Graduate School of Business Administration.

Svensson, R. 1996. Effects of overseas production on home country exports: Evidence based on Swedish multinationals. *Weltwirtschaftliches Archiv* 132 (2): 304–29.

Sweden. 1981. *Effekter av investeringar utomlands.* SOU 1981:33. Stockholm: Liber Förlag.

Swedenborg, B. 1979. *The multinational operations of Swedish firms.* Stockholm: Almqvist & Wicksell International.

———. 1982. *Svensk industri i utlandet: En analys av drivkrafter och effekter.* Stockholm: Industrial Institute for Economic and Social Research.

U.S. Tariff Commission. 1973. *Implications of multinational firms for world trade and investment and for U.S. trade and labor.* Report to the U.S. Senate Committee on Finance, February.

Comment   Guy V. G. Stevens

It is a privilege and a pleasure to participate in this tribute to the career of Robert Lipsey. Bob commented on one of my first published papers back in 1972, and we later collaborated on a study of the interaction between domestic and foreign investments of U.S. multinationals (Stevens and Lipsey 1994). Perhaps more important, over a period now closing in on thirty years, we have participated with a small group of researchers and Department of Commerce officials to improve both the quality and the accessibility of U.S. data on multinational firm operations. No one has contributed more to this effort than Bob.

Data and Findings

Gunnar Fors and Ari Kokko examine a new source of Swedish microeconomic data, exploring some new questions and showing that some old answers depend on the level at which the data are aggregated. The data in question, covering three cross sections (1986, 1990, and 1994), are plant-level data for both parent-firm operations in Sweden and affiliate operations abroad.

Just looking at histograms and averages (table 5.1 and figs. 5.1–5.6) suggests that there is little evidence for some of the worst fears regarding the effects of direct investment. First, there seemed to be no clear pattern of correlation between employment changes for parent operations in Sweden and those for the foreign affiliates: In the initial period (1986–90), domestic employment fell while that in foreign affiliates rose, whereas in the second (1990–94), both fell. Moreover, the earlier period was a boom time in Sweden, so that any reductions in employment in the sample were probably taken up quickly by the rest of the economy. Second, there was no evidence that good jobs were being exported from Sweden to the foreign affiliates; labor productivity in Sweden rose smartly over time, and, with only one exception (which later evaporated), was consistently higher than that in foreign plants. Of course, not all such comparisons are meant to answer definitively such questions as, "What would have happened in the *absence* of the observed changes in foreign affiliate operations?"

The authors' regression analysis attempts to address the "what if" question with respect to the question of changes in Swedish employment.

Guy V. G. Stevens is a senior economist in the International Division of the Board of Governors of the Federal Reserve System, Washington, D.C.

Among other things, here they show that empirical answers to such questions seem to depend on the degree of data aggregation. In what are now fairly well-known regressions of home- or parent-firm employment on domestic and foreign-affiliate net sales (or production), when the firm's data are aggregated over all industries, the sign of the foreign-affiliate sales variable is significantly negative (−0.39). This degree of aggregation corresponds to that of most previous Swedish work using firm data and, as the authors point out, the results are contrary to at least one influential study (Blomström, Fors, and Lipsey 1997). It would appear, then, that Fors finds himself in the enviable position of being able to produce published results arguing for either a significant positive or a negative effect of foreign-affiliate sales on Swedish employment.

However, when the authors use their new data disaggregated by plant, the significant positive effect of foreign-affiliate sales (+0.08) reemerges.[1] I will comment further on these results in the next section.

The authors have just begun to explore their disaggregated data set, but already they are revealing patterns that surprise and intrigue. The turnover in plant ownership shown in figure 5.4 is dramatic—showing, for example, that approximately half of the domestic plants were sold or abandoned in each of the four-year periods studied. This pattern indicates much more flexibility in adjusting the capital stock than I would have imagined. Moreover, there seemed little indication that plants that disappeared were in any way inferior by the measure of labor productivity to those that survived.

Further Comments on the Estimates of the Interactions between Foreign-Affiliate Production and Domestic Variables

Fors and Kokko discuss how the estimated sign of the effect of foreign-affiliate sales or production on domestic employment differs between their two equations, and differs with the results of at least some previous research (e.g., Blomström, Fors, and Lipsey 1997). In their introductory section, they also note the differences of opinion among researchers on the closely related question of the effect of foreign-affiliate production on home-country exports. The resolution of these differences should probably be a priority for future research.

Even if the causes of these different empirical results are identified, I would like to suggest that the best of the resulting equations may not, without something more, be sufficient to throw light on the policy questions they were designed to answer—in this case, the impact of foreign-affiliate production on the demand for domestic (Swedish) labor. Suppose it turns out that the disaggregated equation (2b) is the correct one and that

---

1. The difference in the size of the estimated coefficients for the affiliate sales and other variables concerns me a bit. Perhaps this is a problem of different units of measurement, but the coefficients are 5 to 500 times larger in the equation using the aggregated data.

the coefficient on affiliate sales (ANS_{ijk}) is really 0.08. If we are asked the policy question, "What will be the impact of a one-unit change in ANS on domestic employment (PEMPL)?" we would tend to answer "0.08." This answer assumes not only that a unit of foreign-affiliate sales can be treated as exogenous for purposes of estimation, but also that it can be varied independently of any other variable in the equation. Given that the two variables on the right-hand sides of their equations (foreign-affiliate production and net domestic production) are most likely codetermined, this assumption seems unlikely. In fact, one of the key research questions in the discipline is the degree to which exports from the parent firm, a component of net domestic production, are affected by changes in foreign-affiliate production. For purposes of illustration, assume that, in addition to equation (2b) (see table 5.2), another equation postulates that finished goods exports from the parent, X_S, (subscript "S" for substitutes) plus affiliate production ANS equals a time dependent exogenous variable, D_t (foreign demand). Since X_S plus domestic sales equals parent net sales (PNS) in equation (2b), an exogenous change in ANS would now induce an equal and opposite change in both X_S and PNS. The correct estimate of the overall impact of the change on domestic employment would now be 0.08 − 0.0007.[2]

The foregoing illustrates that, even for plant-level data, an omitted equation can make a crucial difference for the answer to the policy questions that originally motivated the research. This problem becomes even more central when we try to calculate overall country effects of changes in multinational firm activity, necessitating calculations (and probably equations) for interactions with host-country producers in foreign markets and with exporters from third countries. To this problem of selecting properly sized models, one can add the pitfalls of being unsure whether an equation that by necessity involves endogenous variables is truly structural, and of finding adequate instruments to estimate consistent coefficients when simultaneous equation problems do appear.

The citation of this litany of problems perhaps explains the comment in my oral presentation in which, after completing a 1974 paper with Michael Adler on trade and investment, I concluded that this area of study was "too difficult." I am glad that researchers such as the present authors, Bob Lipsey, and others at this conference have continued to labor in this vineyard, despite my timidity at the time. I may have been right that the costs

---

2. The value of 0.0007 seems implausibly small. This is another reason I suspect that the coefficients in equation (2b) might either be implausible or reflect different units of measurement for the two independent variables.

The previous example, for simplicity, ignores exports of intermediate goods from the parent to foreign affiliates. Taking intermediates into account would change the overall result considerably, but would support the main point that it is important not to ignore the other equations in the model that link the endogenous variables appearing in a given equation.

are high, but so are the benefits. The authors further point out that this vineyard is far from picked clean: The wide range in plausible estimates for such questions as the impact of foreign-affiliate production on trade indicates that important policy questions are still open. A useful enterprise, I would venture, would be a study that takes the various contending estimates for the interaction of trade, foreign-affiliate production, and domestic labor demand and tries to understand their differences.

References

Adler, Michael, and Guy V. G. Stevens. 1974. The trade effects of direct investment. *Journal of Finance* 29 (2): 655–76.
Blomström, Magnus, Gunnar Fors, and Robert E. Lipsey. 1997. Foreign direct investment and employment: Home country experience in the United States and Sweden. *Economic Journal* 107:1787–97.
Stevens, Guy V. G. 1972. Capital mobility and the international firm. In *The international mobility and movement of capital,* ed. Fritz Machlup et al., 323–53. New York: National Bureau of Economic Research.
Stevens, Guy V. G., and Robert E. Lipsey. 1994. Interactions between domestic and foreign investment. *Journal of International Money and Finance* 11 (1): 40–62.

III

International Trade
and Exchange Rates

The Optimal Choice of Exchange Rate Regime
Price-Setting Rules and Internationalized Production

Michael B. Devereux and Charles Engel

6.1 Introduction

The modern literature on the choice of fixed versus flexible exchange rate regimes traces back to Friedman (1953). Friedman's contribution emphasized the enhanced flexibility of relative prices afforded by floating exchange rates in a world where nominal goods prices adjust slowly. A country can be insulated to some degree from foreign demand shocks under floating exchange rates because relative price movements absorb some of the changes in demand that would have to be met by changes in quantities produced under fixed exchange rates.

Friedman's early work was supplemented and refined in the 1960s by Mundell (1960, 1961a, 1961b, 1963), who explored the role of capital mobility in the choice of exchange rate regimes. Whether fixed or floating exchange rates are better depends in Mundell's work on whether the source of shocks was monetary or real, on the degree of capital and other factor mobility, and on the relative size of countries.

A large body of literature in the 1970s and 1980s, in turn, extended Mundell's work by incorporating a role for expectations. Contributors include Turnovsky (1976, 1983), Fischer (1977), Hamada and Sakurai (1978), Flood (1979), Flood and Marion (1982), Weber (1981), Kim-

Michael B. Devereux is professor of economics at the University of British Columbia and a research associate of the Centre for Economic Policy Research, London. Charles Engel is professor of economics and public affairs at the University of Wisconsin, Madison, and a research associate of the National Bureau of Economic Research.

The authors thank Anna Schwartz for her thoughtful comments, which point in useful directions for future research. Engel acknowledges funding from a National Science Foundation grant administered by the National Bureau of Economic Research.

brough (1983), Aizenman and Frenkel (1985), and Glick and Wihlborg (1990). These papers evaluated the optimality of exchange rate regimes on ad hoc criteria, generally involving variance of output and inflation.

We investigate the optimality of exchange rate regimes from a welfare maximization standpoint. Others have studied the welfare properties of alternative exchange rate systems, including Lapan and Enders (1980), Helpman (1981), Helpman and Razin (1982), Eaton (1985), Aizenman (1994), Chinn and Miller (1998), and Neumeyer (1998). These papers, however, do not assume any sort of nominal price stickiness, and therefore do not follow directly in the tradition of Friedman and Mundell.

The model we use is a two-country, infinite horizon model of optimization under uncertainty. Consumers get utility from consumption, leisure, and real balances. We assume perfect capital mobility in the model because we allow a complete market of state-contingent nominal bonds. The sources of uncertainty are random monetary shocks at home and abroad. We assume that monopolistic firms must set nominal prices prior to the realization of monetary shocks. Prices adjust fully after one period.

Two important features of the economy that we examine are motivated in part by the empirical research of Robert Lipsey. First is the nature of how price setting affects the optimal choice of exchange rate regime. Friedman and Mundell assumed that producers set prices in their own currencies, and that those prices do not adjust when exchange rates change. Indeed, in their models, the law of one price (LOP) holds for all goods.

Lipsey has demonstrated how poor the LOP assumption is. The seminal paper in this regard is Kravis and Lipsey (1978).[1] That paper demonstrates that prices show substantial deviations from purchasing power parity. Moreover, relative prices move with exchange rates: Countries with weaker currencies have lower prices. These movements appear to be attributable to a large extent to failures of the LOP: "There are reasons for believing that there may be substantial deviations from the law of one price even for traded goods" (p. 227). Furthermore, it appears from microeconomic data that firms set different prices for consumers in different countries. Kravis and Lipsey conclude, "A given seller may charge different prices for a given product to different destinations" (p. 234), and, "Price discrimination is quite common in international trade" (p. 234).

More recent empirical research confirms those findings.[2] Lipsey and Swedenborg (1996) conclude that even for highly tradable food items, a significant temporary factor affecting relative prices across countries is exchange rate movements. We conclude that a better description of price

1. See also Kravis and Lipsey (1987).
2. See especially Engel (1993, 1999), Rogers and Jenkins (1995), and Engel and Rogers (1996).

setting is that nominal prices are sticky in the currency of the consumer; we refer to this type of price stickiness as *pricing-to-market*.

We have argued that the type of price stickiness may be of critical importance in the analysis of fixed versus floating exchange rates (Devereux and Engel 1998). We find that under floating exchange rates and pricing-to-market, foreign monetary shocks do not affect domestic consumption.[3] In contrast, when prices are set in the producers' currencies, the prices paid by home residents for foreign goods change as the exchange rate changes. This introduces a channel through which the foreign monetary shocks can affect domestic consumption. The larger the share of foreign goods in consumption, the more vulnerable consumption will be to foreign money shocks. The type of pricing behavior also influences the average levels of prices, consumption, and leisure under floating exchange rates.

We extend our earlier paper by examining the role of the price-setting behavior of firms when there is internationalized production. Lipsey's empirical work has documented the large and increasing role for multinational corporations (MNCs) in U.S. and world production. Lipsey (1998) finds that internationalized production grew from 4.5 percent of world output in 1970 to 7 percent of world output in 1995. In manufacturing, the share rose from 12 percent in 1970 to 16 percent in 1990 (and probably much higher by 1995). Blomström, Fors, and Lipsey (1997) find that U.S. firms allocated more labor-intensive operations to foreign affiliates. Kravis and Lipsey (1982, 1992) and Lipsey (1988, 1993) document the increasing role of multinational production for U.S. firms.

For purposes of comparison with standard models that assume no internationalized production, we make the extreme assumption that all production for export occurs in foreign affiliates. Kravis and Lipsey (1992) document that by the late 1980s, U.S. multinationals exported more from their foreign affiliates abroad than from the United States.

The model in this paper of floating exchange rates with prices set in the producer's currency is based on Obstfeld and Rogoff (1998). That model, in turn, is influenced by the nonstochastic models of Corsetti and Pesenti (1998) and Obstfeld and Rogoff (1995). These models are examples of recent international models with optimizing agents and prices that are sticky in producers' currencies, and include Svensson and van Wijnbergen (1989), Kollman (1996), and Hau (2000).

Our pricing-to-market model shares some of the characteristics of Bacchetta and van Wincoop's (1998) examination of how exchange rate regime affects the volume of trade and capital flows in a stochastic two-period model of pricing-to-market. Our model of pricing-to-market is also related

---

3. However, we shall see that foreign monetary variance may influence the expected level of home consumption.

to the work of Betts and Devereux (1996, 1998, 2000). Other recent general equilibrium models in which prices are sticky in consumers' currencies include Chari, Kehoe, and McGrattan (1997), Tille (1998a, 1998b), and Engel (1996).

None of the aforementioned models, however, allow for any internationalized production. We believe it is a fitting tribute to Robert Lipsey to demonstrate how some of Lipsey's empirical findings have implications for policy making and for open-economy macroeconomic modeling. Lipsey's work shows clearly the need to abandon the assumption of the LOP, and the increasing importance of allowing for internationalized production in our models.

The general models are laid out in section 6.2. In section 6.3, we investigate the welfare comparisons of fixed versus floating exchange rates under the two models of price-setting behavior. Section 6.4 compares the results with those of Devereux and Engel (1998), so that we can ascertain the role of internationalized production. The concluding section (6.5) points to some potential weaknesses of our analysis and directions for future research.

6.2   The Model

Here we lay out the main features of the models we examine. The model for consumers follows exactly that of Devereux and Engel (1998), which in turn closely follows the model of consumption in Obstfeld and Rogoff (1998). Consumers maximize expected lifetime utility, taking prices and wages as given. Firm managers make production and pricing decisions. Each consumer receives a share of profits from every firm in which he or she owns shares. Monetary authorities in each country let the money supply fluctuate randomly in the floating exchange rate models, and this is the only source of uncertainty in the model. In the fixed exchange rate model, the foreign monetary authority determines the foreign money supply (randomly), while the domestic central bank controls the domestic money supply in order to keep the exchange rate fixed.

Our models include sticky goods prices. Producers must set prices prior to the realization of monetary shocks. One could justify this constraint with an appropriate menu cost model, though we do not model this and simply view the stickiness of prices as an institutional constraint. Prices adjust fully to monetary shocks after one period. There is no persistence to the price adjustment process. We consider two separate types of price setting. In the first type, producers must set prices in their own currencies. For example, the home-currency price of home goods is preset and unresponsive to monetary shocks. This implies that the price for home goods paid by foreign consumers varies when the exchange rate changes in response to monetary shocks. In the other type of model, producers preset prices in consumers' currencies. Home firms set one price for home-country consumers in the home currency and another price for foreign-country consumers in the foreign currency. In the fixed exchange rate model, the currency in which prices are set is irrelevant since the exchange rate is assumed to be fixed permanently. In each of the models, the objective of the firm managers is to maximize the expected utility of the representative owner of the firm.

We shall contrast the choice of exchange rate regime when all production by home firms is accomplished with domestic factors of production (as in Devereux and Engel 1998), with a production configuration in which the domestic firm produces goods for sale to foreigners using foreign factors of production. Similarly, goods sold by the foreign firm to home residents are produced by home-country factors. The sense in which these goods can be classified as *home* and *foreign* becomes ambiguous in this case. Since asset markets are complete, the ownership of the firm is not important. We specify *home* firms as being owned by home residents, but a complete set of contingent claims makes this definition irrelevant. Thus, internationalized production means nothing more or less than the assumption that each monopolistic firm locates production for home-country residents in the home country and for foreign-country residents in the foreign country.

6.2.1   Consumers

The representative consumer in the home country maximizes

$$U_t = E_t \left(\sum_{s=t}^{\infty} \beta^{s-t} u_s \right), \quad 0 < \beta < 1,$$

where

$$u_s = \frac{1}{1 - \rho} C_s^{1-\rho} + \ln\left(\frac{M_s}{P_s}\right) - \eta L_s, \quad \rho > 0.$$

C is a consumption index over home and foreign consumption:

$$C = \frac{C_h^n C_f^{1-n}}{n^n (1 - n)^{1-n}}.$$

There are n identical individuals in the home country, $0 < n < 1$, and $1 - n$ in the foreign country. C_h and C_f, in turn, are indexes over consumption of goods produced at home and in the foreign country, respectively:

$$C_h = \left[n^{-1/\lambda} \int_0^n C_h(i)^{(\lambda-1)/\lambda} di \right]^{\lambda/(\lambda-1)},$$

$$C_f = \left[(1 - n)^{-1/\lambda} \int_n^1 C_f(i)^{(\lambda-1)/\lambda} di \right]^{\lambda/(\lambda-1)}.$$

The elasticity of substitution between any two goods produced within a country is λ, which we assume to be greater than 1. There is a unit elasticity of substitution between the home goods and foreign goods bundles. M/P represents domestic real balances, and L is the labor supply of the representative home agent.

The utility function we consider here is one case investigated by Devereux and Engel (1998). They examine a more general welfare function in which real balances enter as a power function, and labor enters quadratically. We choose this simpler representation for utility here because the model can be solved analytically in closed form for this welfare function, while the more general welfare function requires us to use second-order Taylor series approximations.

We justify the linearity of labor on two grounds. First, some literature has found that when individuals face a discrete choice of working a fixed number of hours or not working at all, the appropriate aggregate representation for leisure in the utility function is linear.[4] Second, we do not believe there is a strong tradition in economics of considering the effects of risk-averse behavior toward uncertainty about consumption of leisure. Risk neutrality toward leisure is probably a plausible assumption.[5]

P, the price index, is defined by

(1) $$P = P_h^n P_f^{1-n},$$

where

$$P_h = \left[\frac{1}{n} \int_0^n P_h(i)^{1-\lambda} di \right]^{1/(1-\lambda)},$$

$$P_f = \left[\frac{1}{1-n} \int_n^1 P_f(i)^{1-\lambda} di \right]^{1/(1-\lambda)}.$$

The preferences of foreign consumers are similar to those of home-country residents. The terms in the utility function involving consumption are identical in the two countries. Note that this implies that if the LOP should hold for both goods, then purchasing power parity obtains $P_t = S_t P_t^*$, where S_t is the home-currency price of foreign currency. The functional

---

4. See Hansen (1985) and Rogerson (1988).
5. The existence of overtime pay, however, suggests that there is some desire to smooth leisure.

form for real balances and labor are also the same, but, for foreign residents, they are functions of foreign real balances and foreign labor supply. The optimal intratemporal consumption choices take on simple forms:

$$C_h(i) = \frac{1}{n}\left[\frac{P_h(i)}{P_h}\right]^{-\lambda} C_h, \qquad C_f(i) = \frac{1}{1-n}\left[\frac{P_f(i)}{P_f}\right]^{-\lambda} C_f,$$

$$P_h C_h = nPC, \qquad P_f C_f = (1 - n)PC,$$

$$\int_0^n P_h(i)C_h(i)di = P_h C_h, \qquad \int_n^1 P_f(i)C_f(i)di = P_f C_f.$$

We assume that there is a set of state-contingent nominal bonds. As Obstfeld and Rogoff (1998) emphasize, the structure of the utility functions ensures that there is complete consumption risk sharing when the LOP holds, regardless of what assets are traded.[6] However, the LOP does not hold in the pricing-to-market model. We consider the assumption of complete asset markets to be convenient, and an approximation to the assumption of perfect capital mobility.

Given the intratemporal consumption choices just given, the budget constraint of the representative home agent is

$$P_t C_t + M_t + \sum_{t+1} q(z^{t+1}, z^t)B(z^{t+1}) = W_t L_t + \pi_t + M_{t-1} + B_t + T_t,$$

where $B(z^{t+1})$ are contingent home-currency denominated nominal bonds whose prices at time t are $q(z^{t+1}, z^t)$, z^t represents the state at time t, π_t is the representative agent's share of profits from all home firms, T_t represents monetary transfers from the government, and W_t is the wage rate.[7]

In addition to the consumption demand equations, we can derive the money demand equation for the representative home-country resident:

(2)
$$\frac{M_t}{P_t} = \frac{\chi C_t^{\rho}}{1 - E_t(d_{t+1})},$$

where $E_t(d_{t+1})$ is the inverse of the gross nominal interest rate, given by

$$d_{t+1} = \beta \frac{C_{t+1}^{-\rho}P_t}{C_t^{-\rho}P_{t+1}}.$$

The trade-off between consumption and leisure is given by

---

6. See Cole and Obstfeld (1991) for an analysis of how the terms of trade changes can serve as a substitute for capital mobility.

7. To avoid excess notation, we will not continue to use this state-contingent notation from here on. The important point to remember is that complete asset markets are necessary to sustain the full risk-sharing condition in equation (4).

(3)
$$\frac{W_t}{P_t C_t^\rho} = \eta.$$

Before turning to the role of government, and the production and pricing decisions of firms, it is convenient to express the equilibrium condition that arises from the complete market in nominal bonds:

(4)
$$\frac{S_t P_t^*}{P_t} = \left(\frac{C_t}{C_t^*}\right)^\rho.$$

There are immediately two important things that arise out of condition (4). First, when the LOP holds (as it does in the PCP and FER models, defined in section 6.2.3), then home consumption always equals foreign consumption: $C_t = C_t^*$.[8]

Second, factor price equalization holds. This arises immediately out of equations (3) and (4), and does not require that the LOP hold for either good. We have

$$W_t = S_t W_t^*.$$

6.2.2   Government

Government alters the money supply with direct transfers. The government budget constraint (in per capita terms) is

$$M_t = M_{t-1} + T_t.$$

6.2.3   Firms

Here we shall discuss the production and pricing decisions for firms with internationalized production. Ultimately we will contrast our welfare results in this model with those in Devereux and Engel (1998). That paper assumes all production by home firms takes place domestically, and all production by foreign firms takes place in the foreign country.

Firms are assumed to be monopolistic competitors. The production function by the home-country firm i for sale to domestic residents is given by

$$X_{ht}(i) = L_t(i).$$

So, total output sold to domestic residents by firm i, $X_{ht}(i)$, is produced using only labor. Similarly, the production function for sales to foreign consumers by firm i is given by

---

8. It is not necessary that markets be complete to sustain this condition in the PCP model.

$$X^*_{ht}(i) = L^*_t(i).$$

The objective of the domestic firms is to set prices to maximize the expected utility of the owners, who are the domestic residents. Firms must set prices before information about the random domestic and foreign money supplies is known. We will consider three models:

PCP: PCP refers to producer-currency pricing. Producers set the price in their own currencies. The price that foreigners pay for home goods, and the price that home residents pay for foreign goods, fluctuates when the exchange rate changes. This model is examined by Obstfeld and Rogoff (1995, 1998).

PTM: PTM refers to pricing-to-market. Producers set the price in the consumers' currency. Prices consumers face do not respond to exchange rate changes. A PTM model was introduced by Devereux and Engel (1998).

FER: FER refers to permanently fixed exchange rates. Prices are set ahead of time, but the choice of currency is irrelevant since there is essentially a single currency.

No state-contingent pricing of goods is allowed in the three models.

The firm owners maximize the expected present value of profits using the market nominal discount factor for the owners of the firm. This is equivalent to maximizing expected utility of the owners. In the PCP model, the firms choose a single price for both markets. Given that there is no intertemporal aspect to the firms' optimization problems (see Obstfeld and Rogoff 1998), for the domestic firm this reduces to maximizing

$$E_{t-1}(d_t\{[P_{ht}(i) - W_t]X_{ht}(i) + [P_{ht}(i) - S_tW^*_t]X^*_{ht}(i)\}).$$

Given that factor price equalization holds in all of our models, this objective function can be simplified to

$$E_{t-1}(d_t\{[P_{ht}(i) - W_t][X_{ht}(i) + X^*_{ht}(i)]\}).$$

Then, using the fact that home and foreign consumption are equal in the PCP model, the optimal price set by the home firm is

$$P_{ht}(i) = P_{ht} = \left(\frac{\lambda}{\lambda-1}\right)\frac{E_{t-1}(C_t^{1-\rho}W_t)}{E_{t-1}(C_t^{1-\rho})}.$$

From equation (3), this price-setting rule can be rewritten as

(5)
$$P_{ht} = \left(\frac{\lambda\eta}{\lambda-1}\right)\frac{E_{t-1}(P_tC_t)}{E_{t-1}(C_t^{1-\rho})}.$$

In a world of certainty, the price would be a markup over unit labor costs. Here, there is a risk premium incorporated in the goods price (as discussed by Bacchetta and van Wincoop 1998, and Devereux and Engel 1998) arising from the covariance of the firm's profits with the marginal utility of consumption.

The LOP holds for the price charged to foreigners by the home firm:

$$(6) \qquad P^*_{ht} = \frac{P_{ht}}{S_t}.$$

Analogous relationships hold for the prices set by the foreign firms:

$$(7) \qquad P^*_{ft} = \left(\frac{\lambda\eta}{\lambda-1}\right)\frac{E_{t-1}(P^*_t C^*_t)}{E_{t-1}(C^{*1-\rho}_t)},$$

$$(8) \qquad P_{ft} = S_t P^*_{ft}.$$

In the PTM model, the firm chooses two different prices—one for residents of its own country, and one for residents of the other country. The typical home firm maximizes

$$E_{t-1}(d_t\{P_{ht}(i)X_{ht}(i) + S_t P^*_{ht}(i)X^*_{ht}(i) - W_t[X_{ht}(i) + X^*_{ht}(i)]\}),$$

where we have used factor price equalization. The price charged by the home firm to the home residents is the same as in the PCP model, and is given in equation (5). But, making use of the risk-sharing condition (4), we find the price charged to foreign residents is given by

$$(9) \qquad P^*_{ht} = \left(\frac{\lambda}{\lambda-1}\right)\frac{E_{t-1}W^*_t C^{*1-\rho}_t}{E_{t-1}(C^{*1-\rho}_t)} = \left(\frac{\lambda\eta}{\lambda-1}\right)\frac{E_{t-1}P^*_t C^*_t}{E_{t-1}(C^{*1-\rho}_t)}.$$

Likewise, the price charged by foreign firms to its own residents is the same as in the PCP model, and is given by equation (7), but the price charged to home-country consumers in the PTM model is

$$(10) \qquad P_{ft} = \left(\frac{\lambda}{\lambda-1}\right)\frac{E_{t-1}(C^{1-\rho}_t W_t)}{E_{t-1}(C^{1-\rho}_t)} = \left(\frac{\lambda\eta}{\lambda-1}\right)\frac{E_{t-1}(P_t C_t)}{E_{t-1}(C^{1-\rho}_t)}.$$

Comparing equation (10) to equation (5), we see that in the PTM model, home residents pay exactly the same price for the home and the foreign good. Likewise, equations (9) and (7) show that the foreign resident pays the same price for the two goods (although the prices do not necessarily equal the price paid by home residents).

In the FER model, the exchange rate is fixed at all times, so the pricing rule is the same whether the firms state prices in their own currencies or the foreign currency.

Equilibrium in the home market for labor requires that labor employed be equal to demand for home goods and foreign goods by home residents:

$$(11) \qquad L_t = n\frac{P_t C_t}{P_{ht}} + (1 - n)\frac{P_t C_t}{P_{ft}}.$$

In both of the models with floating exchange rates, some simplifications of equation (11) are readily derived. In the PTM model, we note that since $P_{ht} = P_{ft} = P_t$, we arrive at

$$(12) \qquad L_t = C_t.$$

The logic of that relationship is straightforward. Since the relative price of home goods to foreign goods is always one, and both goods are produced by domestic labor, then the amount of labor demanded will equal the amount of the good consumed (since the production function is $Y_t = L_t$).

The expectation of equation (11) can be simplified in the PCP model. From equation (5):

$$(13) \qquad E_{t-1}\left(\frac{P_t C_t}{P_{ht}}\right) = \frac{\lambda - 1}{\lambda \eta} E_{t-1}(C_t^{1-\rho}).$$

If we use the facts that $(P_t/P_{ft}) = (P_t^*/P_{ft}^*)$, and $C_t = C_t^*$, then we get, using equation (7),

$$(14) \quad E_{t-1}\left(\frac{P_t C_t}{P_{ft}}\right) = E_{t-1}\left(\frac{P_t^* C_t^*}{P_{ft}^*}\right) = \frac{\lambda - 1}{\lambda \eta} E_{t-1}(C_t^{*1-\rho}) = \frac{\lambda - 1}{\lambda \eta} E_{t-1}(C_t^{1-\rho}).$$

Equations (11), (13), and (14) then tell us in the PCP model

$$(15) \qquad E_{t-1}(L_t) = \frac{\lambda - 1}{\lambda \eta} E_{t-1}(C_t^{1-\rho}).$$

These equations suffice to solve the three models. In the next section, we will analyze welfare under fixed exchange rates, and under the two models of floating exchange rates.

6.3 Welfare Comparisons

We shall assume the money supply follows a random walk:

$$(16) \qquad E_t\left(\frac{M_t}{M_{t+1}}\right) = \mu.$$

Under these assumptions, it is easy to verify from the money demand equation (2) that consumption is a function only of the real money supply:

$$(17) \qquad C_t^p = \left(\frac{1-\mu\beta}{\chi}\right)\frac{M_t}{P_t}.$$

An analogous equation holds for the foreign country.

This equation implies that the home and foreign nominal interest rates must be constant. The ex post real interest rate is determined by the rate of change of consumption: Higher consumption growth is associated with higher real interest rates.

Consider a monetary expansion in the home country under flexible exchange rates. In each of our models, a monetary expansion lowers the real interest rate. Since money is neutral in the long run (i.e., after one period), current consumption must grow. A monetary expansion also leads to expected inflation. The future domestic price level increases more than the current price level in each of our models. When money enters the utility function logarithmically, the increase in expected inflation exactly offsets the decline in the real interest rate, leaving the nominal interest rate unchanged.

It follows immediately that in both the PCP and PTM models, the exchange rate must follow a random walk. In our model, uncovered interest parity may not hold exactly, because there may be a foreign exchange risk premium. However, under assumptions that will be introduced shortly (specifically, that the variance of monetary shocks is constant over time), the risk premium is constant. Since domestic and foreign interest rates are also constant, the expected change in the (log of) the nominal exchange rate must be zero. Because money is neutral in the long run, the current change in the exchange rate is proportional to changes in domestic money (with a positive sign) and foreign money (with a negative sign). In fact, from equations (4) and (17):

$$(18) \qquad S_t = \frac{M_t(1-\mu\beta)}{M_t^*(1-\mu^*\beta)}.$$

We can now derive one of the chief results of this section: In the PTM model, foreign monetary shocks have no effect on domestic consumption, but they do affect home consumption in the PCP model. Recall that $P = P_h^n P_f^{1-n}$. In the PTM model, P is predetermined, so it is not affected by foreign (or domestic) money shocks. It follows from equation (17) that domestic consumption is determined in the short run entirely by the domestic money supply. Changes in the foreign money supply have no effect on domestic consumption. In contrast, in the PCP model, P_f increases when the price of the foreign currency increases, since that price is fixed

Table 6.1   **Variance of Domestic Consumption (holding domestic money supply constant)**

	σ_c^2
PCP	$\sigma_{m*}^2 \cdot (1-n)^2/\rho^2$
PTM	0
FER	σ_{m*}^2/ρ^2

in foreign currency terms; thus, a 1 percent jump in the foreign money supply leads to a 1 percent decrease in S, a 1 percent decrease in P_f, and a $1-n$ percent decline in P. So, a 1 percent increase in the foreign money supply induces a $(1-n)/\rho$ percent increase in C.

We have compared the two floating exchange rate models (PCP and PTM). How do these models compare to the fixed exchange rate (FER) model? To keep exchange rates fixed, the domestic money supply must move in proportion to the foreign money supply (see equation [18]). It follows that in response to a 1 percent shock to the foreign money supply, the domestic money supply must change 1 percent. Since goods prices do not change, equation (17) tells us there must be a $1/\rho$ percent change in domestic consumption.

If our only concern were how the variance of foreign money shocks affected the variance of domestic consumption, it would be clear that floating rates dominate fixed exchange rates. Under fixed rates, a 1 percent shock to foreign money leads to a $1/\rho$ percent change in domestic consumption, compared to a change in domestic consumption of only $(1-n)/\rho$ percent in the PCP model, and 0 percent in the PTM model. Table 6.1 shows how the variance of (the log of) consumption is related to the variance of (the log of) the foreign money supply in each model.[9]

However, the variance of consumption is not the only welfare consideration. Even ignoring the effect on welfare coming from money in the utility function, the variance of foreign monetary shocks has further effects on utility. Leisure enters utility linearly, so greater variance of output (and hence leisure) does not directly influence welfare—but, the variance of foreign monetary shocks has further effects on welfare because it influences the means of both consumption and leisure. This channel arises from the effects that monetary variances have on goods prices.

We assume shocks to money supplies are log-normally distributed. Using equation (16):

$$(19) \qquad m_{t+1} - m_t = -\ln(\mu) + \frac{1}{2}\sigma_m^2 + \upsilon_{t+1},$$

---

9. These results are derived formally in the appendix in equations (A9), (A16), and (A23).

where m_t is the log of M_t (we will follow the convention that lowercase letters are logs of uppercase letters), v_{t+1} is the white noise shock to domestic money, and σ_m^2 is the variance of v_{t+1}. An analogous equation holds for the foreign money supply process.

We can write equations (17) and (18) as

$$(20) \qquad \rho c_t = m_t - p_t + \ln \frac{1 - \mu\beta}{\chi},$$

$$(21) \qquad s_t = m_t - m_t^* + \ln(1 - \mu\beta) - \ln(1 - \mu^*\beta).$$

In log terms, equation (3) can be written as

$$(22) \qquad w_t = p_t + \rho c_t + \ln(\eta),$$

and analogously for the foreign country.

The solutions for goods prices, consumption, and leisure depend on the particular model of price-setting behavior. The appendix derives solutions in terms of the exogenous variables—the domestic and foreign money supplies—for each of our models.

The average levels of consumption and leisure can be different depending on the exchange rate regime. This may seem surprising, since it implies that average long-run consumption depends on a monetary choice—fixed or floating exchange rates. The intuition for this outcome can be seen from equation (3). The level of consumption is related to the markup of prices over wages: When the markup is smaller, the level of consumption is higher. The level of prices is affected by the exchange rate regime because the risk premium incorporated in prices differs between regimes. In turn, since labor is used to produce consumption goods, the expected level of leisure is also different under the different exchange rate regimes.

We compare the influence of the variance of foreign money shocks on the expected level of consumption by setting the variance of domestic money equal to zero in equations (A10), (A18), and (A24). These values are reported in table 6.2.

From table 6.2, the expected level of consumption is higher in the FER model compared to the PCP model when $\rho > (2 - n)/(3 - 2n)$. A sufficient condition is $\rho > 1$. The condition of $\rho > 1$ is necessary and sufficient for expected consumption to be higher in the FER model than in the PTM model. Although there is little agreement empirically about the correct value for ρ, virtually all studies agree that $\rho > 1$. So, while the variance of consumption is higher for fixed exchange rates than in either floating exchange rate model, there is a higher average level of consumption under fixed exchange rates.

Table 6.2   **Expected Level of Domestic Consumption (holding domestic money supply constant)**

	$E(C)$
PCP	$\left(\dfrac{\lambda-1}{\lambda\eta}\right)^{1/\rho} \exp\left(-\left\{\dfrac{(1-n)^2 + \rho(1-n)[1-2(1-n)]}{2\rho^2}\right\}\sigma_{m*}^2\right)$
PTM	$\left(\dfrac{\lambda-1}{\lambda\eta}\right)^{1/\rho}$
FER	$\left(\dfrac{\lambda-1}{\lambda\eta}\right)^{1/\rho} \exp\left[-\left(\dfrac{1-\rho}{2\rho^2}\right)\sigma_{m*}^2\right]$

Table 6.3   **Expected Level of Domestic Employment (holding domestic money supply constant)**

	$E(L)$
PCP	$\left(\dfrac{\lambda-1}{\lambda\eta}\right)^{1/\rho} \exp\left(-\left\{\dfrac{(1-n)(1-\rho)[1-n(1-\rho)]}{2\rho^2}\right\}\sigma_{m*}^2\right)$
PTM	$\left(\dfrac{\lambda-1}{\lambda\eta}\right)^{1/\rho}$
FER	$\left(\dfrac{\lambda-1}{\lambda\eta}\right)^{1/\rho} \exp\left[-\left(\dfrac{1-\rho}{2\rho^2}\right)\sigma_{m*}^2\right]$

This implies a trade-off in utility. Examining (for now) the consumption term alone, using the fact that consumption is log-normal, we can write

$$(23) \qquad \frac{1}{1-\rho}E(C^{1-\rho}) = \frac{1}{1-\rho}[E(C)]^{1-\rho} \cdot \exp\left[\frac{-\rho(1-\rho)}{2}\sigma_c^2\right].$$

Welfare is positively related to the expected level of consumption, but falls with increases in the variance of consumption.

Utility also depends on expected leisure. The greater the average level of employment, the lower the welfare. Table 6.3 reports the expected levels of employment in each model (taken from equations [A12], [A18], and [A26]).

Employment is higher under fixed exchange rates, as compared to floating under PCP, when $1 < \rho < (2-n)/(1-n)$. When n is large (that is, close to one), it is likely that expected employment is higher and expected leisure lower under fixed exchange rates. But for a small country (with n close to zero), average employment under fixed exchange rates will be smaller unless ρ falls in the narrow range between one and two. So, in comparing leisure effects between FER and PCP, the size of the country is quite important. On the other hand, expected employment is higher and expected leisure lower under FER compared to PCP when $\rho > 1$.

In comparing welfare under fixed and floating exchange rates, we look at the effects of the variance of foreign money shocks on domestic welfare. A fixed exchange rate system eliminates the possibility of domestic money shocks, but even under floating rates central banks can choose a zero variance. Thus, we set $\sigma_m^2 = 0$ in our welfare analysis.

Real money balances enter the utility function. It may not be wise to evaluate exchange rate systems in terms of how they affect the real balance part of the utility function. Money in the utility function is a convenient way to create demand for an asset (money) that would otherwise be dominated by other assets. However, there are other ways to model demand for money that may be more realistic (and more complicated) that do not involve welfare's being directly influenced by holdings of real balances. In making welfare comparisons, we will assume real balances are not important in welfare ($\chi \to 0$).

Utility, then, can be expressed in terms of expected consumption, the variance of consumption, and expected leisure. Tables 6.1, 6.2, and 6.3 compare the models for each of these components of utility. The comparisons seem ambiguous: FER is the worst in terms of the variance of consumption, the best in terms of expected consumption, and there is some ambiguity about the ranking in terms of expected leisure. We can further clarify the matter by looking at all three effects together.

6.3.1 PCP versus FER models

In the PCP and FER models we can use equation (15) to write the welfare expression simply as a function of the mean and variance of consumption:

$$(24) \quad E(u) = \frac{1 + \rho(\lambda - 1)}{\lambda(1 - \rho)} E(C^{1-\rho})$$

$$= \frac{1 + \rho(\lambda - 1)}{\lambda(1 - \rho)} [E(C)]^{1-\rho} \cdot \exp\left[\frac{-\rho(1 - \rho)}{2} \sigma_c^2\right].$$

There is a trade-off in choosing between fixed and floating exchange rates. Fixed exchange rates have a higher expected level of consumption (when $\rho > [2 - n]/[3 - 2n]$), but under floating rates the variance of consumption is lower.

We find that welfare is higher under floating rates when $\rho \leq (2 - n)/(1 - n)$. When $\rho \leq 2$, floating rates are always better. As n approaches 1, so that the home country is getting very large relative to the small country, then floating rates dominate. This accords with the intuition that smaller countries may find it desirable to fix their exchange rates to the currency of a larger country, but that large countries are better off with their own independent currencies.

As ρ increases, the fixed exchange rate system's advantage in terms of expected consumption increases. Its disadvantage in terms of variance also falls as the square of ρ increases, although that is offset by the fact that the importance of the variance in welfare rises with the square of ρ (see equation [24]). On net, for large values of ρ, fixed exchange rates become more desirable.

6.3.2   PTM versus FER Models

We have seen from table 6.1 that foreign monetary variance does not affect either the mean or the variance of consumption in the PTM model. Compared to the FER model, the variance of consumption is lower, but the mean of consumption is also lower when $\rho > 1$. The PTM model has the advantage in terms of expected leisure when $\rho > 1$.

As is the case with the PCP and FER models (equation [15]), we have $E(L) = [(\lambda - 1)/(\lambda\eta)]E(C^{1-\rho})$. In the PTM model, this follows from equations (12) and (A14). Thus, conveniently, the analysis simplifies to a comparison of the models in terms of expected consumption and variance of consumption. Equation (24) holds in the PTM model as well as the other two models.

Utility in the PTM model is not influenced by foreign monetary policy shocks. We can derive

$$E(u_{\text{PTM}}) = \left(\frac{\lambda - 1}{\eta\lambda}\right)^{(1-\rho)/\rho}\left[\frac{1 + \rho(\lambda - 1)}{\lambda(1 - \rho)}\right].$$

This can be compared directly to welfare in the FER model:

$$E(u_{\text{FER}}) = \left(\frac{\lambda - 1}{\eta\lambda}\right)^{(1-\rho)/\rho}\left[\frac{1 + \rho(\lambda - 1)}{\lambda(1 - \rho)}\right]\exp\left(\frac{\rho - 1}{2\rho^2}\sigma_{m*}^2\right).$$

It is clear from examination of these equations that any variance in foreign money shocks lowers welfare in the FER model, so that

$$E(u_{\text{PTM}}) > E(u_{\text{FER}})$$

for all admissible parameter values. Even though, when $\rho > 1$, there may be less expected consumption under floating exchange rates and PTM, the fact that home consumption is completely insulated from foreign money shocks is enough to insure that floating rates always dominate fixed exchange rates in this model.

6.4   How Internationalized Production Matters

How do the comparisons between levels of welfare under fixed and floating exchange rates in the models of this paper, with internationalized production, relate to the comparisons in Devereux and Engel (1998) in which there is no internationalized production?

There are surprising similarities in the welfare comparisons. A major reason the welfare comparisons are not very different regardless of whether we assume internationalized production is that there is factor price equalization in our model. Since home-country wages equal foreign-country wages, the prices set by firms are the same whether domestic labor or foreign labor produces output. That is, there is a risk premium incorporated in nominal goods prices arising from the covariance of labor costs with revenues. However, that risk is the same whether domestic or foreign labor is employed because the two types of labor are paid the same wage.

Why is there factor price equalization? From equation (3), the marginal utility of taking one more dollar's worth of leisure, η/W_t, is equal to the marginal utility from one more dollar's worth of consumption, $C_t^{-\rho}/P_t$. That is, each agent works only so much that the last dollar earned creates as much utility from consumption as it does disutility from working; but our assumption of perfect capital mobility and complete nominal asset markets means that the marginal utility of a dollar for the home-country resident is worth the same for the foreign agent: $C_t^{-\rho}/P_t = C_t^{*-\rho}/S_t P_t^*$. Together, these imply that the dollar value of wages must be the same in the two countries: $W_t = S_t W_t^*$. In short, the complete asset market in nominal bonds assures that the marginal value of a dollar spent on leisure is the same in the two countries: $\eta/W_t = \eta/S_t W_t^*$.

Since wage equalization implies that the nominal price set by firms is not affected by the location of production, then neither exchange rates nor consumption levels (from equation [17]) are affected by the location of production. Thus, any welfare comparison involving consumption is not influenced by whether there is internationalized production.

Welfare is also influenced by leisure. One would expect that term to be different depending on where production is located. In Devereux and Engel (1998), domestic workers produce goods consumed by foreigners, so movements in foreign demand for domestic goods change employment. However, in the model of this paper, domestic workers produce only for domestic consumption: They produce both the home and the foreign goods for home consumers.

Surprisingly, in the PCP model, even the leisure term is not affected by the location of production. In the PCP model, as Obstfeld and Rogoff (1998) emphasize, the current account is always balanced. Even though there is perfect capital mobility, the unitary elasticity of demand between foreign and domestic consumption combined with the LOP assumption ensures that the value of goods purchased from abroad by home residents continuously equals the value of goods sold to foreign residents by home firms. However, the prices of home goods and foreign goods are expected to be the same (prior to the realization of monetary shocks). Since the values of exports and imports are equal, and the expected prices are the same, the expected quantity of goods produced by home firms for foreign residents always equals the expected quantity of goods produced by foreign firms for home residents. It does not matter where the goods are produced—expected employment will not be affected by the location of production.

Welfare in the PCP model is not affected by the presence of internationalized production. The same is true for the FER model, since, given the structure of the model, the FER model is identical to the PCP model with $n = 1$. The welfare comparisons for this paper between the PCP and FER worlds are exactly the same as in Devereux and Engel (1998) for these two models.

Expected leisure in the PTM model does depend on where output is produced. In the model of this paper, where domestic labor produces only for home consumers, there is no influence of foreign money shocks on expected employment. In the model of Devereux and Engel (1998), foreign money shocks change domestic employment because they affect foreign demand for home goods (which, in that model, are produced with domestic labor). In that model, when $\rho > 1$, a higher foreign monetary variance raises expected demand for home goods and lowers expected home leisure, so that expected domestic leisure is higher when there is internationalized production. Still, regardless of whether there is internationalized production, floating rates in the PTM model always yield higher expected utility than do fixed exchange rates.

6.5   Conclusions

We find that the hypothesis of how prices are set has implications for the optimal choice of exchange rate regime. If we follow the traditional literature in assuming that prices are set in producers' currencies, and that the law of one price holds, there is no clear-cut answer on which regime is preferable. When a country is small, or very risk averse, it would prefer fixed exchange rates; otherwise, floating exchange rates are preferred.

However, the empirical evidence supports the model of pricing in which producers set different prices in different markets. Prices are set in consumers' currencies and adjust slowly to demand shocks. In that case, we find that floating exchange rates are unambiguously preferred to fixed exchange rates.

That conclusion is not altered by incorporating internationalized production in the model. Indeed, we find under pricing-to-market that the economy is even more sheltered from foreign shocks in a floating exchange rate system than in a world in which all production of the domestic firm takes place in the home country. The reason is straightforward: One potential avenue for foreign shocks to hit the home economy is through employment changes in response to changes in foreign demand for the home good. If a monetary shock abroad changes foreign demand for the home good, that event may alter domestic employment; but, to the extent that the foreign demand is met by production by foreign subsidiaries of the home country, domestic employment is sheltered from the foreign shock. Thus one avenue through which foreign shocks could affect domestic employment and welfare under a floating exchange rate system with pricing-to-market is closed when the home good is produced internationally.

The model considered here is quite simple. We look only at a special case examined by Devereux and Engel (1998), in which real money balances enter the utility function logarithmically and leisure enters linearly. This specification simplifies the analysis considerably—for example, nominal interest rates are constant in equilibrium; yet it also loses some of the interesting and more realistic dynamic behavior of the more complex models. Still, in Devereux and Engel (1998), the flavor of the welfare analysis of exchange rate regimes was not appreciably altered by consideration of the more complex model.

One important extension to this model would allow for price adjustment that lasts longer than a single period. Indeed, it is possible that the speed of price adjustment could differ between exchange rate regimes, altering the welfare analysis. We would also like to consider investment questions. In this study, internationalized production is undertaken using only foreign labor as an input. More interesting would be an analysis that allowed for domestically owned capital to be combined with foreign labor in producing output for sale abroad.

We are not certain in which direction these extensions would tilt the welfare analysis. However, this study has highlighted some differences in the exchange rate systems, and the roles of price setting and internationalized production, that would be important in any extended model.

Appendix

Recall that the pricing formulas for P_{ht} and P_{ft}^* are the same in all three models. Using the fact that prices and consumption will be log-normally distributed in equilibrium, we can write equation (5) as

(A1) $p_{ht} = m_{t-1} - \ln(\mu) + \sigma_m^2 + (1 - \rho)\sigma_{mc} + \ln\left[\dfrac{\lambda\eta(1 - \mu\beta)}{\chi(\lambda - 1)}\right],$

where σ_{mc} is the covariance of m_t and c_t conditional on $t - 1$ information. (In general, we will use the notation σ_{xz} to denote $\text{cov}_{t-1}(x_t, z_t)$, and σ_z^2 to denote $\text{var}_{t-1}(z_t)$.) Similar derivations yield from equation (7):

(A2) $p_{ft}^* = m_{t-1}^* - \ln(\mu^*) + \sigma_{m^*}^2 + (1 - \rho)\sigma_{m^*c^*} + \ln\left[\dfrac{\lambda\eta(1 - \mu^*\beta)}{\chi(\lambda - 1)}\right].$

Equations (A1) and (A2) hold in all three models. We will also use the relationship

(A3) $$p_t = np_{ht} + (1 - n)p_{ft},$$

and the analogous expression for the foreign price level. These equations must be augmented by equations for p_{ft} and p_{ht}^*, as well as equations for output, in order to complete derivations in each model.

The PCP Model

The law of one price holds in this model, so

(A4) $$p_{ft} = s_t + p_{ft}^*,$$

(A5) $$p_{ht}^* = p_{ht} - s_t.$$

Recall, also, the perfect risk-sharing property of this model, so that $c_t = c_t^*$.

Then, using equations (21), (A2), (A3), and (A4), we can derive for the domestic price level

(A6) $p_t = m_t - n\left[v_t - \dfrac{1}{2}\sigma_m^2 - (1 - \rho)\sigma_{mc}\right]$

$\qquad - (1 - n)\left[v_t^* - \dfrac{1}{2}\sigma_{m^*}^2 - (1 - \rho)\sigma_{m^*c}\right] + \ln\left[\dfrac{\lambda\eta(1 - \mu\beta)}{\chi(\lambda - 1)}\right].$

From equations (21) and (A6) we get

(A7) $\rho c_t = n\left[v_t - \dfrac{1}{2}\sigma_m^2 - (1 - \rho)\sigma_{mc}\right]$

$\qquad + (1 - n)\left[v_t^* - \dfrac{1}{2}\sigma_{m^*}^2 - (1 - \rho)\sigma_{m^*c}\right] - \ln\left(\dfrac{\lambda\eta}{\lambda - 1}\right).$

We can derive expressions for σ_{mc} and σ_{m^*c} directly from equation (A7):

$$\sigma_{mc} = \frac{\eta}{\rho}\sigma_m^2,$$

$$\sigma_{m^*c} = \frac{1-n}{\rho}\sigma_{n^*}^2.$$

Plugging these into (A7), we arrive at our expression for domestic consumption:

$$(A8) \quad c_t = \frac{n}{\rho}v_t + \frac{1-n}{\rho}v_t^* - \left[\frac{n\rho + 2n^2(1-\rho)}{2\rho^2}\right]\sigma_m^2$$

$$- \left[\frac{(1-n)\rho + 2(1-n)^2(1-\rho)}{2\rho^2}\right]\sigma_{m^*}^2 - \frac{1}{\rho}\ln\left(\frac{\lambda\eta}{\lambda-1}\right).$$

The variance of domestic and foreign money shocks affects utility also because they affect the variance of consumption. From equation (A7),

$$(A9) \quad \sigma_c^2 = \frac{n^2}{\rho^2}\sigma_m^2 + \frac{(1-n)^2}{\rho^2}\sigma_{m^*}^2.$$

The expected level of consumption is given by

$$(A10) \quad E(C) = \exp\left(Ec + \frac{\sigma_c^2}{2}\right) = \left(\frac{\lambda-1}{\lambda\eta}\right)^{1/\rho}$$

$$\exp\left(-\left[\frac{n^2 + \rho n(1-2n)}{2\rho^2}\right]\sigma_m^2 - \left\{\frac{(1-n)^2 + \rho(1-n)[1-2(1-n)]}{2\rho^2}\right\}\sigma_{m^*}^2\right).$$

Expected utility depends on both the expected level and the variance of consumption:

$$(A11) \quad \frac{1}{1-\rho}E(C^{1-\rho}) = \frac{1}{1-\rho}E\{\exp[(1-\rho)c]\}$$

$$= \frac{1}{1-\rho}\left\{\exp\left[(1-\rho)Ec + \frac{(1-\rho)^2}{2}\sigma_c^2\right]\right\} = \left(\frac{1}{1-\rho}\right)\left(\frac{\lambda-1}{\eta\lambda}\right)^{(1-\rho)/\rho}$$

$$\left(\exp\left\{-\frac{n(1-\rho)[\rho + n(1-\rho)]}{2\rho^2}\sigma_m^2 - \frac{(1-n)(1-\rho)[1-n(1-\rho)]}{2\rho^2}\sigma_{m^*}^2\right\}\right).$$

From equation (15), we can derive the expected level of output easily as

$$(A12) \quad E(L) = \frac{\lambda-1}{\eta\lambda}E(C^{1-\rho}) = \left(\frac{\lambda-1}{\eta\lambda}\right)^{1/\rho}$$

$$\left(\exp\left\{-\frac{n(1-\rho)[\rho + n(1-\rho)]}{2\rho^2}\sigma_m^2 - \frac{(1-n)(1-\rho)[1-n(1-\rho)]}{2\rho^2}\sigma_{m^*}^2\right\}\right).$$

The PTM Model

From equations (5) and (10), we see that P_{ft} and P_{ht} are equal. Using this fact, and the definition of the price index in equation (1), we have

$$(A13) \qquad P_{ft} = P_{ht} = P_t = \left(\frac{\eta\lambda}{\lambda - 1}\right)\frac{E_{t-1}(P_t C_t)}{E_{t-1}(C_t^{1-\rho})}.$$

But, since P_t is in the time $t - 1$ information set, equation (A13) gives us that

$$(A14) \qquad E_{t-1}(C_t^{1-\rho}) = \frac{\eta\lambda}{\lambda - 1}E_{t-1}(C_t).$$

Writing this equation in logs gives us

$$(1 - \rho)E_{t-1}(c_t) + \frac{(1 - \rho)^2}{2}\sigma_c^2 = \ln\left(\frac{\lambda\eta}{\lambda - 1}\right) + E_{t-1}(c_t) + \frac{1}{2}\sigma_c^2.$$

Solving, we find

$$(A15) \qquad E_{t-1}(c_t) = -\frac{1}{\rho}\ln\left(\frac{\lambda\eta}{\lambda - 1}\right) + \frac{\rho - 2}{2}\sigma_c^2.$$

Since P_t is in the time $t - 1$ information set, we have from equation (20)

$$(A16) \qquad \sigma_c^2 = \frac{1}{\rho^2}\sigma_m^2.$$

As compared to the PCP model (equation [A9]), domestic monetary variance has a greater effect on the variance of domestic consumption. Substituting into equation (A15), we get

$$(A17) \qquad E_{t-1}(c_t) = -\frac{1}{\rho}\ln\left(\frac{\lambda\eta}{\lambda - 1}\right) + \frac{\rho - 2}{2\rho^2}\sigma_m^2.$$

The expected level of consumption is given by

$$(A18) \qquad E(C) = \exp\left(Ec + \frac{\sigma_c^2}{2}\right) = \left(\frac{\lambda - 1}{\lambda\eta}\right)^{1/\rho}\exp\left(\frac{\rho - 1}{2\rho^2}\sigma_m^2\right).$$

The expected utility term involving consumption is derived directly from equation (A14) using equation (A18):

$$(A19) \qquad \frac{1}{1 - \rho}E(C^{1-\rho}) = \left(\frac{1}{1 - \rho}\right)\left(\frac{\lambda - 1}{\eta\lambda}\right)^{(1-\rho)/\rho}\left[\exp\left(\frac{\rho - 1}{2\rho^2}\sigma_m^2\right)\right].$$

From equation (12), $L_t = C_t$, so equation (A18) gives us the expression for $E(L)$.

FER Model

We will assume the exchange rate is fixed at 1, so $s_t = 0$ for all t. From equation (21) it follows that

(A20) $m_t + \ln(1 - \mu\beta) = m_t^* + \ln(1 - \mu^*\beta).$

The domestic money supply moves in reaction to foreign money supply shocks in order to keep the exchange rate fixed.

Because exchange rates are fixed, $P_{ft} = P_{ft}^*$ and $P_{ht} = P_{ht}^*$. We can use equations (A1) and (A2) to derive expressions for prices. Noting that all prices are preset, the money demand equation (20) (combined with relation [A20]) tells us

$$\sigma_{mc} = \sigma_{m^*c^*} = \frac{1}{\rho}\sigma_{m^*}^2.$$

We can then derive

(A21) $p_{ht} = p_{ft} = p_t = m_{t-1}^* + \dfrac{1}{\rho}\sigma_{m^*}^2 + \ln\left[\dfrac{\lambda\eta(1 - \mu^*\beta)}{\mu^*\chi(\lambda - 1)}\right].$

Then, using equation (20), we get the expression for consumption under fixed exchange rates:

(A22) $c_t = \dfrac{1}{\rho}v_t^* + \dfrac{\rho - 2}{2\rho^2}\sigma_{m^*}^2 - \dfrac{1}{\rho}\ln\left(\dfrac{\lambda\eta}{\lambda - 1}\right).$

The variance of consumption in the FER model is given by

(A23) $\sigma_c^2 = \dfrac{1}{\rho^2}\sigma_{m^*}^2.$

The expected level of consumption is given by

(A24) $E(C) = \exp\left(Ec + \dfrac{\sigma_c^2}{2}\right) = \left(\dfrac{\lambda - 1}{\lambda\eta}\right)^{1/\rho}\exp\left[-\left(\dfrac{1 - \rho}{2\rho^2}\right)\sigma_{m^*}^2\right].$

The expected utility term involving consumption is

(A25) $\dfrac{1}{1 - \rho}E(C^{1-\rho}) = \dfrac{1}{1 - \rho}E\{\exp[(1 - \rho)c]\}$

$$= \dfrac{1}{1 - \rho}\left\{\exp\left[(1 - \rho)Ec + \dfrac{(1 - \rho)^2}{2}\sigma_c^2\right]\right\}$$

$$= \left(\dfrac{1}{1 - \rho}\right)\left(\dfrac{\lambda - 1}{\eta\lambda}\right)^{(1-\rho)/\rho}\left\{\exp\left[\dfrac{-(1 - \rho)}{2\rho^2}\sigma_{m^*}^2\right]\right\}.$$

We can derive the expected level of output easily as

$$(A26) \quad E(L) = \frac{\lambda - 1}{\eta\lambda}E(C^{1-\rho}) = \left(\frac{\lambda - 1}{\eta\lambda}\right)^{1/\rho}\left\{\exp\left[-\frac{(1 - \rho)}{2\rho^2}\sigma^2_{m^*}\right]\right\}.$$

Given the structure of the model, the fixed exchange rate model simply reduces to the PCP model with $n = 0$.

References

Aizenman, Joshua. 1994. Monetary and real shocks, productive capacity and exchange-rate regimes. *Economica*, no. 244:407–34.

Aizenman, Joshua, and Jacob A. Frenkel. 1985. Optimal wage indexation, foreign exchange intervention and monetary policy. *American Economic Review* 75: 402–23.

Bacchetta, Philippe, and Eric van Wincoop. 1998. Does exchange rate stability increase trade and capital flows? Federal Reserve Bank of New York Working Paper no. 9818.

Betts, Caroline, and Michael B. Devereux. 1996. The exchange rate in a model of pricing-to-market. *European Economic Review* 40:1007–21.

———. 1998. The international effects of monetary and fiscal policy in a two-country model. University of Southern California Department of Economics, working paper.

———. 2000. Exchange-rate dynamics in a model of pricing-to-market. *Journal of International Economics* 50:215–44.

Blomström, Magnus, Gunnar Fors, and Robert E. Lipsey. 1997. Foreign direct investment: Home country experience in the United States and Sweden. *Economic Journal* 107:1787–97.

Chari, V. V., Patrick J. Kehoe, and Ellen McGrattan. 1997. Monetary policy and the real exchange rate in sticky price models of the international business cycle. NBER Working Paper no. 5876. Cambridge, Mass.: National Bureau of Economic Research, January.

Chinn, Daniel M., and Preston J. Miller. 1998. Fixed vs. floating rates: A dynamic general equilibrium analysis. *European Economic Review* 42:1221–49.

Cole, Harold L., and Maurice Obstfeld. 1991. Commodity trade and international risk sharing: How much do financial markets matter? *Journal of Monetary Economics* 23:377–400.

Corsetti, Giancarlo, and Paolo Pesenti. 1998. Welfare and macroeconomic interdependence. Princeton University Department of Economics, working paper.

Devereux, Michael B., and Charles Engel. 1998. Fixed vs. floating exchange rates: How price setting affects the optimal choice of exchange-rate regime. NBER Working Paper no. 6867. Cambridge, Mass.: National Bureau of Economic Research, December.

Eaton, Jonathan. 1985. Optimal and time consistent exchange rate management in an overlapping generations economy. *Journal of International Money and Finance* 4:83–100.

Engel, Charles. 1993. Real exchange rates and relative prices: An empirical investigation. *Journal of Monetary Economics* 32:35–50.

———. 1996. A model of foreign exchange rate indetermination. NBER Working Paper no. 5766. Cambridge, Mass.: National Bureau of Economic Research, September.

———. 1999. Accounting for U.S. real exchange rate changes. *Journal of Political Economy* 107:507–38.

Engel, Charles, and John H. Rogers. 1996. How wide is the border? *American Economic Review* 86:1112–25.

Fischer, Stanley. 1977. Stability and exchange rate systems in a monetarist model of the balance of payments. In *The political economy of monetary reform,* ed. Robert Z. Aliber. Montclair, N.J.: Allanheld, Osmun.

Flood, Robert P. 1979. Capital mobility and the choice of exchange rate regime. *International Economic Review* 2:405–16.

Flood, Robert P., and Robert J. Hodrick. 1986. Real aspects of exchange rate regime choice with collapsing fixed rates. *Journal of International Economics* 21:215–32.

Flood, Robert P., and Nancy P. Marion. 1982. The transmission of disturbances under alternative exchange-rate regimes with optimal indexing. *Quarterly Journal of Economics* 96:43–66.

Friedman, Milton. 1953. The case for flexible exchange rates. In *Essays in positive economics,* ed. Milton Friedman. Chicago: University of Chicago Press.

Glick, Reuven, and Clas Wihlborg. 1990. Real exchange rate effects of monetary shocks under fixed and flexible exchange rates. *Journal of International Economics* 28:267–90.

Hamada, Koichi, and Makoto Sakurai. 1978. International transmission of stagflation under fixed and flexible exchange rates. *Journal of Political Economy* 86:877–95.

Hansen, Gary D. 1985. Indivisible labor and the business cycle. *Journal of Monetary Economics* 16:304–27.

Hau, Harald. 2000. Exchange-rate determination: The role of factor rigidities and nontradeables. *Journal of International Economics* 50:421–47.

Helpman, Elhanan. 1981. An exploration in the theory of exchange-rate regimes. *Journal of Political Economy* 10:263–83.

Helpman, Elhanan, and Assaf Razin. 1982. A comparison of exchange rate regimes in the presence of imperfect capital markets. *International Economic Review* 23:365–88.

Kimbrough, Kent. 1983. The information content of the exchange rate and the stability of real output under alternative exchange-rate regimes. *Journal of International Money and Finance* 2:27–38.

Kollman, Robert. 1996. The exchange rate in a dynamic optimizing current account model with nominal rigidities: A quantitative investigation. International Monetary Fund Working Paper 97/7. Washington, D.C.

Kravis, Irving B., and Robert E. Lipsey. 1978. Price behavior in the light of balance of payments theories. *Journal of International Economics* 8:193–246.

———. 1982. The location of overseas production and production for export by U.S. multinational firms. *Journal of International Economics* 12:201–23.

———. 1987. The assessment of national price levels. In *Real-financial linkages among open economies,* ed. Sven W. Arndt and J. David Richardson, 97–134. Cambridge, Mass.: MIT Press.

———. 1992. Sources of competitiveness of the United States and of its multinational firms. *Review of Economics and Statistics* 74:193–201.

Lapan, Harvey E., and Walter Enders. 1980. Random disturbances and the choice of exchange rate regimes in an intergenerational model. *Journal of International Economics* 10:263–83.

Lipsey, Robert E. 1988. Changing patterns of international investment in and by the United States. In *The United States in the world economy,* ed. Martin Feldstein, 495–545. Chicago: University of Chicago Press.

———. 1993. Foreign direct investment in the United States: Changes over three decades. In *Foreign direct investment,* ed. Kenneth A. Froot, 143–170. Chicago: University of Chicago Press.

———. 1998. Internationalized production in developed and developing countries and in industry sectors. NBER Working Paper no. 6405. Cambridge, Mass.: National Bureau of Economic Research, March.

Lipsey, Robert E., and Birgitta Swedenborg. 1996. The high cost of eating: Causes of international differences in consumer prices. *Review of Income and Wealth,* ser. 42:181–94.

Mundell, Robert A. 1960. The monetary dynamics of international adjustment under fixed and floating exchange rates. *Quarterly Journal of Economics* 74: 227–57.

———. 1961a. A theory of optimum currency areas. *American Economic Review* 51:509–17.

———. 1961b. Flexible exchange rates and employment policy. *Canadian Journal of Economics and Political Science* 27:509–17.

———. 1963. Capital mobility and stabilization policy under fixed and flexible exchange rates. *Canadian Journal of Economics and Political Science* 29:475–85.

Neumeyer, Pablo A. 1998. Currencies and the allocation of risk: The welfare effects of a monetary union. *American Economic Review* 88:246–59.

Obstfeld, Maurice, and Kenneth Rogoff. 1995. Exchange rate dynamics redux. *Journal of Political Economy* 103:624–60.

———. 1998. Risk and exchange rates. University of California–Berkeley, Department of Economics, working paper.

Rogers, John H., and Michael Jenkins. 1995. Haircuts or hysteresis? Sources of movements in real exchange rates. *Journal of International Economics* 38:339–60.

Rogerson, Richard. 1988. Indivisible labor, lotteries, and equilibrium. *Journal of Monetary Economics* 21:3–16.

Svensson, Lars E. O., and Sweder van Wijnbergen. 1989. Excess capacity, monopolistic competition, and international transmission of monetary disturbances. *Economic Journal* 99:785–805.

Tille, Cédric. 1998a. The international and domestic welfare effects of monetary shocks under pricing-to-market. Federal Reserve Bank of New York, working paper.

———. 1998b. The welfare effects of monetary shocks under pricing-to-market: A general framework. Federal Reserve Bank of New York, working paper.

Turnovsky, Stephen. 1976. The relative stability of alternative exchange rate systems in the presence of random disturbances. *Journal of Money, Credit, and Banking* 8:29–50.

———. 1983. Wage indexation and exchange market intervention in a small open economy. *Canadian Journal of Economics* 16:574–92.

Weber, Warren. 1981. Output variability under monetary policy and exchange-rate rules. *Journal of Political Economy* 89:733–75.

Comment   Anna J. Schwartz

I've been delegated to discuss a paper with models that have undergone no empirical testing, in a conference on empirical international economics. The paper discusses the role of price setting in determining the optimality of the exchange rate regime in an environment of uncertainty created by a monetary shock. It is the wrong paper for this conference and I am the wrong person to discuss such a paper. The best I can do to keep to the spirit of this conference is to raise some empirical questions related to the approach the paper takes in dealing with the choice of an exchange rate regime.

Two aspects of the models in the paper are noteworthy. One is that sticky goods prices characterize the models. Prices are sticky for goods that producers price in their own currencies, or for goods that producers price in consumers' currencies. The authors argue that the type of price stickiness "may be of critical importance in the analysis of fixed versus floating exchange rates." The reason is that foreign monetary shocks do not affect domestic consumption under floating rates when producers price in consumers' currencies, but when producers price in their own currencies the prices paid by home residents for foreign goods change as the exchange rate changes. A second aspect of the models is that all production for export occurs in foreign affiliates.

Are Sticky Prices the Norm?

An obvious empirical question to ask is the extent of price-setting behavior of firms and whether the ability to set prices is limited to particular circumstances. During the heyday of the Organization of Petroleum Exporting Countries, they controlled supply and were able to set the price. Currently, crude oil prices are set in auction markets, and producers are unable to manipulate the price (much as they would like to). What is the significance of the fact that the dollar is the currency in which oil prices are set? The dollar is not the producers' currency except for the relatively small share of total oil exports the United States provides. Which of the paper's models fits this case?

Which classes of exports allow producers to set their price? Suppose there is price discrimination in a well-defined set of export goods across countries, but vigorous competition within a country among different exporters of that set of goods. This is no concern of the models.

A feature not present in the models of the paper is a distinction between nontradables and tradables. Instead, there are goods produced at home and goods produced in the foreign country.

Anna J. Schwartz is a research associate of the National Bureau of Economic Research.

Is producer price behavior similar for tradables and nontradables? The usual presumption is that producers have greater monopoly power over nontradables than over tradables. That is the explanation for the higher inflation rate in Hong Kong of nontradables than of tradables. Hong Kong tradable goods prices move with U.S. prices because the Hong Kong dollar exchange rate is pegged to the U.S. dollar.

The sticky prices of the models are nominal prices, whether expressed in the currency of the home country or of the foreign country. A change in the exchange rate times the selling country's price, even if nominally sticky, induces a change in the price faced by the buying country. Such data give an indication of how much cheaper export goods become as a result of the depreciation of a country's currency. The literature on pass-through provides calculations on the extent to which companies pass through into higher export prices the changes caused by exchange rate fluctuations, and the extent to which they have absorbed the changes by either lowering costs or lowering profit margins.

The models do not distinguish countries whose tradables are produced at home from countries whose tradables are produced by foreign affiliates. How important in world trade are countries whose tradables are produced at home compared to countries whose tradables are produced by foreign affiliates? Even countries with some exports produced in foreign affiliates probably also produce some exports at home. How big are the shares of each type of country's world trade?

Wouldn't the optimal exchange rate for countries differ depending on where they produce tradables? Countries whose tradables are produced at home are usually small, commodity exporters, who might be expected to link their domestic currencies to the currencies of their major trading partners. Countries whose exports are produced in foreign affiliates are usually large and might be expected to float.

Price Stickiness and Exchange Rates

It is questionable whether there is empirical support for the authors' belief that the type of price stickiness is the key determinant of whether to fix or to float. The record of the two decades since the end of Bretton Woods suggests that the decision by countries to fix or peg their currencies is made to curb inflation, which is usually produced by imprudent monetary and fiscal policy. The exchange rate regime does not appear to be related to the currency in which exports are invoiced.

According to the model, in countries whose producers set prices in consumers' currencies, domestic consumption is insulated from monetary shocks from abroad. We have an example this year of hot-rolled steel exports to the United States by Japan, Russia, and Brazil at prices that are lower than the production costs of American steel mills. How does such a situation allow domestic consumption to be insulated from foreign monetary shocks?

Factor Price Equalization Abstraction

There is factor price equalization in the models of the paper. Home-country wages equal foreign-country wages, so the prices set by firms are the same regardless of whether domestic labor or foreign labor produces output. This assumption seems to fly in the face of the reason exports are produced in foreign affiliates. It is true that foreign affiliates are sometimes established to counter protectionist tendencies abroad or to take advantage of lower taxes in the foreign jurisdiction; but unquestionably the main reason for moving production of exports abroad is that the cost of hiring foreign labor is lower than the cost of domestic labor.

A conclusion reached in the paper, based on the model in which prices are set in consumer currencies with internationalized production, is that the domestic economy is sheltered from foreign shocks. The reasoning is that when foreign demand for the home good declines, domestic employment is sheltered from the foreign shock because foreign subsidiaries of the home country absorb the decline in demand. Of course, the conclusion holds only if every single export good is produced in foreign affiliates. The spillover from both the Mexican collapse in 1995 and the East Asian crises in 1997–98 on employment in this country is a check on this conclusion.

Models and Empirical Research

Models are often simple in order to develop a tractable analysis of their features. For example, the authors consider a specific utility function, in which real money balances enter logarithmically and leisure enters linearly. What one would like to know is the extent to which the conclusions depend on these specific assumptions. The authors claim that the welfare analysis would not be appreciably altered by a more complex model, but they admit that the assumption of the linearity of labor makes a difference. What would the difference be?

In the welfare analysis, the authors consider the effect on utility only of expected consumption, the variance of consumption, and expected leisure. Real money balances are not considered, although this term is assumed in the utility function. Would it not be more consistent to discuss the effect of real money balances on utility, or to show that the conclusions are not appreciably affected by the omission?

The construction of the models in this paper was inspired by Bob Lipsey's empirical findings that the law of one price does not hold, that price discrimination is quite common for identical goods in international trade, and that internationalized production increased in the past quarter-century. I applaud this homage to Bob's work. However, to build a model in which internationalized production accounts for all exports, when at most it can account for one-fifth of world manufacturing, seems to me to underscore the importance of testing its predictions. Models may be admirable intellectual exercises, but they create a make-believe world. What needs to be established is the relevance of that world to the real world.

Revealing Comparative Advantage
Chaotic or Coherent Patterns across Time and Sector and U.S. Trading Partner?

J. David Richardson and Chi Zhang

7.1 Introduction, Motivation, Novelty, Overview

In this paper we attempt to honor, by mimicry, Bob Lipsey's ongoing life work of innovative and painstaking measurement and analysis.[1]

We do so by mapping and interpreting U.S. comparative advantage across time, trading partners, and sectors at an increasing level of commodity detail. We use Bela Balassa's index of revealed comparative advantage (RCA), measured from U.S. export data. Balassa, like Lipsey, was a master of measurement and analysis (and the early mentor of one of the authors).

To our knowledge, we are among the first to do these mappings simulta-

J. David Richardson is professor of economics and the Gerald B. and Daphna Cramer Professor of Global Affairs at Syracuse University, a research associate of the National Bureau of Economic Research, and a visiting fellow at the Institute for International Economics, Washington, D.C. Chi Zhang is a research associate of the Center for International Security and Cooperation at Stanford University.

Earlier drafts of this paper were presented at the November 1998 Empirical Investigations in International Trade Conference at Purdue University and at Koc University, Istanbul, as well as at the NBER conference. The authors are indebted to the active comments of all the participants there.

1. For example, Bob's early work with Irving Kravis to see how closely the available price indexes of internationally traded goods come to measures that were built up carefully from surveys of actual transactions prices (Kravis and Lipsey 1971), continuing in regular contributions to measures of relative prices through the International Comparisons Project (ICP; most recently Heston and Lipsey 1999, with many references within). Or, for example, Bob's many attempts (with Kravis) to measure the relative importance of MNC production in world trade and production (most recently Kravis and Lipsey 1992, which features the measures of revealed comparative advantage that we use later). We are particular fans of Bob's painstaking efforts to measure what economists really mean by *capital formation* (most recently Kirova and Lipsey 1998, with earlier references within).

neously across time, sectors, and regional markets (groups of trading partners).[2] To coin a term that emphasizes this, we call some of our indexes RRCA indexes—they measure regional revealed comparative advantage by market groups of U.S. trading partners.

We are interested in several patterns of variation. The most novel is the variation in U.S. comparative advantage from region to region. It turns out to be quite diverse; U.S. patterns of comparative advantage seem to be different in different parts of the world, and the differences seem to have changed during the period 1980–95 from which our data come. These differences look different at different levels of aggregation.

Aggregation defines our second pattern of interest. U.S. comparative advantage is naturally quite diverse from sector to sector (by definition), but the advantage differs in interesting ways as sectors are more specifically defined. Sectors in which U.S. exports are typically strong often include disaggregated subproducts in which they are not, and conversely. These patterns, too, change between 1980 and 1995. What accounts for these changes in differences? Why are they important? Our results yield several answers.

Obvious variables, such as proximity, underlie some of our findings, such as the quantitatively sharper (larger) U.S. comparative advantage in exports to the Western Hemisphere and disadvantage in exports to Asia. Less obvious is the apparent influence of per capita income, especially on manufactures; U.S. comparative advantage and disadvantage are quantitatively sharper (larger) in countries that are poorer than they are in richer trading partners.[3] We find this suggestive for evaluating natural regional trading blocs, and for detecting trade diversion, for which there seems to be some evidence with respect to the North American Free Trade Agreement (NAFTA).

Qualitatively, the United States has comparative advantage in differentiated producer goods (e.g., capital equipment) in all regions—though it is less marked in Japan—and comparative disadvantage (except for chemicals) in standardized producer goods (e.g., metals) and consumer goods of all sorts. The producer goods patterns are very stable over time, and

2. Both Kreinin and Plummer (1994a, 1994b) and Hoekman and Djankov (1997) examine the difference between RCA indexes defined for one particular region (East Asia and the European Union, respectively) and normal global-market RCA indexes. Balassa and Bauwens (1988, chap. 3) examine the determinants of regional/bilateral *net* exports, but that is a very different measure of comparative advantage than Balassa's purely export-based measure.

3. Both traditional and modern trade theories allow for this, of course, explaining it by environmental factors that range from cones of diversification (Schott 1998), to global vertical specialization (Hummels, Rapaport, and Yi 1998; Yeats 1998), to two-way trade within a differentiated products sector. In some variants of two-way trade, however (e.g., reciprocal dumping), the very conception of comparative advantage loses relevance, to say nothing of its measurement.

appear in both aggregated and disaggregated data. The consumer goods patterns are, however, both highly volatile and remarkably uneven across groups of trading partners and at different levels of aggregation.

We were far less successful in detecting sectoral niche comparative advantage than geographical niche comparative advantage. We expected increasing specialization as we deepened sectoral disaggregation, rising over time with the advent of vertical specialization (outsourcing or fragmentation), as described in Hummels, Rapaport, and Yi (1998) and Yeats (1998). There was only limited evidence for this among machinery and equipment exports, and none for manufactures in general.

7.2 Background

Indexes of revealed comparative advantage (RCA) have had a checkered history since Bela Balassa developed them decades ago.[4] They are arguably useful as one of the few formal ways of measuring the sector identity and intensity of a country's comparative advantage and disadvantage; yet their consistency with the most familiar theories of trade patterns has not always been clear, despite Balassa's efforts (see also Hillman 1980). Like gravity equations and Grubel-Lloyd indexes, RCA indexes are employed frequently but with little respect.

Even empirical properties of RCA indexes remain unexplored. For example, few researchers have attempted to see if RCA indexes using a country's import data alone suggest similar patterns of disadvantage and advantage as do RCA indexes using the same country's export data alone.[5] Likewise, trade-based RCA indexes could be compared to production-based RCA indexes[6] to see if a consistent story emerges.

Finally, only a few researchers have calculated RCA indexes by regional groupings of a country's trading partners in order to examine similarities and differences in the cross-regional pattern. This, and discovering how these patterns vary with aggregation, are the chief purposes of our paper.

4. Balassa (1965, 1977, 1979, 1989), Balassa and associates (1964), Balassa and Bauwens (1988), Balassa and Noland (1988, 1989).

5. We treat the issue of export-based versus import-based concepts very briefly toward the end of the paper. Balassa (1965), Balassa and Bauwens (1988), and Balassa and Noland (1988, 1989) all use imports to adjust exports either linearly (net exports) or in ratio form. Imports alone, however, give a uniquely different measure of comparative advantage, as we show later.

6. In a world of similar preferences, production-based or value-added-based RCA indexes would be very reasonable measures of comparative advantage. In practice, the requisite data are hard to compile. For recent examples, however, relying on OECD data, see Wolff (1999), using manufacturing production, or Leamer (1997), using value added. For an example using 1963 U.S. data on interstate merchandise shipments, see Greytak, Richardson, and Smith (1999).

7.3   What Do RCA Indexes Measure, Anyway?

RCA indexes measure a country's comparative advantage, and do so in a fairly natural way. One simple explanation is that an RCA index is a ratio of ratios—specifically, that it is relative relative trade shares. The two modifiers *relative* belong in the sentence together because the index is attempting to evaluate comparative advantage, which is itself a relative relative concept: the relative competitiveness of a country's industry to that of its other industries, relative to global norms.

A generic, export-based RCA index is the following (multiplied by 100), using the United States as a focus:

$$\frac{\text{(U.S. exports in sector } i)/(\text{U.S. exports in } \textbf{all} \text{ sectors})}{(\textbf{World} \text{ exports in sector } i)/(\textbf{World} \text{ exports in } \textbf{all} \text{ sectors})}$$

either in a designated importer's **market,** or in a region,
or for the whole world.

As written, the measure corresponds naturally to colloquial and classroom challenges to "tell me what the United States has comparative advantage in!" The answer is sectors in which the index is high. The index itself is the U.S. share of *i* exports in U.S. total exports relative to the world counterpart. Equivalently,[7] it is the U.S. share in world exports of *i* relative to the U.S. share in world exports of everything else (non-*i*). When it is greater than 1 (or 100), the United States is a relatively[8] heavy exporter of *i*, and is said to have revealed comparative advantage in sector *i*; when it is less than 1, it is considered to have revealed comparative disadvantage.

The index is not unique, however. Each boldface word in the definition signals an important choice. Researchers must first define the sectoral boundaries captured by the word *all*. Does it mean all exports of goods and services, a usually troublesome data series to collect? Or does it mean all merchandise exports, a more available series? Or all manufactured exports?[9] Next, researchers must decide how exhaustively they wish to define the world of peer exporters captured by the word *world*—all exporters everywhere in the world, or only a group of close rivals, or perhaps even a particular country against whom a researcher wants to assess U.S. comparative advantage? Finally, researchers must be precise about the customer *market*. Is it U.S. comparative advantage in a single market that interests them? Or is it in a region, or the entire world? If regions are the focus (e.g.,

7. By rearranging the elements of the measure.
8. Relatively relatively.
9. The trouble with these narrower but more widely available measures of *all* exports is that they would fail to record comparative advantage accurately for a country that in reality had its exports principally in unrepresented industries—for example, in various services or raw materials—and had net imports of all sorts of goods, especially manufactures.

Europe and Asia), then researchers must be clear that the group of peer exporters will be different for each region; peer exporters into a unified European market do not include European exporters, and peer exporters into a unified Asian market do not include Asian exporters.[10]

The index is, however, quite robust. Export-based RCA and RRCA measures are not very sensitive to growth and business-cycle differences across trading partners, which tend to affect both the numerator and the denominator in the definition similarly. Nor, for the same reason, are they sensitive to the height of trade barriers, as long as they are across-the-board, nondiscriminatory protection against all exporters into the market of that trading partner. They *are* sensitive to discriminatory barriers against U.S. exports, and may vary also to the degree that U.S. exports vary with U.S. and foreign multinational-firm investment, outsourcing, and so on. Likewise, export-based RCA and RRCA measures are not very sensitive to across-the-board exchange rate strength or weakness of trading-partner currencies, but they are sensitive to unusual strength or weakness against the dollar alone.

7.4 Data and Terminological Conventions

In this paper we compare U.S. export performance in 1980 and 1995 to that of thirty-eight of its largest trading partners and rivals. These thirty-eight also form both the world of U.S. peer exporters and the markets (regional groups) in which U.S. and peer exporters compete.[11] We draw our export data from Statistics Canada's World Trade Data Base, which provides annual trade flow data among countries as reported to the United Nations.

We adopt several conventions in the terms we use. We will refer to cases of large distance from 100 in our RCA measures as *sharp* or *strong* comparative advantage and disadvantage. We will refer to variability over time in our RCA measures as *volatile* comparative advantage and disadvantage, and variability over trading partners and closely related commodity groups

---

10. The same difference exists when single-country markets are the focus. Peer exporters into the Japanese market include everyone *but* Japanese exporters. Production-based RCA indexes, such as those in Leamer (1997) and Wolff (1999), would not be subject to these differences, but neither could they be used to assess the comparative advantage of U.S. production relative to European rivals (e.g., in Japan).

11. Our selection of thirty-eight large partners was only partly dictated by the cumbersomeness of dealing with the universe of U.S. trading partners. But it occasionally causes anomalies, such as a measured U.S. comparative advantage in fuels in Japanese markets—the really big exporters of fuels to Japan (oil producing countries) are not among our thirty-eight country sample. We picked the countries according to several criteria: geographic location, size, and importance in U.S. trade; spectrum of traded merchandise; and change over time. The thirty-eight sample countries represent more than 75 percent of the 1995 U.S. trade. Areas that are not represented are most of Africa, Middle-Eastern oil-exporting countries, Eastern Europe and the former Soviet Union, South Asia, and Central America.

as *geographically diverse* and *sectorally diverse* comparative advantage and disadvantage, respectively.

We will describe the broad commodity classifications of the Standard International Trade Classification (SITC) by nicknames, as follows:[12]

SITC 1–4: primary products
SITC 5–8: manufactures
  SITC 5: chemicals
  SITC 6: manufactured materials
  SITC 7: machinery and equipment
  SITC 8: finished manufactures

We will often find it helpful to describe SITC 5 and 6 as *standardized manufactures* and SITC 7 and 8 as *differentiated manufactures,* although both caricatures do some violence to the diversity of the subproducts therein. We will also find it helpful to describe subaggregates of these broad one-digit classifications as subproducts or subcategories, and to further identify these as consumer goods or producer goods depending on their dominant buyers—wholesalers and retailers on behalf of households, or firms purchasing capital equipment and industrial supplies for themselves.

We explore U.S. export patterns across trading partners, usually aggregating them into regional groups (China and Japan are treated separately). The groups are described by the following nicknames:

EU15: Austria, Belgium, Denmark, Finland, France, Germany, Greece, Ireland, Italy, Luxembourg, the Netherlands, Portugal, Spain, Sweden, and the United Kingdom
NAFTA: Canada and Mexico
Latin6: Argentina, Brazil, Chile, Colombia, Peru, and Venezuela
Tiger: Hong Kong, Korea, Singapore, and Taiwan
OthAs4: Indonesia, Malaysia, the Philippines, and Thailand
China
Others: Australia, Egypt, Israel, New Zealand, South Africa

7.5   Highly Aggregated (One-Digit SITC) Patterns for All Merchandise

We start with a broad overview of U.S. comparative advantage. Table 7.1 records export-based RCA indexes at the one-digit SITC level for 1980 and 1995.

---

12. A more careful description of what belongs in each is as follows:

SITC 1–4: raw materials (fibers, wood, paper) and agricultural and mining products
SITC 5: chemicals, plastics, and pharmaceuticals
SITC 6: iron, steel, and other metals, and products of fiber, wood, paper, rubber, and stone
SITC 7: machinery (for power, industry, and metalworking), office machines, and electrical, telecommunications, and transportation equipment
SITC 8: apparel, footwear, household goods, and scientific and medical instruments

Table 7.1   U.S. Export RCAs, SITC One-Digit Level, Merchandise

		RCA	
SITC		1995	1980
0	Food and live animals used chiefly for food	142.1	128.4
1	Beverages and tobacco	129.9	94.8
2	Crude materials, inedible, except fuels	143.4	137.9
3	Mineral fuels, lubricants, and related materials	43.8	40.2
4	Animal and vegetable oils, fats, and waxes	127.3	135.6
5	Chemicals and related products, n.e.s.	139.3	141.9
6	Manufactured goods classified chiefly by material	85.8	77.1
7	Machinery and transport equipment	97.8	103.1
8	Miscellaneous manufactured articles	78.6	82.2
Weighted correlation[a]		0.88	
Unweighted correlation[b]		0.96	

Note: n.e.s. = not elsewhere specified.

[a]Cross-sectoral correlation coefficient between 1995 and 1980, weighted by export share.

[b]Cross-sectoral correlation coefficient between 1995 and 1980, unweighted.

Table 7.1 reveals the familiar U.S. comparative advantage with the rest of the world[13] in primary products (except fuels) and in manufactured chemicals, and the familiar mixed pattern across other manufactures. In these other manufactures, the United States performs best in machinery and equipment, but shows comparative *dis*advantage in manufactured materials and finished manufactures. Table 7.1 also shows that the worldwide cross-product pattern of broad (one-digit) U.S. comparative advantage did not change much between 1980 and 1995.[14] The correlation between the 1995 pattern and the 1980 pattern is 0.96, though lower (0.88) if the nine observations are weighted by export shares.[15]

In table 7.2, these worldwide patterns are broken down into RRCAs— RCAs across regional trading partners. There are noteworthy subpatterns, which are least parallel across trading partners in the differentiated manufactures sectors (SITC 7 and 8), as might be expected when the aggregates are not very homogeneous.[16] On balance, measures of both comparative advantage and comparative disadvantage are sharper for Asia than for the rest of the world. The United States "wins big" in some sectors and "loses big" in others against its export rivals there.

13. Our "world" is made up of thirty-eight countries.

14. Only food, beverages, and tobacco products show significant growth.

15. Each of our tables provides summary measures for both weighted and unweighted observations. We generally focus on the weighted summary measures in the text summary. Weights are for 1980 and 1995, the same years for which RCAs are calculated. Sectors such as machinery and equipment (SITC 7) and trading partners such as the EU account for disproportionately large shares of U.S. exports.

16. The patterns are also quite diverse across trading partners in fuels, SITC 3.

Table 7.2   **U.S. Export RCAs by Region, SITC One-Digit Level, Merchandise**

SITC	EU15	NAFTA	Latin6	Japan	Tiger	OthAs4	China	Others	Weighted Dispersion[a]	Dispersion[b]	Weighted Correlation[c]	Correlation[d]
1995												
0	130.1	100.4	57.8	271.1	209.3	100.0	213.0	100.1	0.50	0.52	0.91	0.80
1	91.3	45.5	76.8	274.1	231.9	220.8	142.8	120.2	0.61	0.62	0.91	0.69
2	180.6	76.6	76.7	271.4	228.2	127.1	247.3	56.5	0.53	0.61	0.94	0.89
3	86.1	23.6	15.1	228.5	181.8	61.8	36.8	67.0	0.99	0.94	0.87	0.64
4	88.5	124.5	140.1	243.5	232.6	16.0	288.0	146.5	0.58	0.92	0.22	0.91
5	98.9	132.4	156.2	158.5	206.0	217.5	211.7	110.6	0.29	0.30	0.93	0.56
6	64.7	94.4	72.4	102.6	98.0	107.8	63.6	53.7	0.21	0.26	0.22	0.13
7	99.3	106.3	154.3	57.7	96.5	116.2	135.3	122.5	0.23	0.30	0.78	0.89
8	93.3	122.3	100.5	118.4	36.6	37.2	15.9	97.7	0.47	0.74	0.88	0.85
Weighted dispersion[e]	0.22	0.23	0.51	0.69	0.53	0.39	0.71	0.28				
Dispersion[f]	0.29	0.57	0.72	0.55	0.63	0.84	0.99	0.36				

1980

0	137.0	115.7	69.2	233.4	186.7	102.9	122.5	50.2	0.42	0.50
1	69.8	34.2	82.0	238.7	210.6	229.1	21.6	141.4	0.63	0.91
2	150.1	69.1	78.0	246.2	214.7	90.3	115.1	68.0	0.46	0.50
3	84.1	26.9	14.5	241.9	152.0	3.2	1.6	47.3	1.02	1.78
4	135.1	183.7	146.3	230.8	224.2	5.8	125.0	156.2	0.34	1.21
5	107.4	124.8	161.7	185.1	219.1	265.3	101.0	129.4	0.32	0.35
6	76.3	82.6	104.6	56.2	73.0	95.7	83.8	58.0	0.17	0.22
7	90.0	129.2	164.6	37.7	111.1	202.7	126.3	143.3	0.36	0.51
8	95.7	150.2	123.9	79.2	16.1	78.5	17.1	119.1	0.50	0.88
Weighted dispersion[e]	0.24	0.40	0.53	0.80	0.64	0.63	0.30	0.43		
Dispersion[f]	0.27	0.66	0.75	0.74	0.86	1.59	1.48	0.49		
Weighted correlation[g]	0.84	0.78	0.94	0.94	0.96	0.67	0.69	0.92		
Correlation[h]	0.74	0.95	0.99	0.97	0.98	0.75	0.69	0.79		

[a]RCA dispersion across regions by sector, weighted by export share, 1995 and 1980. Dispersion = standard deviation of natural logs of indexes/100.

[b]RCA dispersion across regions by sector, unweighted, 1995 and 1980. Dispersion = standard deviaton of natural logs of indexes/100.

[c]Cross-regional correlation coefficient by sector, weighted by export share, between 1995 and 1980.

[d]Cross-regional correlation coefficient by sector, unweighted, between 1995 and 1980.

[e]RCA dispersion across sectors by region, weighted by export share, 1995 and 1980. Dispersion = standard deviation of natural logs of indexes/100.

[f]RCA dispersion across sectors by region, unweighted by export share, 1995 and 1980. Dispersion = standard deviation of natural logs of indexes/100.

[g]Cross-sectoral correlation coefficient, weighted by export share, between 1995 and 1980.

[h]Cross-sectoral correlation coefficient, unweighted by export share, between 1995 and 1980.

U.S. comparative advantage in primary products and chemicals (SITC 0–4, 5) is especially strong in Asia, far weaker in Europe, and often nonexistent in the Western Hemisphere (where U.S. exports compete against other strong primary product exporters).[17] These regional cross-market patterns are very stable between 1980 and 1995. Five of the first six cross-market correlations at the right of table 7.2 are higher than 0.87.

U.S. *dis*advantage in manufactured materials (SITC 6) is most pronounced in Japanese markets in 1980, but vanishes by 1995, whereas in Latin American markets U.S. disadvantage develops and deepens over the same period. In Europe and China, U.S. disadvantage in manufactured materials is already deep in 1980 and deepens still more by 1995.[18]

In machinery and equipment (SITC 7), U.S. exports are sharply disadvantaged in Japanese markets only, in both 1980 and 1995. In almost every other market the United States is a comparatively competitive machinery and equipment exporter in both years.[19] However, the cross-regional diversity of U.S. machinery and equipment exports was greatly reduced. That is, U.S. RCA indexes moved toward 1 (100) in almost every market between 1980 and 1995. Their weighted dispersion[20] fell by one third, from 0.36 to 0.23.

U.S. disadvantage in finished manufactures (SITC 8) is most pronounced in China and Southeast Asia in both 1980 and 1995, with some shift between the Tiger countries and the near-Tigers (OthAs4).

Regional RCAs can be used to detect trade diversion suggestively, if not definitively. Table 7.2's NAFTA countries column can illustrate how. Trade diversion in Canadian and Mexican markets would imply that each is rely-

---

17. The rival primary-producer exporters would include the Latin6 in NAFTA markets, NAFTA rivals in Latin6 markets, and all other (unmeasured) Western Hemisphere rivals in both markets. In Europe, U.S. export performance is being assessed against Asian and other exporter performances. In Asia, U.S. export performance is being assessed against European and other non-Asian exporters. It may seem paradoxical that U.S. comparative advantage in Asia could be so much stronger than it is in Europe; but there may be no paradox. This relative strength is what we would expect if, for example, U.S. exports were highly competitive against European exports (in Asia and elsewhere), but less competitive against Asian exports (in Europe and elsewhere).

18. One possible cause of the strange pattern of diminishing U.S. comparative disadvantage in Japan in manufactured materials is U.S. bilateral policy activism. Recurrent U.S. pressure on Japan to open its markets to imports in such areas as wood products may have tempted Japanese buyers simply to substitute U.S. suppliers for others. The same pattern is somewhat less pronounced in the Asian Tigers (such as Korea), which were also subject to such policy activism.

19. The United States had very mild 1980 and 1995 disadvantage in Europe and mild 1995 disadvantage in the Asian Tiger markets.

20. Our measures of dispersion are the standard deviations of the natural logarithms of the RCA indexes divided by 100 (so as to be centered symmetrically on zero). See Wolff (1999) or Leamer (1997, 13ff), for views favoring a similar measure of dispersion, using logarithmic transformations of the RCA indexes, in order to avoid the skewness implicit in a ratio of ratios that is centered on 100 or 1, limited in downward variation to zero, but unlimited in upward variation.

ing more on U.S. exporters after NAFTA in products that are better produced in non-NAFTA countries. U.S. comparative advantage in NAFTA markets would thus shift toward middling categories; it would correspondingly decline for categories in which it was strongest before NAFTA.[21] This pattern actually occurs in table 7.2—U.S. RRCA in NAFTA markets is more concentrated on middling categories in 1995 and on the top three RRCAs in 1980; all decline by 1995 in NAFTA markets. This pattern, however, is much less distinct for manufactures alone and within machinery and equipment at the two- and three-digit levels of disaggregation summarized later in tables 7.4 and 7.6.[22]

7.6   Modestly Aggregated (Two-Digit SITC) Patterns for Manufactures

Because the most interesting patterns at the two-digit level are in manufactures, we neglect primary products from here on.

Table 7.3 refines the picture of U.S. worldwide comparative advantage revealed in table 7.1.[23] Virtually all two-digit subproducts show stable comparative advantage over time.[24] For those goods with fairly standardized specifications and production processes (SITC 51–69), U.S. patterns of comparative advantage and disadvantage are also quite uniform across subproducts. However, in differentiated goods (SITC 71–89), U.S. patterns of comparative advantage and disadvantage vary diversely across subproducts. The United States tends to have stable comparative advantage in producer goods subcategories,[25] fairly stable comparative disadvantage in consumer goods subcategories,[26] and reversal of comparative advantage between 1980 and 1995 in the one subproduct on the margin of producer and consumer goods, computers and office machines (SITC 75).

More exactly, table 7.3 reveals remarkable uniformity of comparative advantage across various types of chemical products (SITC 5), and of disadvantage across various types of manufactured materials (SITC 6).

21. The nature of the index is that if competitive advantage rises in some categories compared to others, *comparative* advantage must rise in the first and fall in the second.

22. In table 7.4, although nine of the top eleven NAFTA RRCAs decline by 1995, so do all eleven of the middling RRCAs. In table 7.6, although all twelve of the top NAFTA RRCAs decline by 1995, so do nine of the twelve middling RRCAs.

23. In table 7.3, "all categories" in the definition of the RCA index refers to all manufactured exports; whereas in table 7.1 it refers to all merchandise exports.

24. The correlation coefficients recording this intertemporal stability are about the same or higher at the two-digit level as at the one-digit level. See Hoekman and Djankov (1997, 475) for a similar finding that the intertemporal stability was similar at their four-digit level of disaggregation to that at a two-digit level.

25. Producer goods are taken to include all subcategories of SITC 7 except computers, telecommunications, and road vehicles (SITC 75, 76, 78), plus instruments (SITC 87).

26. Consumer goods are taken to include telecommunications equipment (a large part of SITC 76, though SITC 76 also includes equipment that is a producer good) and autos (the bulk of SITC 78, which also includes trucks, buses, and motorcycles), plus all of SITC 8, except instruments (SITC 87).

	SITC	1995	1980
Organic chemicals	51	135.7	133.0
Inorganic chemicals	52	120.3	114.2
Dyeing, tanning, and coloring materials	53	131.2	117.5
Medicinal and pharmaceutical products	54	120.4	159.1
Essential oils and perfume materials, toilet-cleansing materials	55	138.2	134.9
Fertilizers, manufactured	56	154.4	124.2
Artificial resins, plastic materials, cellulose esters/ethers	58	153.0	161.5
Chemical materials and products n.e.s.	59	153.4	162.6
Leather, leather manufactures n.e.s., and dressed fur/skins	61	86.8	108.4
Rubber manufactures n.e.s.	62	92.5	62.7
Cork and wood manufactures (excluding furniture)	63	73.0	50.9
Paper, paperboard, articles of paper, paper-pulp/board	64	92.3	78.8
Textile yarn, fabrics, made-up articles, related products	65	98.4	116.1
Nonmetallic mineral manufactures n.e.s.	66	74.8	62.9
Iron and steel	67	68.7	48.3
Nonferrous metals	68	86.8	90.2
Manufactures of metal n.e.s.	69	94.5	92.8
Power-generating machinery and equipment	71	111.8	126.3
Machinery specialized for particular industries	72	123.6	133.0
Metalworking machinery	73	102.3	91.3
General industrial machinery, equipment, and parts	74	113.4	137.2
Office machines and automatic data-processing equipment	75	95.2	143.2
Telecommunications and sound-recording apparatus	76	78.8	63.9
Electrical machinery, apparatus, and appliances n.e.s.	77	105.1	104.1
Road vehicles (including air-cushion vehicles)	78	70.9	59.5
Other transport equipment	79	145.6	142.1
Sanitary, plumbing, heating, and lighting fixtures	81	64.9	82.8
Furniture and parts thereof	82	67.2	58.8
Travel goods, handbags, and similar containers	83	15.9	13.3
Articles of apparel and clothing accessories	84	31.0	25.4
Footwear	85	8.5	13.5
Professional, scientific, and controlling instruments	87	145.8	148.0
Photographic apparatus, optical goods, watches	88	70.6	84.9
Miscellaneous manufactured articles n.e.s.	89	92.4	96.5
Weighted correlation[a]			
SITC 51–59			0.77
SITC 61–69			0.96
SITC 71–79			0.91
SITC 81–89			0.99
Correlation[b]			
SITC 51–59			0.35
SITC 61–69			0.80
SITC 71–79			0.85
SITC 81–89			0.97

Note: n.e.s. = not elsewhere specified.
[a]Cross-sectoral correlation coefficient, weighted by export share, between 1995 and 1980.
[b]Unweighted.

Finished manufactures (SITC 8) shows more diversity, as expected of differentiated subproducts, but it is explicable diversity. The United States has strong comparative advantage in instruments (SITC 87), the one producer good among finished manufactures. It has comparative disadvantage in all the consumer goods, with the disadvantage being sharpest in luggage, apparel, and footwear (SITC 83–85), and less sharp in everything else. Machinery and equipment (SITC 7) seems to show even more diversity, but it, too, is explicable, and falls into the same pattern as finished manufactures. The United States has strong comparative advantage in capital equipment—industrial machinery and transport equipment not including road vehicles (SITC 71–74, 77, 79). It has comparative disadvantage in the largely consumer goods categories of household electronics (SITC 76) and road vehicles (SITC 78, largely autos).

These subproduct patterns are very stable between 1980 and 1995 with just a few important exceptions. The most noteworthy is the reversal of U.S. comparative advantage in computers and office machines (SITC 75). U.S. comparative advantage also falls modestly for medicinal and pharmaceutical products (SITC 54) but rises modestly for fertilizers (SITC 56). U.S. comparative disadvantage becomes less marked in iron and steel (SITC 67).

An apparent change between 1980 and 1995 is a moderate evening-out of U.S. comparative advantage across the 34 two-digit manufacturing subsectors. Believers in increasing sectoral niche specialization might expect the opposite.[27] Sectoral niche specialization shows up only a little better at the three-digit level for machinery and equipment (below in table 7.5). Increased subproduct specialization is far less pronounced there, however, than increased *regional* specialization, seen in increased cross-regional dispersion of the RRCA indexes between 1980 and 1995.

When these worldwide patterns are broken down across trading partners in table 7.4, there are noteworthy subpatterns. First, the comparative success of U.S. exporters does differ dramatically from market to market, in ways that do not match simple explanations such as proximity or lingual ties. European economic centrality and preferential trade policies do, however, seem to make typical U.S. RCA indexes lower there than elsewhere. Second, patterns of U.S. comparative advantage sometimes change rapidly over time, especially in China, and especially for consumer goods. Third, the United States has stable global comparative advantage in most varieties of differentiated producer goods, but in Japan it has stable *dis*advantage (as if U.S. exports of differentiated producer goods faced discriminatory market barriers,[28] which is often alleged). Finally, in more standardized producer goods, though U.S. patterns of comparative advantage and disadvantage

27. Proudman and Redding (1997, 23) find a very similar decline in their measure of RCA dispersion for British and German exports from 1970 to 1993.
28. Especially relative to exports back to Japan from Asian affiliates of Japanese companies.

Table 7.4   U.S. Export RCAs by Region, SITC Two-Digit Level, Manufacturing

Category	SITC	EU15	NAFTA	Latin6	Japan	Tiger	OthAs4	China	Others	Weighted Dispersion[a]	Dispersion[b]	Weighted Correlation[c]	Correlation[d]
								A. 1995					
Organic chemicals	51	89.9	129.4	153.1	125.3	210.2	219.8	176.7	112.2	0.35	0.31	0.93	0.61
Inorganic chemicals	52	90.9	83.0	122.2	220.8	223.5	241.9	48.1	72.3	0.51	0.60	0.87	0.94
Dyeing, tanning, and coloring materials	53	81.8	163.0	155.4	101.4	189.8	203.7	102.4	121.8	0.34	0.33	0.98	0.97
Medicinal and pharmaceutical products	54	87.7	160.6	171.7	186.6	191.7	235.0	34.9	98.1	0.38	0.62	0.98	0.97
Essential oils and perfume materials, toilet-cleansing materials	55	79.7	150.4	146.3	229.7	183.1	212.3	95.3	126.0	0.37	0.37	0.94	0.61
Fertilizers, manufactured	56	136.3	40.5	177.0	267.5	241.0	229.3	289.1	144.3	0.62	0.64	0.47	0.90
Artificial resins, plastic materials, cellulose esters/ethers	58	134.0	135.7	163.2	121.6	201.3	232.9	272.0	139.4	0.22	0.29	0.44	0.31
Chemical materials and products n.e.s.	59	118.4	173.0	163.7	155.4	213.4	175.4	182.3	98.0	0.23	0.25	0.72	0.46
Leather, leather manufactures n.e.s., and dressed fur/skins	61	46.8	124.0	8.3	237.0	159.1	128.9	80.0	17.7	0.62	1.16	0.98	0.83
Rubber manufactures n.e.s.	62	76.4	123.1	107.5	55.5	44.3	49.7	12.9	98.3	0.35	0.72	0.58	0.05

Cork and wood manufactures (excluding furniture)	63	123.6	49.1	37.8	270.8	79.3	12.2	40.3	112.1	0.74	0.94	0.64	0.56
Paper, paperboard, articles of paper, paper pulp/board	64	76.6	64.7	138.4	203.2	183.2	220.0	205.3	145.8	0.52	0.47	0.91	0.81
Textile yarn, fabrics, made-up articles, related products	65	76.4	142.6	107.4	98.4	63.7	51.6	22.2	86.6	0.39	0.57	0.95	0.54
Nonmetallic mineral manufactures n.e.s.	66	49.0	109.5	69.6	101.6	121.1	99.5	54.8	29.2	0.50	0.49	0.96	0.73
Iron and steel	67	31.8	97.1	44.5	33.7	108.5	158.4	107.8	35.2	0.52	0.65	0.90	0.76
Nonferrous metals	68	92.3	64.7	31.6	200.8	212.7	195.2	170.5	26.1	0.62	0.85	0.76	0.25
Manufactures of metal n.e.s.	69	71.4	135.8	137.9	58.9	40.3	127.2	31.9	88.7	0.44	0.56	0.96	0.73
Power-generating machinery and equipment	71	94.0	125.6	123.9	60.5	177.1	212.9	214.1	127.4	0.31	0.43	0.85	0.74
Machinery specialized for particular industries	72	73.8	146.1	167.8	58.3	199.5	236.0	261.5	122.5	0.47	0.54	0.93	0.80
Metalworking machinery	73	75.7	154.3	128.6	42.2	158.3	215.5	237.7	118.0	0.51	0.57	0.85	0.84
General industrial machinery, equipment, and parts	74	74.7	135.5	143.6	39.2	155.9	191.8	196.9	132.9	0.39	0.54	0.97	0.80
Office machines and automatic data-processing equipment	75	145.3	122.7	172.6	67.9	46.0	61.1	90.4	129.3	0.46	0.47	0.83	0.10

(continued)

Table 7.4 (continued)

Category	SITC	EU15	NAFTA	Latin6	Japan	Tiger	OthAs4	China	Others	Weighted Dispersion[a]	Dispersion[b]	Weighted Correlation[c]	Correlation[d]
Telecommunications and sound-recording apparatus	76	142.1	79.9	154.5	52.9	67.0	44.8	84.6	100.2	0.41	0.44	0.59	0.44
Electrical machinery, apparatus, and appliances n.e.s.	77	110.3	130.0	164.7	76.7	92.4	127.4	66.4	113.9	0.21	0.30	0.92	0.57
Road vehicles (including air-cushion vehicles)	78	55.7	84.1	147.6	31.5	100.3	169.8	75.7	136.5	0.38	0.56	0.85	0.93
Other transport equipment	79	113.5	90.6	145.0	198.5	221.2	180.7	280.2	120.8	0.36	0.38	0.84	0.39
Sanitary, plumbing, heating, and lighting fixtures	81	68.9	102.1	22.6	44.8	112.6	180.9	15.1	142.6	0.64	0.89	0.76	0.28
Furniture and parts thereof	82	45.1	88.9	23.8	11.5	91.0	168.7	5.6	106.3	0.52	1.20	0.89	0.96
Travel goods, handbags, and similar containers	83	14.3	61.1	3.6	1.1	84.3	266.2	0.2	111.6	1.57	2.50	0.52	0.81
Articles of apparel and clothing accessories	84	44.7	45.3	3.4	1.1	85.1	256.7	1.0	13.9	1.04	2.07	0.26	0.87
Footwear	85	16.2	6.9	1.8	1.0	79.0	273.0	0.4	73.2	1.64	2.32	0.96	0.94
Professional, scientific, and controlling instruments	87	131.5	172.0	169.2	201.0	154.1	137.1	187.4	117.7	0.14	0.18	0.86	0.59

Photographic apparatus, optical goods, and watches	88	84.1	158.3	44.0	46.4	138.1	38.9	16.5	133.9	0.55	0.79	0.96	0.43
Miscellaneous manufactured articles n.e.s.	89	96.0	131.5	47.5	82.7	136.4	134.0	15.2	104.7	0.42	0.75	0.89	0.95
Weighted dispersion[e]		0.32	0.26	0.32	0.62	0.61	0.52	0.78	0.34				
Dispersion[f]		0.54	0.35	0.80	0.70	1.26	1.58	1.81	0.61				
B 1980													
Organic chemicals	51	92.5	134.3	151.7	162.3	218.9	268.1	87.4	147.7	0.33	0.38		
Inorganic chemicals	52	84.5	78.1	158.2	209.4	227.4	266.0	53.7	123.1	0.46	0.58		
Dyeing, tanning, and coloring materials	53	67.4	169.4	153.7	107.2	211.5	265.2	75.3	125.6	0.48	0.48		
Medicinal and pharmaceutical products	54	131.2	172.4	160.5	202.5	211.2	259.7	46.2	150.6	0.21	0.53		
Essential oils and perfume materials, toilet-cleansing materials	55	92.3	168.9	135.9	191.9	203.5	202.6	4.4	146.9	0.34	1.30		
Fertilizers, manufactured	56	144.1	30.5	177.4	244.3	232.9	270.2	128.3	99.8	0.56	0.71		
Artificial resins, plastic materials, cellulose esters/ethers	58	118.6	179.8	177.3	154.6	214.2	265.5	128.3	154.6	0.26	0.26		
Chemical materials and products	59	121.4	171.6	160.2	208.4	222.5	267.3	77.9	103.7	0.34	0.42		

(*continued*)

Table 7.4 (continued)

Category	SITC	EU15	NAFTA	Latin6	Japan	Tiger	OthAs4	China	Others	Weighted Dispersion[a]	Dispersion[b]	Weighted Correlation[c]	Correlation[d]
Leather, leather manufactures n.e.s., and dressed fur/skins	61	88.7	127.0	6.7	174.2	165.0	139.3	126.2	101.0	0.40	1.07		
Rubber manufactures n.e.s.	62	32.1	104.1	170.2	10.0	19.4	196.3	124.6	112.0	0.75	1.10		
Cork and wood manufactures (excluding furniture)	63	113.9	50.1	93.6	76.2	3.9	3.5	30.0	120.4	0.63	1.45		
Paper, paperboard, articles of paper, paper-pulp/board	64	123.2	34.1	164.3	212.9	181.2	269.8	126.7	154.6	0.74	0.62		
Textile yarn, fabrics, made-up articles, related products	65	104.4	170.3	125.5	60.2	53.7	115.0	63.4	139.9	0.35	0.43		
Nonmetallic mineral manufactures	66	40.7	132.3	123.9	58.9	126.6	126.1	9.5	22.2	0.69	0.98		
Iron and steel	67	30.8	100.9	91.1	4.4	54.6	262.1	128.2	33.5	0.72	1.24		
Nonferrous metals	68	111.8	51.1	60.6	153.9	131.4	31.3	47.5	56.4	0.43	0.56		
Manufactures of metal n.e.s.	69	83.8	137.7	136.3	33.7	42.4	245.8	82.2	113.0	0.45	0.65		
Power-generating machinery and equipment	71	87.2	146.2	155.7	96.6	194.8	268.9	127.1	150.4	0.33	0.36		

Machinery specialized for particular industries	72	78.0	152.8	176.2	87.9	212.0	266.9	127.9	150.0	0.37	0.42
Metalworking machinery	73	58.1	159.9	156.7	32.4	129.5	269.7	104.0	144.5	0.57	0.66
General industrial machinery, equipment, and parts	74	94.8	162.0	171.4	79.6	184.3	267.6	121.7	147.8	0.32	0.39
Office machines and automatic data-processing equipment	75	138.7	140.7	166.5	110.6	110.2	264.7	128.2	146.3	0.11	0.28
Telecommunications and sound-recording apparatus	76	117.2	131.2	161.2	12.1	33.8	178.9	122.9	140.9	0.71	0.95
Electrical machinery, apparatus, and appliances n.e.s.	77	108.2	165.0	156.3	59.0	69.0	83.8	114.8	142.9	0.36	0.38
Road vehicles (including air-cushion vehicles)	78	23.6	103.9	160.1	3.9	80.5	268.4	128.1	149.4	0.66	1.37
Other transport equipment	79	117.1	130.7	159.7	174.1	176.2	268.6	128.3	120.8	0.25	0.28
Sanitary, plumbing, heating, and lighting fixtures	81	67.2	156.2	47.9	212.0	139.9	127.1	34.8	21.2	0.60	0.82
Furniture and parts thereof	82	43.5	119.2	10.6	9.5	99.5	88.2	3.2	113.2	0.59	1.40
Travel goods, handbags, and similar containers	83	12.7	33.1	3.5	38.7	151.6	62.7	0.4	116.1	1.44	2.01

(*continued*)

Table 7.4 (continued)

Category	SITC	EU15	NAFTA	Latin6	Japan	Tiger	OthAs4	China	Others	Weighted Dispersion[a]	Dispersion[b]	Weighted Correlation[c]	Correlation[d]
Articles of apparel and clothing accessories	84	76.6	112.3	1.2	2.1	135.2	71.8	0.0	49.5	0.81	2.94		
Footwear	85	22.6	11.1	0.5	1.7	65.4	120.5	0.0	132.9	0.90	2.18		
Professional, scientific, and controlling instruments	87	120.9	170.2	178.5	260.5	166.0	155.8	127.1	141.6	0.19	0.24		
Photographic apparatus, optical goods, watches	88	101.6	174.8	46.0	229.3	150.1	38.0	105.4	144.5	0.50	0.63		
Miscellaneous manufactured articles n.e.s.	89	99.5	147.8	20.3	98.9	155.6	81.5	8.3	118.2	0.43	1.05		
Weighted dispersion[e]		0.36	0.31	0.22	0.82	0.69	0.44	0.38	0.38				
Dispersion[f]		0.59	0.47	0.75	1.06	1.61	1.45	1.85	0.53				
Weighted correlation[g]		0.89	0.93	0.76	0.82	0.79	0.43	0.51	0.87				
Correlation[h]		0.85	0.88	0.92	0.73	0.92	0.83	0.79	0.56				

Note: n.e.s. = not elsewhere specified.

[a] RCA dispersion across regions by sector, weighted by export share, 1995 and 1980. Dispersion = standard deviation of natural logs of indexes/100.

[b] RCA dispersion across regions by sector, unweighted, 1995 and 1980. Dispersion = standard deviation of natural logs of indexes/100.

[c] Cross-regional correlation coefficient by sector, weighted by export share, between 1995 and 1980.

[d] Cross-regional correlation coefficient by sector, unweighted, between 1995 and 1980.

[e] RCA dispersion across sectors by region, weighted by export share, 1995 and 1980. Dispersion = standard deviation of natural logs of indexes/100.

[f] RCA dispersion across sectors by region, unweighted, 1995 and 1980. Dispersion = standard deviation of natural logs of indexes/100.

[g] Cross-sectoral correlation coefficient, weighted by export share, between 1995 and 1980.

[h] Cross-sectoral correlation coefficient, unweighted, between 1995 and 1980.

are stable over time, they are more mixed across trading partners, with comparative advantage in some markets and disadvantage in others, depending on product group.

In standardized manufactures (SITC 5 and 6), U.S. patterns of comparative advantage are surprisingly different, both qualitatively and quantitatively, across trading partners. In chemical subproducts (SITC 51–59), U.S. comparative advantage is strong across the board in both 1980 and 1995, except in Europe. It is exceptionally strong in Asia (except in China),[29] often ranging above 200. U.S. comparative advantage in paper and wood products (SITC 63 and 64) and in nonferrous metals (SITC 68) is also exceptionally strong in Asia—in 1995 especially—and usually nonexistent (U.S. disadvantage) elsewhere. In iron and steel (SITC 67), U.S. export performance in both 1980 and 1995 ranges from strong comparative advantage (in OthAs4) to strong comparative disadvantage (in Europe and Japan).

In differentiated manufactures (SITC 7 and 8), there are several varieties of pattern. The first two varieties characterize producer goods and seem very stable over time; the second two characterize consumer goods and are chaotic.

Variety 1: Stable Patterns across Time, Common across Trading Partners. Instruments (SITC 87) shows strong patterns of U.S. comparative advantage for every set of trading partners in both 1980 and 1995.

Variety 2: Stable Patterns across Time, Diverse across Trading Partners. Producer goods other than instruments show stable comparative advantage over time, but diversity across trading partners. Nonelectrical industrial machinery (SITC 71–74) shows strong patterns of U.S. comparative advantage in both 1980 and 1995 for every set of trading partners except Europe and Japan.[30] Electrical machinery (SITC 77) shows reasonably strong U.S. comparative advantage in both 1980 and 1995 everywhere except Asia. In Asia, the main exception to temporal stability is China, where U.S. comparative advantage in electrical machinery in 1980 becomes strong *dis*advantage by 1995.[31]

Variety 3: Changing Patterns across Time, Diverse across Trading Partners. Computers and office equipment (SITC 75) shows strong patterns of U.S. comparative advantage for every set of trading partners in 1980, but the

29. In China, U.S. chemicals comparative advantage is quite different across subproducts and quite volatile over time.

30. This pattern is consistent with both Japan's and Europe's importing preferentially from other countries in our data set. For Japan, such preferential spheres of influence seem likely to include most other Asian exporters; for Europe, such preferential patterns might be seen with exports from former colonies.

31. This pattern might occur, for example, if U.S. foreign investors in China displaced their previous exports to China faster than rival exporters did.

comparative advantage remains in 1995 only for non-Asian regions; in Asia, U.S. advantage has turned to marked disadvantage.

Variety 4: Chaotic Patterns across Time and Trading Partners. Consumer goods categories (SITC 76, 78, 81–84) all reveal quite erratic patterns, with the exception of footwear and photographic apparatus (SITC 85, 88).[32]

7.7 Less Aggregated (Three-Digit SITC) Patterns for Machinery and Equipment

To see whether patterns of comparative advantage become even more interesting at the three-digit level, we selected machinery and equipment (SITC 7) for deeper analysis. That sector is both large and tempting as a venue for national industrial policies. The very disaggregated region-by-region export data are, however, unfortunately suspect in the early years for China and emerging Asia, and also for office equipment (SITC 75) and road vehicles (SITC 78).

Table 7.5 refines the picture of U.S. worldwide comparative advantage in machinery and equipment.[33] The United States has strong and consistent comparative disadvantage in the three consumer goods categories (SITC 761–762, radios and televisions, and 775, other household equipment). Among producer goods, the United States has strong, stable comparative advantage in some categories, but not in others. RCAs are high and stable for power-generating equipment (except standard internal combustion engines), pumps, heating and cooling equipment, agricultural and specialized machinery, and aircraft; but RCAs are lower and less stable for machine tools, electrical equipment, and producer goods for more mature, standardized industries (textiles, paper, printing, railways, and shipping).[34]

Across trading partners, the patterns in table 7.6 for machinery and equipment exports recall those of table 7.4 for all manufactures.

Producer goods subproducts mimic variety 2 (mentioned previously) because they are stable over time[35] (with some exceptions), but are very

---

32. Footwear (SITC 85) shows enormous U.S. comparative disadvantage, except in Asian near-Tigers (OthAs4) and Tigers. U.S. comparative advantage in photographic apparatus, optical goods, and watches (SITC 88) varies dramatically across trading partners, but is reasonably stable except in Japan, where it declines precipitously from strong advantage to strong disadvantage.

33. In table 7.5, "all categories" in the definition of the RCA index refers to all selected three-digit categories of machinery and equipment, whereas in table 7.3 it refers to all manufactured exports, and in table 7.1 to all merchandise exports.

34. Moenius and Riker (1998) find that sectoral patterns of U.S. trade in machinery and equipment (SITC 7) are far more volatile over time than in other sectors. Intervening years between 1980 and 1995 may indeed reveal patterns of similar volatility, especially because those years marked a period of exceptionally strong real exchange values for the dollar and exceptionally weak Latin American markets relative to those elsewhere in the world.

35. The correlations between 1980 RRCAs and 1995 RRCAs drop considerably from their two-digit counterparts.

Table 7.5　　　　**U.S. Export RCAs, SITC Three-Digit Level, Machinery and Equipment**

	SITC	1995	1980
Steam and other vapor-generating boilers and parts	711	169.4	141.7
Steam and other vapor power units, steam engines	712	185.0	152.0
Internal-combustion piston engines and parts	713	94.0	119.7
Engines and motors, nonelectric	714	131.9	126.9
Rotating electric plant and parts	716	105.2	138.3
Other power-generating machinery and parts	718	94.6	107.4
Agricultural machinery and parts	721	152.7	123.5
Tractors fitted or not with power take-offs, etc.	722	95.3	129.8
Civil engineering and contractor's plant and parts	723	142.3	157.3
Textile and leather machinery and parts	724	69.3	89.6
Paper and pulp-mill machinery, machinery for manufacture of paper	725	117.3	99.3
Printing and bookbinding machinery and parts	726	91.5	118.6
Food-processing machines and parts	727	120.2	141.7
Machinery and equipment specialized for particular industries	728	130.8	130.1
Machinery and tools for working metal and metal carbides, and parts	736	103.3	90.6
Metal-working machinery and parts	737	80.5	125.1
Heating and cooling equipment and parts	741	143.1	156.8
Pumps for liquids, liquid elevators, and parts	742	126.1	136.8
Pumps and compressors, fans and blowers, centrifuges	743	114.6	147.3
Mechanical handling equipment and parts	744	120.9	146.7
Other nonelectrical machinery, tools, apparatus, and parts	745	120.8	134.6
Ball, roller, or needle-roller bearings	749	84.4	107.2
Television receivers	761	33.0	84.4
Radio broadcast receivers	762	22.7	14.8
Telecommunications equipment and parts	764	94.0	69.7
Electric-power machinery and parts thereof	771	81.4	95.1
Electrical appliances such as switches, relays, fuses, plugs, etc.	772	104.8	121.3
Equipment for distributing electricity	773	99.6	129.6
Electric apparatus for medical purposes (e.g., radiology)	774	114.1	87.0
Household-type electrical and nonelectrical equipment	775	70.3	72.3
Thermionic, cold, and photo-cathode valves, tubes, parts	776	114.3	88.7
Electrical machinery and apparatus, n.e.s.	778	93.5	120.3
Railway vehicles and associated equipment	791	93.8	88.3
Aircraft and associated equipment and parts	792	156.2	150.8
Ships, boats, and floating structures	793	64.5	69.9
Weighted correlation[a]		0.86	
Correlation[b]		0.81	

Note: n.e.s. = not elsewhere specified.

[a]Cross-sectoral correlation coefficient, weighted by export share, between 1995 and 1980.

[b]Cross-sectoral correlation coefficient, unweighted, between 1995 and 1980.

Table 7.6 U.S. Export RCAs by Region, SITC Three-Digit Level, Machinery and Equipment

	SITC	EU15	NAFTA	Latin6	Japan	Tiger	OthAs4	China	Others	Weighted Dispersion[a]	Dispersion[b]	Weighted Correlation[c]	Correlation[d]
						A. 1995							
Steam and other vapor-generating boilers and parts	711	125.3	65.5	180.0	254.7	240.4	249.9	288.0	151.8	0.51	0.49	0.25	0.10
Steam and other vapor power units, steam engines	712	108.8	125.4	176.8	221.8	223.4	250.4	289.2	145.5	0.29	0.35	0.79	−0.09
Internal-combustion piston engines and parts	713	69.7	134.7	99.8	10.9	192.1	246.2	181.4	146.1	0.49	0.99	0.92	0.84
Engines and motors, nonelectric	714	104.9	107.7	140.6	237.3	185.9	214.8	234.6	110.5	0.34	0.36	0.97	0.30
Rotating electric plant and parts	716	84.5	109.0	141.5	45.9	121.3	170.8	144.0	131.6	0.29	0.41	0.78	0.75
Other power-generating machinery and parts	718	48.7	146.7	142.3	26.3	198.0	248.5	254.5	126.8	0.60	0.80	0.99	0.93
Agricultural machinery and parts	721	132.9	140.9	164.0	179.0	198.9	247.3	251.6	126.0	0.16	0.27	0.60	0.10
Tractors fitted or not with power take-offs, etc.	722	73.3	109.2	161.6	10.7	208.2	250.6	202.7	151.5	0.51	1.02	0.78	0.91
Civil engineering and contractor's plant and parts	723	81.5	173.6	167.2	18.6	178.0	249.7	282.4	146.5	0.44	0.87	0.89	0.29

Textile and leather machinery and parts	724	32.6	193.0	141.1	16.1	85.8	235.5	153.7	134.8	0.87	0.94	0.99	0.89
Paper and pulp-mill machinery, machinery for manufacture of paper	725	52.3	155.1	170.6	91.3	199.1	248.1	241.8	144.7	0.54	0.53	0.98	0.62
Printing and bookbinding machinery and parts	726	54.9	137.0	175.7	39.8	220.4	241.8	280.4	60.9	0.67	0.76	0.87	0.42
Food-processing machines and parts	727	56.4	156.2	171.9	142.8	202.6	239.8	282.8	129.8	0.57	0.49	0.92	0.25
Machinery and equipment specialized for particular industries	728	81.7	141.4	172.6	82.3	210.8	228.4	272.7	117.2	0.44	0.46	0.82	0.21
Machinery and tools for working metal and metal carbides, and parts	736	77.5	159.4	128.7	42.9	158.4	214.2	235.2	116.6	0.51	0.56	0.86	0.70
Metal-working machinery and parts	737	37.9	98.1	122.7	9.3	151.6	249.8	284.5	148.6	0.72	1.12	0.59	0.61
Heating and cooling equipment and parts	741	93.0	152.5	163.6	75.2	196.1	175.8	277.1	134.1	0.33	0.41	0.87	-0.06
Pumps for liquids, liquid elevators, and parts	742	84.6	170.0	111.3	48.2	193.1	246.6	229.3	141.3	0.43	0.55	0.92	0.89

(*continued*)

Table 7.6 (continued)

	SITC	EU15	NAFTA	Latin6	Japan	Tiger	OthAs4	China	Others	Weighted Dispersion[a]	Dispersion[b]	Weighted Correlation[c]	Correlation[d]
Pumps and compressors, fans and blowers, centrifuges	743	60.8	163.6	85.8	31.1	162.5	155.5	205.4	147.1	0.47	0.64	0.82	0.25
Mechanical handling equipment and parts	744	81.6	128.6	168.9	28.9	163.0	245.3	181.2	142.5	0.40	0.67	0.98	0.63
Other nonelectrical machinery, tools, apparatus, and parts	745	85.6	156.8	170.8	66.0	115.5	231.2	248.6	137.8	0.37	0.46	0.96	0.18
Ball, roller, or needle-roller bearings	749	52.8	113.8	135.4	22.5	109.8	162.0	79.5	104.1	0.45	0.64	0.98	0.93
Television receivers	761	89.1	26.3	180.1	10.5	82.7	4.4	7.1	134.4	0.90	1.44	−0.47	0.15
Radio broadcast receivers	762	61.3	78.2	32.0	10.8	5.2	0.7	0.1	17.3	0.89	2.33	0.93	−0.01
Telecommunications equipment and parts	764	143.8	99.5	178.1	58.6	80.0	65.7	127.1	105.7	0.36	0.39	0.79	0.53
Electric-power machinery and parts thereof	771	81.8	105.3	159.5	52.5	46.1	65.6	32.6	119.1	0.38	0.53	0.69	0.60
Electrical appliances such as switches, relays, fuses, plugs, etc.	772	101.9	133.6	153.4	38.8	94.0	83.9	94.8	83.1	0.31	0.41	0.89	0.60

Equipment for distributing electricity	773	135.7	97.7	146.4	75.8	91.3	67.1	111.5	137.4	0.18	0.29	-0.72	-0.18
Electrical apparatus for medical purposes (e.g., radiology)	774	76.2	167.9	177.8	142.4	234.0	246.7	286.3	112.7	0.47	0.44	0.90	0.56
Household-type electrical and nonelectrical equipment	775	72.0	118.8	171.7	116.0	20.0	31.3	4.4	142.2	0.64	1.26	0.83	0.24
Thermionic, cold, and photo-cathode valves, tubes, and parts	776	126.2	163.8	176.0	90.8	103.4	137.0	176.0	123.2	0.22	0.24	0.77	0.34
Electrical machinery and apparatus n.e.s.	778	107.6	112.9	164.4	48.9	75.2	123.0	64.1	112.5	0.30	0.39	0.65	0.86
Railway vehicles and associated equipment	791	46.2	91.9	123.4	32.4	227.8	249.8	252.3	127.1	0.36	0.77	0.47	0.88
Aircraft and associated equipment and parts	792	119.8	97.2	143.3	227.4	233.1	179.8	281.4	119.9	0.36	0.38	0.87	0.01
Ships, boats, and floating structures	793	51.0	53.5	166.5	50.3	21.2	216.2	209.8	129.5	0.61	0.84	0.25	0.47
Weighted dispersion[c]		0.28	0.25	0.19	0.68	0.46	0.39	0.48	0.17				
Dispersion[b]		0.37	0.39	0.32	0.97	0.83	1.23	1.58	0.38				

(*continued*)

Table 7.6 (continued)

SITC		EU15	NAFTA	Latin6	Japan	Tiger	OthAs4	China	Others	Weighted Dispersion[a]	Dispersion[b]	Weighted Correlation[c]	Correlation[d]
	B. 1980												
711	Steam and other vapor-generating boilers and parts	63.2	146.8	175.5	130.7	226.8	270.2	64.2	156.7	0.41	0.53		
712	Steam and other vapor power units, steam engines	107.4	145.4	178.7	62.8	232.9	270.2	64.2	156.7	0.41	0.54		
713	Internal-combustion piston engines and parts	69.5	155.6	131.8	27.8	215.4	269.8	64.2	153.1	0.43	0.75		
714	Engines and motors, nonelectric	95.3	112.4	174.2	242.0	188.3	267.2	64.2	146.8	0.37	0.48		
716	Rotating electric plant and parts	106.5	171.8	176.7	40.3	159.1	269.5	64.2	151.9	0.34	0.62		
718	Other power-generating machinery and parts	54.6	181.5	172.0	65.7	202.5	270.2	n.a.	114.1	0.55	0.60		
721	Agricultural machinery and parts	111.8	119.4	176.8	152.6	206.1	270.2	64.2	139.8	0.15	0.43		
722	Tractors fitted or not with power take-offs, etc.	41.8	170.3	176.7	21.6	231.7	262.3	128.3	156.9	0.49	0.88		
723	Civil engineering and contractor's plant and parts	112.0	162.1	177.6	101.3	227.8	268.0	64.2	153.6	0.28	0.46		
724	Textile and leather machinery and parts	50.8	168.4	163.5	29.7	105.4	260.9	64.2	142.8	0.64	0.73		

Paper and pulp-mill machinery, for manufacture of paper	725	55.4	123.1	174.1	86.7	229.8	270.2	64.2	155.9	0.50	0.58
Printing and bookbinding machinery and parts	726	90.4	125.8	179.0	72.7	226.2	267.9	64.2	154.3	0.34	0.52
Food-processing machines and parts	727	86.2	175.5	177.2	174.4	204.9	266.4	64.2	145.2	0.36	0.47
Machinery and equipment specialized for particular industries	728	76.8	161.9	175.6	144.4	218.2	266.8	64.2	135.4	0.43	0.49
Machinery and tools for working metal and metal carbides, and parts	736	59.0	162.1	155.4	32.0	128.2	269.6	64.2	144.5	0.58	0.69
Metal-working machinery and parts	737	91.2	139.8	179.1	51.0	226.1	270.2	64.2	144.8	0.29	0.59
Heating and cooling equipment and parts	741	113.1	174.5	174.2	132.9	229.1	268.9	64.2	152.5	0.27	0.44
Pumps for liquids, liquid elevators, and parts	742	81.6	171.1	167.4	92.3	203.1	269.8	n.a.	139.2	0.39	0.42
Pumps and compressors, fans and blowers, centrifuges	743	99.6	184.2	174.7	100.3	167.8	269.2	64.2	147.3	0.32	0.45

(*continued*)

Table 7.6 (continued)

	SITC	EU15	NAFTA	Latin6	Japan	Tiger	OthAs4	China	Others	Weighted Dispersion[a]	Dispersion[b]	Weighted Correlation[c]	Correlation[d]
Mechanical handling equipment and parts	744	110.5	151.6	177.4	68.5	191.8	265.3	64.2	155.2	0.26	0.50		
Other nonelectrical machinery, tools, apparatus, and parts	745	98.0	156.8	173.0	104.6	200.3	268.6	64.2	146.3	0.29	0.45		
Ball, roller, or needle-roller bearings	749	69.6	150.1	159.5	40.2	125.6	264.3	64.2	134.0	0.45	0.61		
Television receivers	761	34.1	177.3	179.1	2.2	27.8	270.2	64.2	157.0	0.64	1.58		
Radio broadcast receivers	762	51.0	154.2	54.2	0.0	1.0	77.9	64.2	66.7	0.88	2.95		
Telecommunications equipment and parts	764	119.7	119.1	177.7	17.2	43.9	189.2	64.2	142.7	0.63	0.82		
Electric-power machinery and parts thereof	771	70.2	129.7	166.5	39.9	79.3	230.8	64.2	143.6	0.45	0.58		
Electrical appliances such as switches, relays, fuses, plugs, etc.	772	106.3	167.7	163.7	75.5	133.5	69.9	64.2	145.4	0.29	0.39		
Equipment for distributing electricity	773	114.3	144.1	122.4	59.8	163.4	269.6	64.2	149.0	0.25	0.49		
Electrical apparatus for medical purposes (e.g., radiology)	774	38.6	135.1	179.0	193.8	225.6	264.4	64.2	82.4	0.74	0.68		

Household-type electrical and nonelectrical equipment	775	58.9	176.5	168.1	18.0	20.2	268.0	64.2	154.1	0.80	1.02
Thermionic, cold, and photo-cathode valves, tubes, parts	776	115.1	156.4	130.5	62.4	82.6	71.1	64.2	150.5	0.33	0.38
Electrical machinery and apparatus n.e.s.	778	104.0	180.1	148.1	51.1	103.3	239.6	64.2	144.6	.39	.52
Railway vehicles and associated equipment	791	16.8	108.1	83.9	9.8	230.4	270.2	64.2	96.4	0.50	1.16
Aircraft and associated equipment and parts	792	120.6	136.2	170.5	230.8	204.6	268.6	64.2	123.4	0.32	0.46
Ships, boats, and floating structures	793	93.8	130.4	132.5	6.4	47.1	268.1	64.2	88.7	0.54	1.11
Weighted dispersion[e]		0.25	0.14	0.13	0.86	0.56	0.44	0.08	0.10		
Dispersion[f]		0.44	0.15	0.24	1.62	1.05	0.37	0.12	0.20		
Weighted correlation[g]		0.76	0.29	0.50	0.94	0.86	0.55	-0.29	0.28		
Correlation[h]		0.48	0.15	0.74	0.56	0.92	0.49	0.06	0.60		

Note: n.e.s. = not elsewhere specified. n.a. = not available.

[a]RCA dispersion across regions by sector, weighted by export share, 1995 and 1980. Dispersion = standard deviation of natural logs of indexes/100.

[b]RCA dispersion across regions by sector, unweighted, 1995 and 1980. Dispersion = standard deviation of natural logs of indexes/100.

[c]Cross-regional correlation coefficient by sector, weighted by export share, between 1995 and 1980.

[d]Cross-regional correlation coefficient by sector, unweighted, between 1995 and 1980.

[e]RCA dispersion across sectors by region, weighted by export share, 1995 and 1980. Dispersion = standard deviation of natural logs of indexes/100.

[f]RCA dispersion across sectors by region, unweighted, 1995 and 1980. Dispersion = standard deviation of natural logs of indexes/100.

[g]Cross-sectoral correlation coefficient, weighted by export share, between 1995 and 1980.

[h]Cross-sectoral correlation coefficient, unweighted, between 1995 and 1980.

diverse across regional markets. That cross-regional diversity seems to be increasing. The dispersion of U.S. comparative advantage across trading partners increases between 1980 and 1995 for twenty out of thirty-two producer goods categories.[36]

The three consumer goods subproducts mimic variety 4 in that they are chaotic over time and regional market. In fact, the dispersions of U.S. comparative advantage across trading partners for radio and television exports are larger than those for any of the thirty-two producer goods, and the cross-regional dispersion for household equipment is sixth highest among the thirty-five categories.

There is some, though very limited, evidence of sectoral niche specialization. The cross-product dispersion indexes rise between 1980 and 1995 in five of the eight regional markets for U.S. exports, but several (especially China's) are suspect due to the poor quality of the 1980 data. And though U.S. comparative disadvantage becomes sharper for machinery and equipment in the Asian Tigers between 1980 and 1995 (part of a niche specialization story), U.S. comparative advantage does not. Nor is there any evidence of increasing sectoral niche specialization in U.S. exports of machinery and equipment to Europe or Japan.

7.8   Addendum: Using Import Data Alone

Our RCA indexes in this paper are based on U.S. export data alone. Comparative advantage is measured by U.S. versus rival export performance in world and regional markets. Comparative advantage is signaled by indexes that are greater than 100.

However, comparative advantage might also be signaled by RCA indexes based on U.S. import data alone. In contrast to export-based measures, these would measure the relative competitiveness of foreign exporters in U.S. markets. By way of an analogy to this construction, the import-based measure would be the share of industry i in total U.S. imports divided by the share of industry i in the rest of the world's total imports. U.S. comparative advantage would be signaled by RCA indexes that were less than 100. If the rest of the world in these measures were to include only a subset of peer importer countries, then we would have the import-based counterpart to the focus of this paper, our RRCAs (regional RCA indexes). For example, relative to its NAFTA partners, the United States would be said to have comparative advantage in sector i if its import shares of i were lower than those of Canada and Mexico (relative to its import shares of everything else).

It is not clear that the export-based and import-based measures would

36. In table 7.4, only 18 of the 34 two-digit submanufactures showed increasing cross-regional dispersion between 1980 and 1995.

(or should) parallel the underlying reality of U.S. comparative advantage. The most important reason is that the markets in which U.S. comparative advantage is being measured differ—non-U.S. markets in one case, U.S. markets in the other. Therefore, export-based U.S. RCA measures would be expected to differ from import-based U.S. RCA measures, for precisely the same reasons that RRCA measures differ across the various trading-partner markets. Furthermore, with a trading partner with which two-way trade is high, both the export-derived RCA and the import-derived RCA might be above 100, signaling simultaneous comparative advantage and disadvantage. The problem is actually in the concept, not in the measure; the apparently anomalous measures are accurately reflecting the intrinsic ambiguity of any concept of comparative advantage in which two-way trade is high.

References

Balassa, Bela. 1965. Trade liberalization and "revealed" comparative advantage. *Manchester School of Economic and Social Studies* 33 (May): 90–123. Reprinted as chap. 4 of Balassa (1989).

———. 1977. "Revealed" comparative advantage revisited. *Manchester School of Economic and Social Studies* 45 (December): 327–44. Reprinted as chap. 5 of Balassa (1989).

———. 1979. The changing pattern of comparative advantage in manufactured goods. *Review of Economics and Statistics* 61 (May): 259–66. Reprinted as chap. 2 of Balassa (1989).

———. 1989. *Comparative advantage, trade policy, and economic development.* New York: New York University Press.

Balassa, Bela, and associates. 1964. *Studies in trade liberalization: Problems and prospects for the industrial countries.* Baltimore: Johns Hopkins University Press.

Balassa, Bela, and Luc Bauwens. 1988. *Changing trade patterns in manufactured goods: An econometric investigation.* Contributions to Economic Analysis no. 176. Amsterdam: North-Holland.

Balassa, Bela, and Marcus Noland. 1988. *Japan in the world economy.* Washington, D.C.: Institute for International Economics.

———. 1989. The changing comparative advantage of Japan and the United States. *Journal of the Japanese and International Economies* 3 (June).

Greytak, David, J. David Richardson, and Pamela J. Smith. 1999. *Intra-national, intra-regional trade in manufactures: What can we learn from the "51" United States in 1963?* Maxwell School, Syracuse University. Unpublished.

Heston, Alan, and Robert E. Lipsey, eds. 1999. *International and interarea comparisons of income, output, and prices.* Studies in Income and Wealth, vol. 61. Chicago: University of Chicago Press.

Hillman, Arye. 1980. Observations on the relation between revealed comparative advantage and comparative advantage as indicated by pre-trade relative prices. *Weltwirtschaftliches Archiv* 116 (2): 315–21.

Hoekman, Bernard, and Simeon Djankov. 1997. Determinants of the export structure of countries in Central and Eastern Europe. *World Bank Economic Review* 11 (3): 471–87.

Hummels, David, Dana Rapaport, and Kei-Mu Yi. 1998. Vertical specialization and the changing nature of world trade. *Economic Policy Review* 4 (2): 79–99.

Keller, Wolfgang. 1998. Product differentiation, scale economies, and foreign trade. Paper presented at the Fifth Annual Empirical Investigations in International Trade Conference, Purdue University, 13–15 November.

Kirova, Milka S., and Robert E. Lipsey. 1998. Measuring real investment: Trends in the United States and international comparisons. NBER Working Paper no. 6404. Cambridge, Mass.: National Bureau of Economic Research, February.

Kravis, Irving B., and Robert E. Lipsey. 1971. *Price competitiveness in world trade.* New York: Columbia University Press.

———. 1992. Sources of competitiveness of the United States and of its multinational firms. *Review of Economics and Statistics* 74 (2): 193–201.

Kreinin, Mordechai, and Michael G. Plummer. 1994a. "Natural" economic blocs: An alternative formulation. *International Trade Journal* 8 (2): 193–205.

———. 1994b. Structural change and regional integration in East Asia. *International Economic Journal* 8 (2): 1–12.

Leamer, Edward E. 1997. Evidence of Ricardian and Heckscher-Ohlin effects in OECD specialization patterns. In *Quiet pioneering: Robert M. Stern and his international economic legacy,* ed. K. E. Maskus, P. M. Hooper, E. E. Leamer, and J. D. Richardson. Ann Arbor: University of Michigan Press.

Maskus, Keith E., Peter M. Hooper, Edward E. Leamer, and J. David Richardson, eds. 1997. *Quiet pioneering: Robert M. Stern and his international economic legacy.* Ann Arbor: University of Michigan Press.

Moenius, Johannes, and David Riker. 1998. Trade barriers and the volatility of comparative advantage. Paper presented at the Fifth Annual Empirical Investigations in International Trade Conference, Purdue University, 13–15 November.

Proudman, James, and Stephen Redding. 1997. Persistence and mobility in international trade. Bank of England Working Paper Series no. 64, June.

Schott, Peter K. 1998. One size fits all? Theory, evidence, and implications of cones of diversification. Paper presented at the Fifth Annual Empirical Investigations in International Trade Conference, Purdue University, 13–15 November.

Wolff, Edward N. 1999. Specialization and productivity performance in low-, medium-, and high-tech manufacturing industries. In *International and interarea comparisons of income, output, and prices,* ed. A. Heston and R. E. Lipsey. Studies in Income and Wealth, vol. 61. Chicago: University of Chicago Press.

Yeats, Alexander. 1998. Just how big is global production sharing? World Bank Working Paper no. 1871, January.

Comment   Kei-Mu Yi

Since Bela Balassa first developed a convenient way of measuring comparative advantage almost thirty-five years ago, there have been advances in

Kei-Mu Yi is senior economist in the International Research Department at the Federal Reserve Bank of New York.

raw data collection, in matching/linking trade, production, and endowment data, in computation technology, and in the theory of international trade with many goods and factors. We now have the tools and technology to calculate comparative advantage in a variety of economic contexts. Nevertheless, it is still the case that these calculations are usually limited to a few countries, a few sectors, and a few years. Hence, despite the well-known theoretical limitations of Balassa's revealed comparative advantage (RCA) measure, its simplicity and broad applicability—because it requires data on trade flows only—makes it useful in building a set of stylized facts. These facts have the potential to inform our theoretical and theory-based empirical research.

In this paper, David Richardson and Chi Zhang extend the dimensionality of RCAs by constructing indexes with respect to particular geographic regions. The regional revealed comparative advantage (RRCA) index for the United States with respect to Japan, for example, is the U.S. share of world exports of industry i's goods to Japan relative to the U.S. share of world exports of all goods to Japan. Richardson and Zhang calculate RCAs and RRCAs for U.S. exports at the one-digit, two-digit, and three-digit levels for 1980 and 1995. The RRCAs are computed across eight geographic regions.

Relation to Robert E. Lipsey's Research

As Richardson and Zhang note, Bela Balassa "was a master of measurement and analysis," or, in other words, very much in the mold of Robert Lipsey. Lipsey, of course, has made important contributions in the measurement of international prices and quantities throughout the last forty years. From his 1963 book *Price and Quantity Trends in the Foreign Trade of the United States*—which pushed back the frontier of measurement of import and export prices and quantities in several directions, including constructing a complete and accurate time series for 1879–1923, as well as providing more detailed disaggregation—to his more recent work documenting the extent of internationalized production in the world economy, all of his research has been the definitive work in the field.

This paper's broad connection to Lipsey's work is clear: The paper deals with the measurement of exports; it also deals with assessing comparative advantage, which ideally requires accurate measurement of (autarky) relative prices. More specifically, Lipsey himself has calculated RCAs. For example, in Kravis and Lipsey (1992), RCAs are calculated for U.S. multinational exports over time and disaggregated into high technology, medium technology, and low technology. In this work, Kravis and Lipsey find that U.S. multinational RCAs are much higher than overall U.S. RCAs in the high technology and medium technology sectors.

Theoretical Background of RCAs

Revealed comparative advantage for the U.S. in sector i is measured as

$$\frac{X_{\text{U.S.},i}/X_{\text{U.S.}}}{X_{\text{W},i}/X_{\text{W}}},$$

where $X_{j,i}$ denotes exports by country j (U.S. or World) in sector i and X_j denotes total exports by country j. RRCAs are RCAs where exports are defined as exports to a region. Hence, the RRCA for Latin America is U.S. exports of sector i's goods to Latin America (relative to total U.S. exports to Latin America), relative to world (excluding Latin America) exports of sector i's goods to Latin America (relative to total world exports to Latin America).

When does RCA reveal comparative advantage and when does it not? This question has been addressed rigorously elsewhere; I will mention a few cases in which RCA does and does not reveal comparative advantage. Under the classical $2 \times 2 \times 2$ Heckscher-Ohlin model with free trade and identical preferences, RCA does indeed reveal comparative advantage. This is true in the classical Ricardian model with two goods and identical preferences, as well. However, in more general settings, RCA does not reveal comparative advantage. For example, the generalized Heckscher-Ohlin framework with more goods than factors implies

$$p_{a,\text{U.S.}}M \geq 0,$$

$$p_{a,\text{r.o.w.}}(-M) \geq 0,$$

$$(p_{a,\text{U.S.}} - p_{a,\text{r.o.w.}})M \geq 0,$$

where $p_{a,j}$ refers to autarky prices in country j (U.S. or rest-of-world [r.o.w.]), and M denotes the U.S. vector of net imports. On average, the United States will export goods that have lower relative autarky prices, but there is no prediction for particular goods. In other words, it is possible that it will export some goods that have higher autarky prices than that of the rest of the world.

RCAs also do not reveal comparative advantage when tariffs, transportation costs, other nontariff trade barriers and other distortions, or home bias in preferences affect the pattern of exports. In addition, vertical specialization, in which countries import inputs and use them to make export goods, may lead to misleading inferences. For example, Mexico and Spain are major motor-vehicle producers and exporters, which would yield a large RCA or RRCA number for motor vehicles; however, both countries tend to specialize only in motor vehicle assembly.

It is perhaps more appropriate to think of RCA as telling us about competitiveness rather than about comparative advantage. Indeed, Kravis and Lipsey (1992) often refer to their RCA numbers as measures of competitiveness.

Results

The results are presented in six tables, starting with the one-digit SITC trade data, and continuing to the three-digit SITC data, although the latter is only for SITC 7 (machinery and equipment). In all cases, the United States is the reference country. One property of RCAs (and RRCAs) to remember is that at least one sector must have an RCA (or RRCA) < 1 and at least one sector must have an RCA (or RRCA) > 1. In addition, the RCAs can be thought of as weighted averages of the RRCAs, in which the weights are complicated functions of the industry-level and aggregate export shares to the region and to the world.

The major results are summarized as follows:

1. There is very little variation in RCAs or RRCAs over time, at all levels of disaggregation. This means that changes over time in U.S. export patterns tend to be mirrored by changes in world export patterns.

2. There is wide variation in RRCAs across regions, at all levels of disaggregation. This means, for example, that a good that the U.S. exports (relatively) intensively is exported particularly intensively to particular regions, and is not exported intensively to other regions.

3. The machinery and equipment industry (SITC 7) tends to exhibit wider variation in RCAs than do other sectors as the data become more disaggregated—but a similar pattern does not hold for the RRCAs. This means that machinery and equipment contain many different niche goods in which different countries specialize, but that geography exerts an independent effect on export patterns regardless of whether the goods are machinery-and-equipment goods or other goods.

Result 1 is understandable in a context where the major changes in the world tend to be uniform across countries, such as GATT-induced tariff reductions. To the extent that changes tend to be country specific, such as the structural transformation occurring in China between 1980 and 1995, one would expect larger variation over time, and indeed this is present in these tables.

The most interesting aspect of the paper is the breakout into geographic destination. U.S. (relative to world) exports to a country or region exhibit a great deal of variation across one-digit, two-digit, and three-digit SITC sectoral breakouts. This suggests the importance of industry-level, bilateral-partner-specific factors such as transportation costs, regional trade agreements, common resources, and so forth. Were it not for these factors, the RRCAs would equal the RCAs across all geographic destinations. It would be interesting to try to study more formally the linkages between these factors and the RRCAs.

One particular pattern seems curious. Tables 7.4 and 7.6 indicate that the RRCAs involving NAFTA declined for many industries between 1980 and 1995. This is a period during which *maquiladora* trade soared and the United States–Canada Free Trade Agreement was implemented. For example, *maquiladora* exports as a share of Mexico's total exports increased from about 15 percent to more than 30 percent. These exports have tended to concentrate in textiles and apparel, in transportation equipment, and in electronics. In all three industries, most of the gross production is derived from imported inputs; that is, only about 20 percent of the value of gross production represents value added. Most of the imported inputs are from the United States; hence, high *maquiladora* exports in (for example) electronics also mean high U.S. exports of electronic components. Yet in all three industries, the RRCAs declined. This implies that world exports to Mexico in these industries increased by more than U.S. exports to Mexico in these industries. It would be good to try to reconcile the results in this paper with the facts of rapid U.S. export growth to Mexico and Canada.

As just mentioned, it would be useful to tie the RRCA measures formally to possible explanatory factors, such as industry- and bilateral-partner-specific transportation costs, industry-specific regional trade agreements, and so on. Further, just as trade theories and models have been developed to rationalize the gravity equation (indeed, there is now a surplus of such theories), it would be nice to do the same for the RCAs and RRCAs. While it may be true that RCAs do not truly reveal comparative advantage, it is still the case that they may be useful in helping to establish the important forces behind observed trade patterns. Finally, I would suggest including oil-producing countries in the sample, to help remove some of the apparent anomalies in the oil related data.

References

Kravis, Irving B., and Robert E. Lipsey. 1992. Sources of competitiveness of the United States and of its multinational firms. *Review of Economics and Statistics* 74 (2): 193–201.
Lipsey, Robert E. 1963. *Price and quantity trends in the foreign trade of the United States.* Princeton, N.J.: Princeton University Press.

U.S. Trade and Other Policy Options and Programs to Deter Foreign Exploitation of Child Labor

Drusilla K. Brown, Alan V. Deardorff,
and Robert M. Stern

8.1 Introduction

Our paper deals with the increasingly important issue of the exploitation of child labor in developing countries. This has in recent years attracted considerable attention and debate in trade policy circles in the United States and elsewhere. While child labor around the world is an acknowledged fact, its magnitude and characteristics are imperfectly measured. Notwithstanding this, our focus here is primarily analytical insofar as we attempt to model family labor supply decisions in the context of an open economy. This enables us to examine a number of policy options and programs for dealing with child labor exploitation. Hopefully, our work will motivate others to take the next important measurement and empirical steps that are needed to assess the current state of affairs and to devise methods for improving the work and living conditions of children and their families in developing countries.

We begin in section 8.2 with a discussion of the determinants of child labor and selected information on the global, national, and sectoral employment of children. In section 8.3, we discuss the range of policies and programs used in the United States to help effect a reduction in foreign child labor. With the foregoing as background, we turn in section 8.4 to conceptual considerations, using a framework that we have developed to analyze the economic determinants of child labor and the expected conse-

Drusilla K. Brown is associate professor of economics at Tufts University. Alan V. Deardorff is the John W. Sweetland Professor of International Economics and professor of economics and public policy in the Department of Economics and Gerald R. Ford School of Public Policy at the University of Michigan. Robert M. Stern is professor emeritus of economics and public policy in the Department of Economics and Gerald R. Ford School of Public Policy at the University of Michigan.

quences of alternative measures that are designed to reduce child labor. Conclusions and implications for further research and policy are presented in section 8.5.

8.2   Determinants, Magnitudes, and Characteristics of Child Labor

It is useful to begin by considering what is meant by *child labor*. In western societies, chronological age is customarily used to separate childhood from adulthood. In other societies, however, the way childhood is viewed will often be determined by societal factors, including (1) the level of economic development; (2) the level and composition of social expenditures; (3) cultural considerations; and (4) the phase of demographic transition.

The distinction between work and education is also less clear in developing countries. There may be sectors in which children are apprenticed for long periods of time in exchange for benefits that may come later, after they are trained and have acquired on-the-job experience. Child labor can also be difficult to detect—for example, few child workers can be found in the export sectors. According to the U.S. Department of Labor's Bureau of International Labor Affairs (1994, 2) only about 5 percent of employed children work in the export industries in manufacturing and mining. Rather, children are usually found in family-based agriculture, in such services as domestic help, restaurants, and street vending, in prostitution, and in such small scale manufacturing as carpets, garments, and furniture.

As a consequence, there is a wide range of uncertainty about the actual magnitudes involved. Grootaert and Kanbur (1995, 188–89) report results from an International Labour Organization (ILO) survey that concludes that there were approximately 78.5 million economically active children under the age of fifteen years in 1990. Similarly, UNICEF reports 80 million children aged ten to fourteen whose work is characterized as "so long or onerous that it interfered with their normal development" (Grant 1991). However, the total number of working children worldwide is thought to be far greater. The ILO places the figure closer to 100–200 million (U.S. Department of Labor, Bureau of International Labor Affairs 1994, 2). An even larger estimate of child labor is found when the work of younger children is included. For children between ages five and fourteen, the ILO estimates that 250 million are working, of which 120 million are working full time (U.S. Department of Labor, 1998, 1).[1]

In addition to the incidence of child labor, it is worthwhile to consider the conditions under which children work. There is a wealth of information provided by various sources concerning the nature of child labor. For example, the Department of Labor's Bureau of International Labor Affairs

---

1. See Kruse and Mahony (1998) for estimates of the number of children and youth working under conditions that violate U.S. federal and state child labor laws.

(1995, 2–5) describes work for children employed in commercial agriculture:

Large numbers of children may be found toiling in the fields and fisheries from daybreak until dusk. Many of these children work for commercial farms and plantations or fishing operations. Plantations, which produce commodities exclusively for export, employ 20 million persons, or 2 percent of the persons working in the agricultural sector in developing countries. Children make up an estimated 7 to 12 percent of the work force on plantations. . . . Among the products produced by children are cocoa, coffee, coconuts, cotton, fruit and vegetables, jasmine, palm oil, rubber, sisal, sugar cane, tea, tobacco, and vanilla. Children also dive for fish, work on fishing platforms and boats, and work in factories that process fish. . . . The great majority of children in agriculture work as part of a family unit. . . . Workdays can be extremely long. . . . Children in agriculture face many safety and health risks. . . . Regular exposure to dangerous chemical fertilizers and pesticides poses another threat to children.

Children delivered into bonded labor for the purposes of intergenerational debt servitude perhaps suffer most of all. Human Rights Watch (1996, 54) has documented bonded child labor in the Indian footwear industry. They estimate that between 2,000 and 20,000 bonded child laborers as young as six or seven years old are trafficked from the rural villages of Rajasthan to Mumbai annually. Further, Human Rights Watch (1996, 104–5) estimates that 10 to 20 percent of child laborers in the Indian handknotted carpet industry are bonded workers. Generally, these children are trafficked from Bihar or Nepal; a similar situation exists in Nepal itself. Brokers known as *naikes* offer rural families loans in exchange for their children. The children are then sent to Kathmandu to discharge the families' debts by working in carpet factories.

Working conditions for bonded child laborers can be horrific. The Bureau of International Labor Affairs (1995, 2–5) reports that

. . . Forced and bonded child labor can be found in all sectors of the economy. Bonded children working in the carpet industries of India, Pakistan, and Nepal may work up to 20 hours a day. They often sleep, eat and work in the same small, damp room, and are sometimes locked in at night. . . . Many of the children suffer from skin ailments, chronic colds, respiratory problems, spine deformities, and weakened eyesight. . . . In the jungle of south-eastern Peru, children recruited by contractors to work for nine months in gold mines find they must continue to work well beyond that period to pay [what] . . . they owe the contractors. . . . The forced labor of children occurs in the fishing industries of Indonesia, Sri Lanka, the Philippines, India, and Pakistan. . . . Forced child labor is also widespread in the informal service sector, particularly in the employment of child domestic servants and in the sex industry. . . . A different form of child labor in the service sector is the use of young boys, usually kidnapped from southern Asia, as camel jockeys in Persian Gulf States.

Similarly, Human Rights Watch (1996, 104, 109) documents cases in the Indian hand-knotted carpet industry in which children are "forced to work long hours . . . for no wages or nominal wages . . . some being ill-treated, beaten, tortured, abused, branded, and kept half fed, half clad." Children working with sharp instruments frequently cut themselves. The wounds may be treated by "putting sulphur from match heads into the cuts and then lighting them on fire, thereby sealing the wound" and avoiding infection. As adults, these former child workers suffer from badly damaged hands and eyes and stunted growth.

8.3 Policies and Programs for Reducing Foreign Child Labor

Having discussed some of the characteristics of child labor, we now consider the policies and programs used in the United States to deter the foreign employment and exploitation of children. These include (1) U.S. trade policies, (2) economic and technical assistance provided through the ILO, (3) supranational measures, (4) codes of conduct for U.S. firms engaged in foreign production, and (5) consumer labeling. We briefly discuss each of the foregoing.

8.3.1   U.S. Trade Policies

Elimination of child labor exploitation is considered to be a core international labor standard, the others being prohibition of forced labor, freedom of association, the right to organize and bargain collectively, and nondiscrimination in employment. For some time, the United States has had a number of policies and programs designed to achieve these core standards and other standards that bear upon conditions of work; these are summarized in table 8.1. The most recent measure is one sponsored by Congressman Bernard Sanders (I-Vt.) in October 1997 as a rider to the fiscal year 1998 Treasury Appropriations Act, which was approved by voice vote in Congress and signed by President Clinton. Section 1307 of the U.S. Tariff Act of 1930 provides authority for the U.S. Customs Service to prohibit "importation of products made, in whole or in part, with use of convict, forced, or indentured labor under penal sanctions." The Sanders Amendment makes it "explicit that merchandise manufactured with 'forced or indentured child labor' falls within the prohibition of this statute."[2] With funding made available by Congress, the U.S. Customs Service is currently attempting to devise and implement monitoring and inspection

---

2. For further details, see http://www.customs.ustreas.gov/enforce, childfi2.htm. See also "Customs walks tightrope on new child labor law" (1997).

Table 8.1   **Evolution of Labor Standards in U.S. Trade Policy Legislation**

Year	Act	Labor Standards Provisions
1890	McKinley Act	Prohibited imports made by convict labor.
1930	Tariff Act, Section 1307	Prohibited imports of goods made by convict labor, forced labor, or indentured labor under penal sanction.
1933	National Industrial Recovery Act (judged unconstitutional by U.S. Supreme Court in 1935)	Permitted imports only if produced according to U.S. domestic fair labor standards, including the right to organize and bargain collectively, limits on maximum hours of work, and minimum wages.
1974	Trade Act	Directed the President to seek the adoption of fair labor standards in the Tokyo Round of GATT negotiations.
1983	Caribbean Basin Economic Recovery Act	Extended criteria for eligibility as a beneficiary country to include the degree to which workers are afforded reasonable workplace conditions and enjoy the right to organize and bargain collectively.
1984	Generalized System of Preferences Renewal Act	Extended criteria for eligibility as a beneficiary country to include whether the country has taken, or is taking, steps to afford its workers internationally recognized worker rights, defined as including freedom of association; the right to organize and bargain collectively; freedom from forced labor; minimum age for the employment of children; and acceptable conditions of work with respect to wages, hours of work, and occupational safety and health.
1985	Overseas Private Investment Corporation Amendments Act	Required the corporation to insure, reinsure, guarantee, or finance a project in a country only if the country is taking steps to adopt and implement internationally recognized worker rights as defined for GSP purposes above.
1986	Anti-Apartheid Act	Made it incumbent on U.S. firms employing more than twenty-five persons in South Africa to follow a code of conduct that includes fair labor standards.
1987	U.S. participation in Multilateral Investment and Guarantee Agency of World Bank	Made U.S. participation conditional on countries' affording internationally recognized worker rights to their workers.
1988	Trade Act (Omnibus Trade and Competitiveness Act)	Made the systematic denial of internationally recognized worker rights (as defined above) by foreign governments an unfair trade practice and liable for U.S. countermeasures where such denials cause a burden or restriction on U.S. commerce.
1997	Sanders Amendment to 1930 Tariff Act, Section 1307	Included prohibition of merchandise manufactured with forced or indentured child labor.

Source: Adapted in part from Alam (1992, p. 25).

procedures to ban imports produced by forced child labor in response to complaints filed.[3]

The United States also uses preferential tariff treatment of exports to induce developing country trade partners to reduce child labor under the U.S. Generalized System of Preferences (GSP). Since 1984, the GSP program specifies a number of labor rights violations that might be cause for suspension of GSP privileges. Evidence of a change in policies is a condition for the preferences to be reinstated.[4]

8.3.2 Economic and Technical Assistance Provided through the ILO

The United States provides a significant amount of economic and technical assistance to developing countries through its bilateral foreign aid programs and its contributions to multilateral institutions. For our purposes here, we wish to call attention to U.S. assistance to address issues of child labor that are channeled through the ILO. Thus, as noted in U.S. Department of Labor (1998), President Clinton proposed in his fiscal year 1999 budget "a new initiative to fight abusive child labor. The initiative builds on the administration's record of reporting on child labor, aiding the private sector in the development of codes of conduct and labeling efforts, pressing successfully for a greater ILO focus on exploitative child labor, leveraging change in the domestic garment industry through the use of 'hot goods' [sic] laws, and using U.S. laws to suspend trade benefits in response to persistent exploitative child labor practices."

What is especially noteworthy in particular is the U.S. assistance provided to the ILO International Programme for the Elimination of Child Labor (IPEC):[5] "The President's FY 99 . . . budget proposes that the U.S. contribute a total of $30 million—*a 10-fold increase*—to IPEC in support of programs aimed at reducing the most intolerable forms of child labor—forced or indentured work, work by very young children, and work in the most hazardous occupations. The U.S. funds will support multi-dimensional programs including key elements such as in-country ownership, innovative partnerships between governments, workers, and NGOs [nongovernmental organizations], development of reasonable educational alternatives, monitoring, creative use of media, and documentation."

U.S. contributions/pledges to IPEC as of March 1998 are indicated in table 8.2. The total U.S. contribution of $8.1 million to IPEC since its

---

3. According to the *New York Times,* the International Labor Rights Fund filed a complaint to ban imports of South Asian carpets under the provisions of the Sanders Amendment (see "Ban sought on South Asian rugs" 1997). This complaint is presently under investigation by the U.S. Customs Service. See also "Citrus squeeze" 1998.

4. Further details can be found in Brown, Deardorff, and Stern (1996, 234–36).

5. IPEC (International Labour Organization [ILO] 1996a) identifies three conditions that characterize "intolerable" child labor: children working under forced labor conditions and in bondage; children in hazardous working conditions and occupations; and very young children (under the age of twelve).

Table 8.2   U.S. Contributions/Pledges to IPEC as of March 1998

Country	Program	Amount	Comments
Bangladesh	Phase 1 of project to remove children from garment factories and place them in schools	$867,273	Approximately 10,000 children have been phased out of factories and placed in 315 schools.
	Phase 2 of project: funding for continuation of monitoring and verifications project	$840,779	Monitoring continues.
Philippines	Statistical survey on child labor in the Philippines	$268,465	Completed.
Africa	Regional workshop on child labor in commercial agriculture	$170,381	Completed.
	Protection of children from hazardous work in plantations in selected countries in Africa (pledged)	$1,000,000	Project proposal underway.
	Funding of Uganda's participation in IPEC (pledged)	$1,500,000 over three years	
Brazil	Combating child labor in the shoe industry of Vale dos Sinos	$308,958	Ongoing.
Thailand	Phase 1 of Northern program to prevent children from being lured into exploitative child labor and prostitution	$484,923	Completed.
	Phase 2 of program	$261,070	Project underway.
Pakistan	Phasing children out of soccer ball industry; providing educational opportunities; internal and external monitoring	$755,744	Project underway.
Nepal	Elimination of girls' trafficking and of commercial sexual exploitation of children; includes children trafficked into India	$192,809	Project underway.
Central America	Combating child labor in selected Central American countries (specifics TBD; pledged)	$1,000,000	Awaiting project proposal.

Source: U.S. Department of Labor (1998).

inception in 1992 will be increased significantly by the funds appropriated in the FY 99 U.S. budget. Twenty donor countries are presently providing IPEC support to twenty-nine developing countries, with an additional twenty-four developing countries preparing to participate. The U.S.-supported IPEC programs noted in table 8.2 evidently address many different aspects of child labor. As noted in U.S. Department of Labor (1998, 3), this range of programs "suggests that interventions need to be made on all fronts and that no single type of intervention is sufficient in itself. It is exactly this type of broad based multi-sectoral action that ILO-IPEC is promoting." It is also noteworthy that IPEC strives to involve trade unions and NGOs in its programmatic activities. Thus (p. 6), "In recent years, a broad social alliance involving governments, NGOs, workers, and employers' organizations, media, academic institutions and various other actors has emerged in many countries—often as [a] result of the catalytic and facilitating role IPEC has played."

8.3.3 Supranational Measures

It should be clear from the preceding discussion that the ILO is the main international organization concerned with labor standards. Established in 1919, the methods and principles set out in the ILO constitution deal with all conceivable aspects of labor standards. The ILO is primarily concerned with (1) the definition of worker rights, especially through the adoption of ILO conventions and recommendations;[6] (2) measures to secure the realization of worker rights, especially by means of international monitoring and supervision, but not by imposition of trade sanctions; and (3) assistance in implementing measures, especially through technical cooperation and advisory services.

8.3.4 Codes of Conduct

On the domestic side, the Clinton administration has sought to work with U.S. firms to develop codes of conduct that would limit imports of goods produced by children as a matter of corporate policy. As noted by the Bureau of International Labor Affairs (1996, 12), "Corporate codes of conduct are policy statements that define ethical standards for companies. Corporations voluntarily develop such codes to inform consumers about the principles that they follow in the production of goods and services they manufacture or sell. Corporate codes of conduct usually address many

---

6. It is interesting that formal ratification of ILO conventions differs considerably among ILO members, apparently because particular conventions may be at variance with national laws and institutional practices. Thus, for example, as Rodrik (1996, 15–16) notes, the United States has ratified only 11 of the 176 ILO conventions, whereas several other industrialized and developing countries have ratified a significantly larger number. Ratification of ILO conventions may therefore not be an accurate indicator of existing national regulations governing labor standards, and there are many cases in which ratified conventions are not enforced.

workplace issues—including child labor—and, according to some observers are part of a broader movement toward corporate social responsibility." Codes of conduct have become more widespread in recent years, especially in the apparel industry. Firms in industries such as apparel that rely heavily on foreign production may have a strong incentive to articulate and carry out codes of conduct. By doing so, the firms can reassure consumers that they are making serious efforts to upgrade foreign labor standards and working conditions for both adults and children.[7] However, the degree of meaningfulness and effectiveness that the codes of conduct will achieve depends above all on their credibility. Of particular importance are the transparency of the codes of conduct, monitoring, and enforcement.

8.3.5 Consumer Labeling

Several American and European importers have recently attempted to go beyond a corporate code of conduct to communicate standards of employment to consumers. Many firms have adopted the strategy of labeling products with statements that are intended to give the impression that child labor was not employed during production.

Product labeling intended to combat illegal child labor began in earnest in the 1990s. A brief summary of existing programs in hand-knotted carpets, footwear, and soccer balls is provided in table 8.3. A thorough description of each program can be found in U.S. Department of Labor, Bureau of International Labor Affairs (1997). The programs differ dramatically in their structures, underlying philosophies, and objectives. However, all of them state either on the product label or in the program's literature that the objective is to produce goods that are not manufactured with illegal child labor.

Labeling as a strategy for reducing child labor has received analytical support from Freeman (1994), but it is not without its critics. First and foremost, any campaign that removes a child from the workplace is vulnerable to the charge that the welfare of the child has not necessarily been improved. Work may simply be the difference between life and death for some children. Eliminating jobs could easily leave child workers with greatly worsened choices. In fact, some of the labeling programs (such as for hand stitched soccer balls) that appear to have the greatest success in credibly eliminating child workers have, in fact, the worst record in demonstrating that children's lives have been improved. More effective may be

---

7. According to the *New York Times,* a presidential task force comprising human rights groups, labor unions, and apparel industry giants reached an agreement that seeks to end sweatshops by means of a code of conduct for wages and working conditions in foreign apparel factories used by American companies (see "Apparel industry group" 1997). Subsequently, it turned out that it was not possible for all parties concerned to reach agreement on the link between wages and the basic needs of workers. For this reason, some of the participating labor unions and labor rights groups declined to support the agreement.

Table 8.3   Product Labeling Programs Claiming Nonuse of Illegal Child Labor

Program	Country	Year	Fees	Monitoring	Child Development	Label	Penalty
				A. Hand-Knotted Carpets			
Rugmark (private)	India Nepal Pakistan	1994 1995 In process	Importers: 1–1.75% of carpet value Exporters: 0.25% of carpet value	Licensing, random inspection, carpet tracking, loom registration	Five schools for weavers' children and former child weavers, funded from importer fees	On carpet	License revoked after second violation
Kaleen (quasi-governmental)	India	1995	Exporters: 0.25% of carpet value	Registration of carpets and looms, random inspection	Contributions to fund twelve schools in rugmaking region	On carpet	License revoked after third violation
STEP (Swiss industry group)	India Nepal Pakistan	1995	Importers: $2.40 per square meter	None; few site visits	Support to child care center, health education, two schools	Retailer display	Deregistered after one violation
Care and Fair (German industry group)	India Nepal Pakistan	1994	Importers: $125 + 1% of carpet value Exporters: 0.25% of carpet value	Self-monitoring	Support to thirty-five projects in India and Nepal, one school in Pakistan	Retailer display	Placed on list of noncompliant firms
Jackciss (carpet weaving collective)	Pakistan	1987		Supervisor inspections	Contributes to schools or builds schools where nonexistent	On carpet	

	Country	Year	Payment	Method	Program	Label	Enforcement
B. Leather Footwear							
Abrinq Foundation (nonprofit)	Brazil	1990	none	Commitment letter, background check, self-monitoring	Individual members undertake child development projects	On product and retailer display	30 days to correct violation, followed by decertification
Pro-Child Institute (nonprofit)	Brazil	1995	$50–200/month	Commitment letter, self-monitoring		On shoes	30 days to correct violation, followed by decertification
C. Soccer Balls							
Reebok (firm)	Pakistan	1996		Centralized production in one facility, guarded entrance and exit, external monitoring by human rights activist	Educational project targeting displaced child workers	On balls	
Baden Sports (firm)	China Pakistan	1977		Centralized production, automation, switching of production from Pakistan to China		On balls	
Dunkin' Donuts (firm)	Pakistan			Detailed records on sites and workers, random inspection by labor rights activists		On balls	
Seneca (firm)	Pakistan			Centralized production facility			
Franklin Sports (firm)	Pakistan			Centralized production			

Source: U.S. Department of Labor, Bureau of International Labor Affairs (1997).

greater attention to educational opportunities, and/or a subsidy that can replace a child's contribution to family income if the child attends school.[8] The rehabilitation programs maintained by some labeling programs are clearly an attempt to improve the options for children while eliminating or reducing work. However, many child welfare projects associated with labeling programs have encountered difficulties in providing services to children. In the case of Rugmark Internationale (in table 8.3), resources for supporting former child workers are inadequate. In other cases, the administrators of labeling programs find that they lack the expertise or legal authority to administer child care programs.

Product labeling programs have also been criticized on grounds of the credibility of the claims made on their labels. In order to address these criticisms, elaborate monitoring procedures have been adopted. However, some organizations believe that credible monitoring is simply an impossible task. Licensed employers have been quite skillful in undermining the effectiveness of even the most carefully designed monitoring effort, and it is not uncommon for many of them to counterfeit labels.

8.4   Conceptual Considerations and Analysis of Alternative Measures to Reduce Child Labor

In order to shed some light on possible effects of various policies regarding child labor, we use this section of the paper to examine the issue in the context of a theoretical model. We will first use the model to demonstrate analytically the conditions under which child labor exploitation might occur. We then use the model to analyze the impact of three policies intended to deter child labor, which are a complete ban on child labor, a nonprohibitive tax on child labor, and a subsidy for education.

The model consists essentially of a microeconomic model of labor supply by a family—parent and child—embedded in a standard Heckscher-Ohlin (HO) general equilibrium model of production and trade. For both, we draw upon more detailed work that has been done elsewhere, contenting ourselves here with giving only the flavor of some of the results that can be obtained, together with the intuition behind them.[9]

---

8. An educational subsidy program targeted at the children of Brazilian orange pickers has produced very suggestive results. Citrovita Agro Industrial Ltd., the largest juice producer in the town of Catanduva, funds an educational center for underprivileged youth. In addition, the local government gives needy parents whose children maintain a specified school attendance record a stipend of $45 per month per child. The stipend roughly equals the child's forgone earnings as an orange picker while in school. In the year since the program has been in effect, truancy in Catanduva has dropped from 18 percent to less than 1 percent. The success of the program in Catanduva clearly stems from two characteristics. First, the subsidy is paid only in lieu of work by the child; and, perhaps more importantly, the program designers are willing to accept the parents' decisions as to how each family's subsidy is spent. As a consequence, the community has replaced work with school as a way for the child to bring resources into the household.

9. For related work, see Basu and Van (1998) and Basu (1999).

8.4.1   The HO Model

We use a two-cone version of the HO model, which most closely and simply captures the large differences that exist between the developed and developing parts of the world.[10] That is, while we assume that countries everywhere share the same constant-returns-to-scale technologies for producing several goods from primary inputs of capital and labor, the factor endowments of countries are sufficiently diverse as to prevent factor price equalization (FPE) among all of them. Instead, the world is divided into two cones of factor proportions. In the more capital-abundant cone of the North, we find the factor endowments of the rich developed countries. Within that cone, these countries have FPE among themselves, and they produce and collectively export goods from the capital-intensive end of the factor intensity spectrum. At the same time, the less capital abundant countries of the South occupy a more labor abundant/intensive cone. They too have FPE among themselves, and they specialize in labor-intensive goods. Factor prices can differ markedly between these two parts of the world, with the South having much lower wages (and higher returns to capital) than the North.

For the most part, too, the South produces different goods than the North, while within the South countries specialize further among the various labor-intensive goods depending on their factor endowments relative to other countries in the southern cone. The countries with the smallest endowments of capital per worker, which will be the focus of our attention here, will pay the same wages as other countries in the same cone, due to FPE among them. However, they will tend to produce and export a different selection of goods, concentrating on the most labor-intensive of the larger group of labor-intensive goods produced in the South.

For simplicity and concreteness of results, we allow only two factors in our discussion, capital and labor. One may think of human capital as being implicit in the model but aggregated together with capital. One could also allow some exogenous variation in the amount of effective labor per worker, especially across countries. More importantly, we explicitly allow the labor factor in the South to encompass both adult and child labor as perfect substitutes, with children contributing only a constant fraction of the effective labor input of an adult.

Before moving on to the micromodel of labor supply, several familiar properties of this HO trade model may be noted. First, as long as world prices of all goods remain unchanged, factor prices of countries within a cone will not change with variations in their factor supplies. This is the lesson of FPE,[11] and it applies within a cone of a multicone model as much

---

10. See Deardorff (1979).
11. Causing Leamer and Levinsohn (1995) to call it the "Factor Price Insensitivity Theorem."

as in the more familiar textbook model with a single cone. Second, if prices of goods change, as they will when large changes in factor supplies cause changes in world supplies of goods, then factor prices change in accordance with the Stolper-Samuelson theorem. However, that theorem must be interpreted within the context of a cone of specialization. That is, when the relative price of a good goes up, the effect on factor prices within a cone—say, the South—depends on whether that good is produced there at all, and, if it is produced, on the factor intensity of the good relative to that of others in the same cone.[12] If the good is not produced, then its higher relative price simply lowers the real wages of all factors in the cone; but if it is produced, then this raises the real return to the factor used intensively in its production, relative to other goods in the same cone.

These familiar properties of the HO model, in their perhaps unfamiliar guises in the multicone model, will be useful later, when we discuss the general equilibrium and world market implications of various policies for dealing with child labor.

8.4.2   Parent and Child Labor Supply

Unlike most applications of the HO trade model, ours will assume variable labor supply, and in particular we will make a distinction between supply of adult labor and supply of child labor. Our model of a family has just two people, a parent and a child, with a single utility function that is intended to reflect the interests of both. Both members of the family can potentially contribute to that utility by three means: leisure, home production, and market production. The model is static, but the leisure of the child can be taken to include time spent in school, and the contribution of the child's leisure to family utility can therefore encompass the future return to education. Home production represents whatever the family member can contribute directly to the family's welfare by working in the home (or on the family's land) to produce goods and services for the family's own consumption. It does not include work he or she may do at home to produce goods for sale or in a subcontracting arrangement with a firm. Such work, although done at home, is part of market production, which of course may also be done elsewhere (in a factory or on a plantation).

Family utility depends on these three arguments—leisure, home consumption, and market consumption—each of which may be contributed by one or both family members. These three arguments in the utility function are not, in general, perfect substitutes, and indeed we will further specify the pattern of substitution among them shortly. The contributions of parent and child to each of these arguments, however, are taken to be perfect substitutes for each other, though not on a one-for-one basis. Thus, each hour of home production by the parent will yield some fixed amount of home consumption, while each hour of home production by the child

---

12. See Davis (1996).

will yield a similarly fixed, but presumably smaller, amount of home consumption. Likewise, working in the market, each family member earns a fixed wage, again with the child's wage presumably being smaller than the parent's. The contributions of each family member's leisure time to family utility are similarly fixed per hour, although here we presume (and hope) that the family places a higher value on the child's leisure than on the parent's. If the family does not, then we may get what we take to be the pathological (but perhaps all too common) case of true exploitation of child labor.

We will not attempt here to explore this model in full detail and rigor, but it may nonetheless be useful to lay it out formally.

8.4.3   The Model

The notation in the model is as follows:

C_h, C_m	Consumption of home produced and market purchased goods
T_i, H_i, L_i	Time allocated to leisure, home production, and market production by family member, $i = p, c$ for parent and child respectively
v_i, a_i, w_i	Productivity of time allocated to leisure v_i (in terms of utility), home production a_i (in terms of home produced consumption), and market production w_i (the wage) for family member i
C, T	Effective total consumption (CES aggregate) and leisure
$\overline{T}_p$, $\overline{T}_c$	Time available for parent and child respectively (excludes biologically necessary leisure)
$\rho_j = (\sigma_j - 1)/\sigma_j$	CES utility parameters, $j = U, C$

The equations for the model are as follows. The family is assumed to choose T_i, H_i, L_i, $i = p, c$, to solve the following maximization problem:

$$(1) \qquad \max[C^{\rho_U} + T^{\rho_U}]^{1/\rho_U},$$

subject to

$$(2) \qquad C = [C_h^{\rho_C} + C_m^{\rho_C}]^{1/\rho_C},$$

$$(3) \qquad T = v_p T_p + v_c T_c,$$

$$(4) \qquad C_h = a_p H_p + a_c H_c,$$

$$(5) \qquad C_m = w_p L_p + w_c L_c,$$

$$(6) \qquad H_p + L_p + T_p = \overline{T}_p,$$

$$(7) \qquad H_c + L_c + T_c = \overline{T}_c.$$

If home and market consumption are relatively close substitutes, such that $\sigma_c > 1$ as we assume, and if consumption and leisure are not close substitutes, such that $\sigma_U < 1$ as we also assume, then this formulation yields a backward-bending supply curve of labor. That is, if we raise both wages while keeping their proportions fixed, total labor supply first rises with the wage at low wages, but falls thereafter with further increases in wages.

Exactly who does what within this family depends both on the level of the wages and on the productivities of the parent and child in satisfying their various needs. Because the formulation here is linear, it is convenient to think in terms of parents' and children's each having comparative advantage in one or another activity, much as in a Ricardian trade model with three goods. That is, we can order the three activities—leisure, home production, and market production—by the ratio of the parent's and the child's productivity, to get a chain of comparative advantage. It follows, exactly as in a Ricardian trade model, that neither family member will engage in any activity in which he or she has a comparative disadvantage unless the other family member is already devoting all of his or her time to it as well.

To illustrate, we will assume throughout most of our discussion that the following ordering prevails:

$$(8) \qquad \frac{w_c}{w_p} < \frac{a_c}{a_p} < \frac{v_c}{v_p}.$$

The motivations here are (1) that the child is less productive than the adult at both home and market production, so that the first and second ratios are both less than one; (2) that the family sees greater utility value in the child's leisure than in the parent's, partly out of care for the child and partly because the child's leisure includes the benefits of education, so that the third ratio is greater than one; and (3) that the child's greatest comparative disadvantage is in market production. With this assumed ordering, the child will never engage in market production unless the parent is already devoting all of his or her time to market production as well; but this can happen, if the wages of both are low and productivity of home production is even lower.

In general, under the assumptions in equation (8), the only patterns of intrafamily specialization that can be observed are those depicted in table 8.4. Which of these patterns is chosen then depends upon all of the parameters, including the market wage rates.

For our purposes here, we care most about the implications of the model for labor supply. Two aspects of this will be of interest: how the total labor supply of the family varies when wages of parent and child move together, and how they vary when the wage of only one family member changes while the other is fixed. The first case is depicted in figure 8.1.

Table 8.4   **Patterns of Intrafamily Specialization**

T Leisure	H Home Production	L Market Production
C,P	P	P
C	P	P
C	C,P	P
C	C	P
C	C	C,P

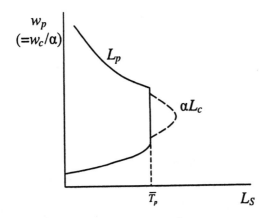

Fig. 8.1   **Family labor supply as wages vary together**

Here it is assumed that the parent's and the child's wages move together, as they would (and will in our discussion) if the child's productivity in market production is some fixed fraction of an adult's while both become more or less valuable with varying market conditions. Letting $\alpha = w_c/w_p$ < 1 be that fraction, we graph the family's total effective labor supply in units of the parent's labor, $L_S = L_p + \alpha L_c$, as a function of the parent's wage. When both wages are very low, even the parent provides very little market production, since the parent can use his or her time more productively at home. As the wages rise, the parent increases his or her labor supply, but because of the child's comparative disadvantage in market production, the child remains at home, engaged in leisure and probably home production. Only when the rising wage has drawn the parent into market production full time does the family even consider putting the child to work as well, and even then the wages must rise a bit more before that happens. Now, as wages rise further, we finally do see child labor, its amount increasing, for a time, with the wage.

With the assumed elasticities of substitution, however, there comes a point at which further increases in both wages cause the family to reduce labor supplied to the market, and with the assumed pattern of comparative advantage, it is the child's labor that is withdrawn first. Only when the wages have risen to the point that the child no longer works in the market does the parent's labor supply begin to decline as well.

We can also ask how labor supplies vary if we change one wage while holding the other fixed. Of greatest interest will be changes in the child's wage, so that is the case we consider here. Suppose, starting from some point on the labor supply curve in figure 8.1, that the child's wage now changes while the parent's does not. (Of course, if the child was not working initially, then a small change in the child's wage will not change the child's employment status. Most interesting therefore are cases in which we start with the child already working.) Two such cases are shown in figure 8.2.

Here we have magnified the portion of the family labor supply curve along which the child works, shown as the solid curve L_S. Then for two arbitrary points selected on this curve, marked A and B, we draw portions of the labor supply curves that would be observed if only w_c were then to change. In both cases, the broken curves show what would happen if w_c were to vary (as it does along L_S) but w_p were to remain fixed at w_A and w_B, respectively. In both cases, because a fall in the child's wage is now not accompanied by the income loss of a fall in the parent's wage as well, the family cuts back more on the child's labor supply than it does along L_S. Thus, where the labor supply was positively sloped as at A, its response to a fall in only the child's wage is more elastic than if both wages fell together; if the labor supply was negatively sloped as at B, the response becomes less elastic.

From this we see something like a trade-off between the income of the family and the effect that can be obtained on child labor by changing the child's wage. If the family is very poor, as at point A, then a reduction in the child's wage rate will discourage the family from having the child work, at the cost, of course, of reducing the family's income still further. On the other hand, if wages are somewhat higher to start with, as at B, so that the family has reached the point at which further wage increases will reduce child labor, a fall in the child's wage will have the perverse effect of causing him or her to work more. As we will see, this case may have some relevance for policy.

Not depicted previously but always true under the assumed pattern of comparative advantage is the effect of a change in the parent's wage on child labor. Starting again from a situation in which the child is already working, a rise in the parent's wage has the same effect on the family as an increase in the family's wealth, since it simply raises the income from the maximum number of hours that the parent is already working. Because the utility function is homothetic in consumption and leisure, this can only reduce the amount of market production that the family asks the child to provide, and this increases the child's leisure. By the same token, a fall in

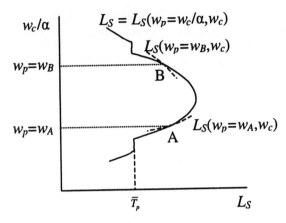

Fig. 8.2   **Family labor supply as child's wage varies**

the parent's wage will increase child labor supply if it is already positive, and it may well put the child to work if he or she was not already there.

What our model cannot tell us very clearly is the effect of any of these changes on the welfare of the child alone. We have chosen to model the utility of only the family unit, not of the individuals within it. Certainly a rise in either wage benefits the family as a whole, even though a rise in the child's wage may cause the child to work longer hours. That this may nonetheless benefit the child, however, is quite possible, since the family enjoys greater market consumption as a result.

8.4.4   The Bad Parent

The case we have considered so far, with equation (8), provides the most favorable interpretation of child labor, in which children work only if their parents are already working the maximum that they biologically can, and the family acknowledges the high cost to the child (in forgone leisure) of working. The family nonetheless sends the child to work if the need for what the child can earn is large enough due to both low wages overall and low productivity at home. Based on the evidence we have described earlier in the paper, we believe that this captures reasonably well a large fraction of the child labor observed in the world.

It does not capture all of it, however. As we have discussed, many children are trapped in situations so harsh that it is implausible that they are benefiting at all from the arrangement. When children are essentially sold, as bonded laborers or in other similar arrangements, and when they live apart from their families with their wages given to the family instead of to them, then it seems clear that only the parents are benefiting, and at the children's expense.

Our model can capture at least one aspect of such behavior by simply reducing the utility value that the family unit places on the child's leisure, v_c. Reduced sufficiently, this will alter the ordering in equation (8), putting the child's comparative advantage in leisure below that of both kinds of work. The possible patterns of specialization that one may now observe are altered from those previously laid out. It is now easy to generate a scenario in which it is the child who works the maximum that is physically possible, either at home (Cinderella) or in the market (as essentially slave labor). Indeed, if we completely reverse the ordering of equation (8), the same graphs of labor supply that we used before will apply, but with the identification of parent and child labor supply reversed. It is worth noting that, even in this case, a reduction in the wage of the child worker may induce the parent to force the child to work more, not less, though only if the child is not already working the maximum.

8.4.5   Policies toward Child Labor

We turn now to a discussion of several policies that might be used to discourage child labor, in the hope that our model may help to illuminate their effects. We will consider three policies: a complete ban on child labor, a nonprohibitive tax on child labor, and a subsidy to education. In each case we consider first the effects if the policy is applied "in the small" (to a small enough part of the developing world that it will not change world prices), and second if it is applied "in the large" (to all less developed countries [LDCs] as a group).

Ban on Child Labor

Suppose first that child labor is simply and effectively banned within a single small LDC. If that does not alter wages of parents, then under the assumptions of our model the families of child workers are unambiguously made worse off. They lose the income of the children, and we know from their choice to put the children to work in the first place that they view the benefits of that income as exceeding its costs. We can question whether the children themselves are worse off, of course, but only if we doubt the goodwill of the parents.

But won't the ban in fact alter the parent's wage? With less labor supplied by children, then one might expect the wages of the remaining workers to be bid up. That would be true in a closed economy, but in the small open economy, as assumed here, it is not. As long as factor price equalization holds, the wages of parents—which are determined by unchanged world prices of goods—will not be changed by the ban on employing their children.

Thus it is only when we expand the ban on child labor to much or all of the developing world that we can expect to find an effect on adult wages. In that case, the ban reduces labor supply in enough of the world to reduce the supply in world markets of the most labor intensive goods, and the prices of these will rise as a result. It is through this mechanism—the Stolper-Samuelson theorem in action—that we can expect to see the ban on child labor improving the wages of the parents. This is hopeful, but there is still no assurance that the increased wage of a parent more than makes up for the lost wage of the child and thus that families or their children are made better off. This will depend on many things, including the elasticity of demand for labor-intensive goods.

A Nonprohibitive Tax on Child Labor

We next consider a nonprohibitive tax on child labor. We do this not because anyone has proposed this as a desirable policy, but because many policies that have been proposed and used have effects similar to such a tax. A campaign of opprobrium, for example, leveled against employers of child labor, implicitly raises the cost to them of that employment, but it may not raise it enough to stop their doing it. A well-advertised program of labeling can have a similar effect, by causing unlabelled merchandise to sell at a discount.

Suppose then that such a tax is implemented, again in the small to start with. The productivity of children's labor is not altered by the tax, and therefore potential employers will continue to be willing to employ them for a wage equal to that productivity minus the tax. In other words, the effect of the tax is simply to lower the wage received by child workers. Since it does not alter the wage of their parents (FPE again), the scenario is exactly that of figure 8.2. The tax may therefore either increase or decrease the hours worked by children, depending on which portion of the labor supply curve they were in; but unambiguously the welfare of the children's families is reduced. Thus the tax almost certainly does not make the children better off (except perhaps in the case of the bad parent), and it may even cause them to work more.

As in the case of the ban on child labor, the tax may possibly become beneficial if it is levied in the large, on enough of the developing world to alter world prices. Note in this case, however, that labor supply may rise, not fall, such that the effect on world prices would be opposite that of a ban and could lower prices of unskilled-labor-intensive goods and thus the implied unskilled wage.

Of course, the analysis of a tax is not complete without an accounting for how the revenue from it is used, but that is an issue only if it really is a tax. If costs are increased by other means, as suggested previously, then there is no revenue, even potentially, to offset the adverse effects on the child workers and their families.

A Subsidy to Education

We noted earlier the recent moves that have been made toward pulling children out of work instead of pushing them into not working. By offering families a cash subsidy to send their children to school, one can obviously alter in an important way the calculus of their decision making. In the previous model, this would alter equation (5) to include the market consumption that can be financed by the subsidy:

$$(5')   \qquad C_m = w_p L_p + w_c L_c + s_e T_c,$$

where s_e is the education subsidy. If $s_e > w_c$, then the effect is extreme, since the family would never then send the child to work. Even with a smaller subsidy, however, the change in incentives can have important effects, and it seems clear that this can only reduce child labor. Furthermore, and unlike the other policies, this subsidy can only benefit the families, not harm them.

This is true in the small, when wages are fixed by FPE, and it is equally true in the large—for once again, by reducing the supply of child labor, a broadly used education subsidy has the potential to reduce the world supply of unskilled labor. This in turn can raise the world prices of goods that these workers produce, as well as their wages.

This all sounds fine, but of course we have not accounted for the very real cost of financing the subsidy. As usual in matters of this sort, unless a market failure is being corrected, a subsidy will itself distort markets and cause a net reduction in overall economic welfare. In this case, because the gains to the poor families of the child workers seem clear, these gains are smaller than the cost of the subsidies. It probably would not be hard to dream up market failures to justify this cost, but we do not view that as necessary. Redistribution of world income toward the poor is sufficiently difficult that advocates of redistribution would not condemn a policy such as this on the grounds of a little economic inefficiency. On the contrary, if the world can harness the righteous indignation over child labor to the cause of truly helping these children and their families, many would view the effort as worth the cost.

8.5   Conclusions and Implications for Policy

In section 8.3 we noted five kinds of policies and programs that have been suggested or used for deterring the employment of children. We conclude by revisiting them, providing our assessment of their desirability from the perspectives both of our analysis in section 8.4 and of broader considerations. To avoid repetition, we address the policies and programs in three groups.

8.5.1   Trade Policies

As might be expected from trade theory, the case for the use of trade restrictions to deter child labor has several analytical weaknesses. Objections could arise partly from the usual distortions that trade intervention causes or from a concern that the real motivation for such policies is the protection of domestic interests of the developed countries rather than the welfare of exploited children. It is also the case that if such protection is the actual objective, then there are forms of intervention other than trade restrictions that provide higher welfare for all concerned.

More importantly, however, is the welfare of the exploited children themselves, and whether they are truly helped by, say, a boycott of the goods they are employed to produce. If such a boycott were truly complete, then the effect would be that of a ban on child labor, as discussed earlier. Such a ban would indeed reduce the employment of children, but except perhaps in the case of bad parents, it would hurt the children rather than helping them. Furthermore, if trade restrictions effect only a partial boycott—being implemented by some importing countries rather than all—or if they merely lower the net prices of imported goods that continue to be produced with child labor, then the effect will be similar to that of a tax on child labor. Here, as we saw, the children are hurt while their employment may actually rise.

8.5.2   ILO Assistance and Other Supranational Measures

We have already noted that funds have been contributed by the United States and other developed countries to the ILO's IPEC for improving labor standards. These funds can be used in a variety of ways, and they are not without their pitfalls; but they potentially provide the means for truly alleviating the plight of working children and not just removing them from view. To the extent that such funds are used to subsidize the education of poor youth, and in particular to provide them and their families an incentive to remove them from more arduous activities, these programs act much like a subsidy to education. It is notable that the amount of money contributed to these programs by the United States, though laudable, is miniscule compared to what the United States contributes to many other domestic and even international initiatives.

8.5.3   Codes of Conduct and Labeling

Neither codes of conduct nor consumer labeling (which in effect simply helps producers to gain a marketing advantage from their codes of conduct) unambiguously improve the welfare of children. To the extent that they only reduce the demand for child labor or, equivalently, raise its perceived cost to potential employers, these initiatives cater more to the sensitivities of western firms and their customers than to the needs of the children who are said to be their focus. Indeed, simply to stop employing an impoverished child could be viewed in some cases as more harmful than employing the child—again with perhaps the exception of children of bad parents or children in forced or bonded labor.

The welfare impact of a code of conduct or of any labeling cannot be evaluated simply by determining whether the affected children are still working. Rather, the outcomes for children should also be measured in terms of standard of living, educational attainment, and so forth. As we have discussed, the more carefully constructed codes and labeling schemes have in fact devoted some of their revenues to educating, feeding, and housing former child workers. So far, this role has been a very limited one—limited by the licensing fees that labelers can collect and by the generosity of corporations.

The role for consumers in improving the welfare of children hinges on the need to identify the fundamental sources of child poverty (not merely child labor) and to make their product choices accordingly. Perhaps the pursuit of profits by corporations can be harnessed to this end, but the benefits will accrue to child workers only if they and their families actually receive additional resources.

References

Alam, Asad. 1992. *Labor standards and comparative advantage.* Ph.D. diss., Department of Economics, Columbia University.

Apparel industry group moves to end sweatshops: Agreement to bring worldwide inspection. 1997. *New York Times,* 9 April, A11.

Ban sought on South Asian rugs in campaign against child labor. 1997. *New York Times,* 6 November, 12.

Basu, Kaushik. 1999. Child labor: Cause, consequence and cure, with remarks on international labor standards. *Journal of Economic Literature* 37:1083–119.

Basu, Kaushik, and Pham Hoang Van. 1998. The economics of child labor. *American Economic Review* 88:412–27.

Brown, Drusilla K., Alan V. Deardorff, and Robert M. Stern. 1996. International labor standards and trade: A theoretical analysis. In *Fair trade and harmonization: Prerequisites for free trade?* ed. Jagdish N. Bhagwati and Robert E. Hudec, 227–80. Cambridge, Mass.: MIT Press.

Citrus squeeze: U.S. child labor law sparks a trade debate over Brazilian oranges. 1998. *Wall Street Journal,* 9 September, A1.

Customs walks tightrope on new child labor law. 1997. *Journal of Commerce,* 14 October, 1A.

Davis, Donald R. 1996. Trade liberalization and income distribution. NBER Working Paper no. 5693. Cambridge, Mass.: National Bureau of Economic Research, August.

Deardorff, Alan V. 1979. Weak links in the chain of comparative advantage. *Journal of International Economics* 9 (May): 197–209.

Freeman, Richard B. 1994. A hard-headed look at labor standards. In *International labor standards and global economic integration: Proceedings of a symposium.* Washington, D.C.: U.S. Department of Labor, Bureau of International Labor Affairs.

Grant, James. 1991. *The state of the world's children 1991.* Oxford: Oxford University Press for UNICEF.

Grootaert, Christiaan, and Ravi Kanbur. 1995. Child labour: An economic perspective. *International Labour Review* 134:187–203.

Human Rights Watch. 1996. *The small hands of slavery: Bonded child labor in India.* New York: Human Rights Watch.

International Labour Organization (ILO). Directorate of Labour Welfare and the International Programme on the Elimination of Child Labour (IPEC). 1996a. *Child labour in the football manufacturing industry.* Geneva: ILO.

International Labour Organization (ILO). 1996b. *Economically active populations: Estimates and projections, 1950–2010.* Geneva: ILO.

———. 1996c. *International Programme on the Elimination of Child Labor (IPEC).* Brochure. Geneva: ILO.

Kruse, Douglas, and Douglas Mahony. 1998. Illegal child labor in the United States: Prevalence and characteristics. NBER Working Paper no. 6479. Cambridge, Mass.: National Bureau of Economic Research, March.

Leamer, Edward E., and James Levinsohn. 1995. International trade theory: The evidence. In *Handbook of international economics,* vol. 3, ed. Gene Grossman and Kenneth Rogoff, 1339–93. Amsterdam: North-Holland.

Organization for Economic Cooperation and Development (OECD). 1996. *Trade, employment and labour standards: A study of core workers rights and international trade.* Paris: OECD.

Rodrik, Dani. 1996. Labor standards in international trade: Do they matter and what do we do about them? In *Emerging agenda for global trade: High stakes for developing countries,* ed. Robert Lawrence, Dani Rodrik, and John Whalley, 35–79. Washington, D.C.: Overseas Development Council.

U.S. Department of Labor. 1998. The role of governments and non-governmental organizations in combating child labor: ILO-IPEC experience. Public hearing. 13 February.

U.S. Department of Labor. Bureau of International Labor Affairs. 1994. *By the sweat and toil of children.* Vol. 1, *The use of child labor in American imports.* Report prepared for the Committee on Appropriations. Cong. Washington, D.C.: U.S. Department of Labor.

———. 1995. *By the sweat and toil of children.* Vol. 2, *The use of child labor in U.S. agricultural imports & forced and bonded child labor.* Report prepared for the Committee on Appropriations. Cong. Washington, D.C.: U.S. Department of Labor.

———. 1996. *By the sweat and toil of children.* Vol. 3, *The apparel industry and codes of conduct: A solution to the international child labor problem?* Washington, D.C.: U.S. Department of Labor.

———. 1997. *By the sweat and toil of children.* Vol. 4, *Consumer labels and child labor.* Washington, D.C.: U.S. Department of Labor.

Comment   Robert W. Staiger

Brown, Deardorff, and Stern have written a very useful paper on an important topic. The topic is child labor, and the first thing the paper does is to provide a very thoughtful survey of existing research with regard to the determinants, magnitudes, and characteristics of child labor. This survey

Robert W. Staiger is professor of economics at the University of Wisconsin, Madison, and a research associate of the National Bureau of Economic Research.

is especially valuable in serving at a broad level to remind the reader of two important points. First, the magnitude of the problem in developing countries is huge (tens and possibly hundreds of millions of children working under conditions that "interfere with their normal development"). And second, developed countries will face severe limitations if they seek to address this problem directly by withholding market access for goods produced with child labor (evidently only a very small percentage of all child workers are employed in the export industries of developing countries).

The second thing the paper does is to provide a description of the various programs and policies used in the United States to deter child labor in foreign countries. These include unilateral actions taken by the U.S. government, actions taken by the U.S. government that work through international agencies, attempts by the U.S. government to facilitate corporate codes of conduct, and private sector attempts to engineer product labeling programs. An important issue associated with the last two mentioned programs concerns monitoring, and the paper elaborates, from the perspective of a simple theoretical model, on a number of the problems involved with monitoring.

The third thing the paper does is to develop a simple general equilibrium model to examine the impacts of various policies on the use of child labor. A model of family labor supply is embedded in a traditional two-cone Heckscher-Ohlin model. Within the family, the parent and the child can allocate their time to leisure, home production, and/or market production, and children are assumed to have a comparative disadvantage in market production. With appropriate elasticity assumptions, family labor supply will eventually become "backward bending": that is, fixing the relative wages of parent and child, rising wages will first lead to greater family labor supply but eventually to reductions in family labor supply. Given the comparative disadvantage of the child in market production, family labor is supplied to the market first by the parent, and only as the wages rise further (in fixed proportion) will the child eventually be pulled into market employment. As wages rise further still, and the backward-bending portion of the family labor supply curve is reached, child labor supply to the market is reduced.

If, after the description of the complexities associated with the problem of child labor contained earlier in the paper, any reader still believes that policy responses to the problem should be obvious, then this simple model should dispel that view. Consider, for example, the relatively straightforward goal of reducing child labor (and forget about the far more subtle task of attempting to ensure that child welfare is actually enhanced). The model nicely illustrates how the supply of child labor to market production will be a non-monotonic function of wages, and this result is most evident when only the child's wage is varied: As the child's wage is reduced, very poor families (on the upward-sloping portion of the family labor supply) will reduce child labor supply to the market, while better-off families (on the backward-bending portion of the family labor supply) will increase child labor supply to the market. Hence, whether aggregate child labor rises or falls as the market wage of children is reduced depends on, among other things, the distribution of family income across the economy. The broader implication is that it may be extremely difficult for the developed world to find simple policies that reliably reduce child labor in the developing world if these policies work through their effects on prices and wages.

The Heckscher-Ohlin features of the model are also nicely put to work in the analysis of the effects on family welfare of an outright ban on child labor. Unless the ban applies to significant portions of the developing world, it will not significantly affect the prices of internationally traded goods, and hence factor prices in a developing country to which the ban applies will not be affected (factor price insensitivity), and the impact on family income will simply be the lost income of the child. Only if goods prices are altered by the ban will family incomes in the developing world also be affected by changes in the wages of parents, with the direction of these changes predicted by the Stolper-Samuelson theorem.

My discussion thus far has focused on things that are in the paper which I like, and there are many of these. There are also things that are not in the paper which I would like to have seen the authors discuss (of course, I can always hope that these things will be the topic of some of their future work). In particular, I think that to make much more progress on the issue of child labor in the developing world, we are going to have to begin to confront in a systematic fashion a number of questions that the paper doesn't really raise, though these are questions that to some extent lurk around the edges of the discussion. The first question to which I refer is simply this: Why is the developed world unhappy with the treatment of child labor in the developing world? (I.e., What is the problem?) Only after we are comfortable with our answer to this first question can we seek answers to the second: What should be done about the treatment of child workers in the developing world? (I.e., What is the solution?) The remainder of my comments will focus on a number of possible answers to these questions.

Why is the developed world unhappy with the treatment of child labor in the developing world? One possible answer is the "race-to-the-bottom" fear that low-cost products of child labor will erode the living standards of workers in the developed world, who must compete with these developing country exports. For example, the additions to the labor force of the developing world that are implied by the lax or nonexistent child labor laws in these countries may affect living standards of workers in the developed world through the greater availability of labor-intensive exports from developing countries. According to this answer, the developed world cares about the treatment of child labor in the developing world because of the resulting *trade effects,* and a pecuniary externality of international dimensions is thereby created through the impact of child labor laws on exporter prices.

Whether this externality leads to inefficient policy choices, and hence to a "problem" that all governments could in principle agree to "solve" through negotiations of some kind, depends at least in part on whether countries can affect exporter prices through their policy choices. But even if there is an inefficiency of this type, it is tied fundamentally to concerns over market access (i.e., trade effects), and this has important implications for answers to the second question raised earlier. In particular, as I have argued in other work (Bagwell and Staiger 2000 and forthcoming), this problem can be handled at least in theory with market access negotiations under existing GATT rules (appropriately modified). Hence, if this is the problem, then GATT's existing principles may be well equipped to provide the solution, and as a consequence there may be no need to embark on a major shift of approach to find solutions to the problem of child labor in the developing world.

However, there are other possible answers to this first question. The mere fact that the United States has federal child labor standards of its own suggests the possibility that, as a country, we are uncomfortable with the child labor outcomes that an unconstrained market would deliver. Perhaps, if we want to answer the question of why we care about the labor standards of other countries, we might seek answers through national introspection: Why do we perceive the need to adopt labor standards of our own? I can think of at least three distinct answers (and I am sure there are many more).

First, a national child labor standard may provide parents with a commitment device with respect to their children, and hence solve an intrafamily time-consistency problem. For example, a parent may hope to induce his or her child to expend effort throughout the school year by announcing that the child will have to continue to attend school the following year, regardless of this year's performance; but at year's end, if the child is failing school, the parent may well have reason to rethink his or her announced policy, perhaps allowing the child to quit school and enter the workforce after all. If the child anticipates this, he or she may be less inclined to expend effort at school, and the parent may then encounter difficulties achieving the desired educational goals for the child. In this situation, a federal child labor standard, which keeps children below a specific age out of the workforce and in school and is enforced by sanctions, can help parents achieve a desired degree of credibility with respect to their children. Notice, however, that while this argument might provide a rationale for a country to adopt a child labor standard of its own, it does not by itself provide a separate reason why one country might care about the labor standards of another country.

Second, a national child labor standard may be in place to prevent an influx of low wage child labor from undercutting the wages of adult workers. Under this logic, if we choose to prevent our own children from undercutting the wages of our adult workers, we might well wish to prevent the children from developing countries from doing this as well. Notice, however, that this simply gives a reason for the developed world to care about the trade effects of the developing world's child labor standards, and thus this is a special case of market access concerns generated by an international pecuniary externality, as just noted. Hence, this would not by itself provide a separate reason why one country might care about the labor standards of another country.

Third, a national child labor standard may be in place to correct a nonpecuniary externality that each family's child labor supply decision exerts on others. In this case, the key question is whether this externality is national or international in scope. For example, if the externality related to child labor supply decisions concerns the impact of these decisions on the likelihood of criminal activity later in life, then this is likely to be an externality of national scope, and as such it would not provide a separate rationale for why one country might care about the labor standards of another country. On the other hand, perhaps we care directly about the welfare of children other than our own *and* we don't trust all parents to make decisions that serve the welfare of their children. For example, it may be that most parents are well equipped to solve on their own the time-consistency problem noted earlier, but that as a nation we support the cost of administrating federal child labor standards because some parents are not so equipped, and we care about the welfare of their children. In this case, our direct concern for the welfare of children might extend as well to the children of the developing world, and then we would be directly affected by the child labor standards chosen by a developing country. Here is a reason, separate from market access concerns, why one country might care about the labor standards of another country.

I don't know which, if any, of these cases is relevant in practice, and it may well be that I have left out entirely the most important reason or sets of reasons for why the developed world cares about the labor standards chosen by the developing world. It seems clear, however, that identifying the possible reasons for the problem is a crucial step in finding a solution. For example, if the sources of the problem can be tied to market access concerns, as in the race-to-the-bottom sort of fears described previously, then GATT's market access focus can probably be utilized to provide the solution. On the other hand, if the source of the problem is not tied to market access concerns, but reflects instead international externalities of a nonpecuniary nature as in the final case described previously, then solutions might be better found outside of GATT, perhaps utilizing instead the ILO.

In any event, let me summarize. The paper written by Brown, Deardorff, and Stern has contributed to the important task of characterizing the facts of child labor in the developing world, and it has also taken an important step in showing how our familiar models of international trade can help to illuminate the impacts of various policy options on the supply of child labor in the developing world and on the welfare of child workers. What is now needed is to take a step back, and to ask why the developed world cares.

References

Bagwell, Kyle, and Robert W. Staiger. 2000. The simple economics of labor standards and the GATT. In *Social dimensions of U.S. trade policies,* ed. Alan V. Deardorff and Robert M. Stern. Ann Arbor: University of Michigan Press.
———. Forthcoming. Domestic policies, national sovereignty and international economic institutions. *Quarterly Journal of Economics.*

Contributors

Robert E. Baldwin
Department of Economics
Social Science Building 7321
University of Wisconsin–Madison
1180 Observatory Drive
Madison, WI 53706

Magnus Blomström
European Institute of Japanese Studies
Stockholm School of Economics
Post Office Box 6501
Sveavagen 65
S-113 83 Stockholm, Sweden

Bruce A. Blonigen
Department of Economics
1285 University of Oregon
Eugene, OR 97403

Drusilla K. Brown
Department of Economics
Tufts University
Braker Hall
Medford, MA 02155

Alan V. Deardorff
Department of Economics and
    Gerald R. Ford School of Public
    Policy
University of Michigan
458 Lorch Hall
611 Tappan Street
Ann Arbor, MI 48109

Michael B. Devereux
Department of Economics
University of British Columbia
997-1873 East Mall
Vancouver, BC V6T 1Z1 Canada

Charles Engel
Department of Economics
1180 Observatory Drive
University of Wisconsin
Madison, WI 53706

Gunnar Fors
National Board of Trade
Box 6803
113 86 Stockholm, Sweden

Linda Goldberg
Research Department, 3rd Floor
Federal Reserve Bank-New York
33 Liberty Street
New York, NY 10045

James Harrigan
International Research Function
Federal Reserve Bank of New York
33 Liberty Street
New York, NY 10045

Ann E. Harrison
Graduate School of Business
Columbia University
615 Uris Hall
3022 Broadway Street
New York, NY 10027

Michael M. Knetter
Amos Tuck School of Business
100 Tuck Drive
Dartmouth College
Hanover, NH 03755

Ari Kokko
European Institute for Japanese Studies
Stockholm School of Economics
PO Box 6501
Sveagvagen 65
S-113 83 Stockholm, Sweden

Edward E. Leamer
John E. Anderson Graduate
School of Management
University of California, Los Angeles
Box 951481
Los Angeles, CA 90095

James R. Markusen
Department of Economics
University of Colorado
Boulder, CO 80309

Keith E. Maskus
Department of Economics
University of Colorado
Boulder, CO 80309

J. David Richardson
Department of Economics
347 Eggers Hall
Syracuse University
Syracuse, NY 13244

Anna J. Schwartz
National Bureau of Economic
Research
365 Fifth Ave., 5th Floor
New York, NY 10016

Matthew J. Slaughter
Department of Economics
Dartmouth College
Hanover, NH 03755

Robert W. Staiger
Department of Economics
University of Wisconsin
1180 Observatory Drive
Madison, WI 53706

Robert M. Stern
Gerald R. Ford School of Public
Policy
413 Lorch Hall
University of Michigan
Ann Arbor, MI 48109

Guy V. G. Stevens
Board of Governors of the Federal
Reserve
20th and Constitution Avenue, NW
Washington, DC 20551

Birgitta Swedenborg
Center for Business and Policy Studies
(SNS)
Box 5629
114 86 Stockholm, Sweden

Kei-Mu Yi
International Research
Federal Reserve Bank of New York
33 Liberty Street
New York, NY 10045

Chi Zhang
Center for International Security and
Cooperation
Institute for International Studies
Stanford University
Stanford, CA 94305

Author Index

Subject Index